FIFTY
MILLION
RISING

FIFTY MILLION RISING

The New Generation *of*
Working Women Transforming
the Muslim World

SAADIA ZAHIDI

NATION
BOOKS
New York

Nation Books
116 East 16th Street, 8th Floor
New York, NY 10003
www.publicaffairsbooks.com/nation-books
@NationBooks

Printed in the United States of America

First Edition: January 2018

Published by Nation Books, an imprint of Perseus Books, LLC, a subsidiary of Hachette Book Group, Inc. Nation Books is a copublishing venture of the Nation Institute and Perseus Books.

The publisher is not responsible for websites (or their content) that are not owned by the publisher.

PRINT BOOK INTERIOR DESIGN BY LINDA MARK

Library of Congress Cataloging-in-Publication Data
Title: Fifty million rising : the new generation of working women transforming the
    Muslim world / Saadia Zahidi.
Description: First edition. | New York : Nation Books, [2018] | Includes bibliographical
    references and index.
Identifiers: LCCN 2017029076 | ISBN 9781568585901 (hardcover) |
    ISBN 9781568585918 (ebook)
Subjects: LCSH: Women—Employment—Islamic countries. | Muslim women—
    Employment. | Muslim women—Economic conditions. | Feminism—Islamic countries. |
    Economic development—Islamic countries.
Classification: LCC HD6206.5 .Z34 2018 | DDC 331.40917/67—dc23
LC record available at https://lccn.loc.gov/2017029076

ISBNs: 978-1-56858-590-1 (hardcover), 978-1-56858-591-8 (ebook)

LSC-C

10 9 8 7 6 5 4 3 2 1

Contents

Khadija's Daughters

O NE AFTERNOON WHEN I WAS NEARLY TEN YEARS OLD, MY father, a geophysicist, took me and my younger sister along on one of his regular work trips to a gas field in northern Punjab, a few hours' drive from the capital, Islamabad, where I grew up. Pakistan doesn't have much oil or gas, and most exploration of its limited supply is done by the national oil and gas development corporation, which my father worked for in the first half of his working life. It was a blistering hot summer day in a barren landscape of dry, sepia-colored rocks. Dotting this desolate landscape at regular intervals were scores of men placing seismometers into the ground. These small machines read sound waves to develop a picture of the formation of rocks thousands of meters below the surface.

I had been to my father's office in Islamabad many times before, spending an hour or two there after school while he finished up his work, but it was my first time at the field. At the office were many "uncles," friends and colleagues of my father's who sent their children to the same schools and often socialized together with their families in the evenings and on weekends. This wholly male community of geologists, geophysicists, and engineers and their families made up a small, middle-class urban tribe.

Several of those uncles were at the field that day. One of them announced very proudly that the firm had just finished building a women's bathroom and my sister and I could now use it. I was mildly surprised that they had bothered to build a women's bathroom out here, but didn't think more of it and the conversation moved on. As a young science aficionado, I was more interested in an explanation of how the seismometers worked. My father, perhaps without knowing the revolution he was about to start in his daughter's mind, took me over to one of the cabins and knocked on the door. Out came a woman carrying a long roll of seismic graphs. Her name was Nazia, and she was one of the company's first female field engineers. I was dumbstruck as she greeted us and remained so as she explained how the seismometers worked. I didn't ask any follow-up questions on the technology, as I normally would have, to the misery of most adults. Instead, my mind was buzzing with questions about *her*—but I was too shy to ask them directly. I spent the rest of the visit waiting impatiently to get back to the car.

When we did finally start driving back, I launched into a stream of questions. How come Nazia was a field engineer? Despite growing up around geophysicists, geologists, and field engineers, I had never heard of a woman in these professions, and I'd certainly never seen one. How come she was allowed to be at the field? I didn't know women could work in a place full of men or live in a gas field trailer alone. What did her parents or husband think? I didn't think a woman could make such a bold choice without someone granting her permission. How could she wear *shalwar kameez*—the long shirt and loose trousers that most women in Pakistan wear—with a hard hat and boots? The only outdoorsy type of women I had ever seen were women working in rice fields, who dressed in traditional local outfits, or adventurous women in Western books and movies who wore

Western clothes. A Pakistani white-collar woman in local clothes working in a gas field and using the safety equipment required in such an environment was more cognitive dissonance than my ten-year-old mind could handle.

My questions and the assumptions and biases behind them were a product of the time and place I grew up in. In 1990, only 2 percent of college-age women in Pakistan actually went to university, and barely 13 percent went to high school. Fewer than four million adult women—just 14 percent of the total adult female population—were part of the Pakistani workforce. Of course I had met educated, working women. There were my teachers in school, and my mother and grandmother were teachers. The latest doctor I had visited had been a woman, and one of my aunts was a doctor. Yet, despite their proximity to my life, and even with a child's eye, I knew that working women were very rare in the society around me and that teaching and medicine were among the very few professions in which women's work was socially sanctioned.[1]

But a woman who studied to become a field engineer and then chose to practice her profession on a gas field full of men—her image is burned into my mind to this day because of all that she represented. A woman who held her own in a man's world. An educated woman who earned her own money. A woman who made her own independent choices. A woman who was respected professionally by men like my father and his colleagues. She was a type of woman I had never before seen in my young life. The type of woman most girls in Pakistan didn't get to see. But once seen, she could not be unseen.

For men like my father, who was already convinced that women should be able to study, having these early pioneering female colleagues showed them firsthand that their daughters might have a viable path for professional fulfillment too, even in fields that men of my father's generation had never considered. As the first in his family to go to university, my father saw education as a path to the middle class. But he also enjoyed learning, and so he was always trying to expand our minds with talk of science, math, and politics, subjects he loved to discuss. Soon after that trip to the gas field—and soon after Nazia's start in the company—he began to speculate excitedly about all the things we could do with our future acquired knowledge. In one such chat, he proposed that my sister could become a pilot, because the Pakistan Air Force had just started to train women. Another time he speculated that I could become a news anchor, because Pakistan Television, the state-owned television network, had starting recruiting more women. At first, I was surprised, just as I was when I met Nazia. I had never imagined that these were possibilities for us, because, well, we were girls and I thought our options were limited. We could go into teaching or even medicine perhaps, if we were lucky. But before long I too caught his enthusiasm and was imagining a new future for myself. Change was in the air.

That change has accelerated very rapidly since the turn of the millennium. Since 1990, when there were fewer than four million working women in a Pakistani population of 107 million, the population has almost doubled, but the number of working women has nearly quadrupled, and much of that acceleration happened in the last decade. Fifteen million women now participate in Pakistan's labor force.[2] Working women are still a small percentage of the adult female population—around 25 percent—but the increase in their numbers represents an economic and cultural shift of enormous magnitude.

Fifteen million women are renegotiating their own and their families' norms and values. They are setting out of the house for reasons their mothers never had. They are earning an income, as only their fathers, husbands, and brothers may have done in the past. They are spending their new income in new ways, exercising power over markets that may have ignored them in the past or simply never existed without their purchasing power. They are shaping their workplaces—schools, hospitals, corporate offices, armies, factories, and yes, gas fields—in unprecedented ways. They are envisaging a different future for their daughters and changing their sons' preconceptions of women's role in society as limited just because of who they are. And by planting the seed of an idea in the minds of millions of other little girls, the daughters of their neighbors, friends, and relatives—the idea that they too can work someday—they are spreading a movement from one generation to another.

This shift has not been limited to Pakistan. A quiet but powerful tsunami of working women has swept across the Muslim world. In all, 155 million women work in the Muslim world today, and fifty million of them—a full third—have joined the workforce since the turn of the millennium alone, a formidable migration from home to work in the span of less than a generation.

As a result, more young Muslim women work and earn an income than ever before in the history of Islam. Through this simple but unprecedented act, they have changed their own destiny, the future of their economies, the shape of their societies, and perhaps even the world.

A Role Model at the Origin

The first convert to Islam was a businesswoman.

She was a wealthy trader who inherited her father's business and later expanded it into an even more impressive enterprise. At one point, she offered a job to a man. He accepted, and then conducted a trading mission from Mecca to Syria under the tutelage of his female CEO.

Her name was Khadija, he was the Prophet Muhammad, and the two later married.

Khadija's personal loyalty and dedication to the Prophet were essential pillars of support in their early days of spreading the message of Islam. So too was the safety net of wealth and financial independence she was able to provide for him and early converts in a hostile environment.

These details were taught so dryly and rapidly in my childhood schools—and indeed even in schools today—that it took me until now, while researching this book, to realize how much subtle power they might hold in shaping the minds of Muslim women. For many Muslim girls and young women, Khadija is one of the few influential female role models they learn about through their own religion. She, perhaps more than anyone else in the history of the religion, legitimizes the possibility of Muslim women's independence, both economically and socially.

The epic battle between work, professional fulfillment, and selfhood, on the one hand, and marriage and motherhood, on the other, plays out in many cultures around the world. Although scholars and religious authorities' interpretations of Islam on the matter of women's education, work, and family roles vary vastly by sect and geography, there is near-universal reverence among Muslims for Khadija, who is often referred to as the Mother of the Believers. This reverence sends a powerful if implicit signal, to ordinary men and women alike, that women who work and earn money can also be *good* wives and mothers. It underscores that women's economic independence can be good for all without being in conflict with their family roles.

Today Khadija's legacy is reflected in the fifty million women who are emerging as new economic actors. These entrepreneurs, employees, and CEOs are redefining what it means to be a woman in the modern Muslim world.

There is an untold and still unfolding story hidden in the lives of these women, and it started in their classrooms. In just a generation or two, a widespread education movement has elevated the prospects of women in Muslim countries, especially in the Arab states of the Persian Gulf, parts of North Africa, the newly industrializing countries of Southeast Asia, and Central and Western Asia. Most of these governments, especially those that possess oil wealth, have made massive investments in education over the last decades, rapidly lifting primary and secondary education rates from abysmally low starting points only forty years ago. Progress in sub-Saharan Africa and South Asia has been slower.

The shift has also occurred for women in higher education. In twothirds of the Muslim-majority countries covered here (see the next section), university enrollment rates for women now exceed those for men, in part owing to investments put in place several decades ago. In Algeria, Bahrain, Kazakhstan, Kuwait, Kyrgyzstan, Qatar, Tunisia, and the United Arab Emirates, women's university enrollment rates are higher than those of men by double digits. In many countries of the Muslim world, these education revolutions are much bigger than in other emerging markets. In Bahrain, Iran, Kazakhstan, Kyrgyzstan, Turkey, and Saudi Arabia, university enrollment of college-age women *exceeds* rates in Mexico, China, Brazil, and India.

With female education becoming deeply rooted and normalized within family structures, the next wave of change has started to build: women are going to work. Where are these fifty million women? Over nine million new women have entered the labor force in the Middle East and North Africa (MENA) region, over ten million in Indonesia, over ten million in Bangladesh, over eight million in Pakistan, nearly three million in Turkey, over two million in Iran, and over a million each in Malaysia, Sudan, and Uzbekistan.

These ordinary women have made conscious, and often deeply personal and brave, decisions to do something—*work*—that is at once mundane and yet utterly profound. This extraordinary shift is at its heart a dramatic human movement in which economics trumps culture.

And it has happened at unprecedented speed. The changes in women's employment that took place over the course of half a century in the United States have been compressed into just a little over a decade in today's Muslim world, where they are set to continue at a significantly faster pace. Imagine if the United States had been transformed in just a few years from the era of the "Feminine Mystique" in the 1960s to the "Lean-In" era of the 2010s. In essence, that is the magnitude of the change sweeping the working women of the Muslim world today. The context, however, for this exponential change—the economic drivers, the use of technology, the globalization of goods and ideas, the cultural caution, and the societal adaptation—is entirely unique to this moment in the Muslim world.

The Muslim World

Today's Muslim world comprises 1.6 billion people, one-fifth of the world's population. Half of these people are women: one in every ten of us on the planet, or eight hundred million women in all. That's more than the combined populations of the United States, Russia, and Brazil. Or put another way, there are more Muslim women in the world than there are Chinese women or Indian women, who hail from the two most populous countries in the world.

The oft-uttered phrase "the Muslim world" suggests a monolithic body but in fact covers a vast spread of geographies, cultures, and economies. Most of the world's Muslims live in over fifty countries where they are the majority. These include the oil-rich states of the Arabian Gulf—Bahrain, Kuwait, Oman, Qatar, Saudi Arabia, and the United Arab Emirates (UAE)—which boast very high per capita incomes and relatively small populations.[3] Countries such as Malaysia, Turkey, Iran, Jordan, and Tunisia have upper-middle-income levels, with annual income per capita between US$4,000 and US$12,000. The nations where the per capita income falls in the lower-middle range include Morocco, Pakistan, Indonesia, Egypt, Bangladesh, and Tajikistan. Finally, the Muslim countries with low income per capita include economies and cultures as diverse as Afghanistan, Mali, and Niger. Many Muslims also live in countries where they are not a majority but their absolute numbers are still in the millions, like India, Nigeria, and Ethiopia.

This book looks at thirty countries in particular for data: those with at least 60 percent Muslim citizens, populations over one million, and an average annual income of US$1,026 per capita or higher.[4] Sixteen are in the MENA region—Algeria, Bahrain, Egypt, Iran, Iraq, Jordan, Kuwait, Libya, Morocco, Oman, Qatar, Saudi Arabia, Syria, Tunisia, the United Arab Emirates, and Yemen. Two are in sub-Saharan Africa—Sudan and Mauritania. Eight are in Europe and Central Asia—Azerbaijan, Kazakhstan, Kosovo, Kyrgyzstan, Tajikistan, Turkey, Turkmenistan, and Uzbekistan. Finally, two are in South Asia—Pakistan and Bangladesh—and two are in East Asia—Indonesia and Malaysia. Six of these economies are high-income, ten are upper-middle-income, and fourteen are lower-middle-income. In all, they account for 1.2 billion Muslims.

The combined gross domestic product (GDP) (adjusted for purchasing power parity [PPP]) of these thirty Muslim-majority countries, at nearly US$14 trillion, represents almost 12 percent of global GDP. This percentage of GDP is nearly as high as that of the two largest economies in the world, the United States (over US$18 trillion) and China (over US$19 trillion), according to 2015 figures. Since the turn of the millennium, half of these thirty countries have had average growth rates of 5 percent or more. In that same fifteen-year period, the United States grew by 2 percent, Brazil by slightly more than 3 percent, China by over 9 percent, and India by 7 percent.[5]

Many of these Muslim economies continue to be a source of international interest, owing to their large market size, natural resources, agricultural production, manufacturing, and tourism and other services—or their geopolitical relevance. The high-income, oil-producing Muslim countries have provided the fuel base for much of the world's energy needs during the last decades; even as oil prices have plunged, they remain attractive markets. The middle-income group includes some of the highest-potential markets in the Muslim world. Six of them—Bangladesh, Egypt, Indonesia, Iran, Pakistan, and Turkey—were identified by Goldman Sachs as among the "Next 11" economies with promising outlooks for investment and future growth.[6] Most of them have in fact lived up to their promises for growth, despite the global economic crisis and the political instability several of them have experienced recently.

According to the data, each of these economies has already experienced major changes in women's education and employment—and they are poised for more. This is not to suggest that the work is complete, nor that the advent of "womenomics" in the Muslim world has led to gender equality or even debate over the desirability of gender equality, in the economy or otherwise.[7] The gaps between women's and men's labor force participation remain large across most Muslim-majority countries. Many women are still held back by cultures, norms, and religious interpretations that diminish their opportunity to learn or earn—and that sometimes even curtail their basic safety, identity, and dignity. Many live in countries where poor governance, conflict, or economic downturns, rather than culture, hold back generations of both women and men from education and jobs.

But in the aggregate, the change under way today is unleashing a domino effect that may well be unstoppable. As more and more girls go to school and university, and as more and more women join the workforce, they change the world around them through their new-found agency. Their talents, skills, spending power, and ideas are a vital fuel for the economies of their countries. In the Middle East alone, if female labor force participation rose to its full potential by 2025, the GDP of the region would spike by 47 percent.[8] Even if female participation across the MENA region were to rise only to the same levels as the best-performing country in the region by 2015, estimates suggest an 11 percent increase in GDP. The simple and yet extraordinarily complex phenomenon of *women working* can lead to economic prosperity—and strengthen the conditions for greater societal stability—in the Muslim world.

Businesses and policymakers are starting to notice, and what they do next will guide some of the most important change the Muslim world has ever seen. If they begin in earnest the broader regulatory work of eliminating barriers to women's participation in their companies and economies, they will unleash the power of the new female economy. And that matters not only to the eight hundred million women in the Muslim world but to the world at large.

Although the majority of their populations identify as Muslim, the countries covered in this book are by no means economically, racially, and culturally homogenous. Far from it. Interpretations and sects of Islam also vary greatly across and within these economies. Some people are deeply pious, others are nominally practicing, and some practice not at all. But these countries all share the common thread of Muslim identity, however weak or strong it may be in each society. And the same forces that are exposing the Western world and the Muslim world to each other are also leading to more exchange and exposure *within* the Muslim world, including among working women who are noticing the diversity of ways in which different types of Muslim women are reconciling work, family, and faith.

Untold Stories

I love data. Data reveal fascinating patterns that allow us to see that large numbers of people are making new decisions. It's what first got me excited about writing this book.

But while data reveal trends, they do not tell us why trends occur. To understand what these numbers about Muslim women's employment meant, I needed to learn more about the lives of the women who represent them. I spoke to 200 women, as well as some men, from different classes, countries, and professions to understand the factors that led fifty million Muslim women to the workforce, an act with scant precedent in their own families and little public backing in their societies. I reported from inside their homes to understand individual and household decisions, from inside the businesses that sought their skills and their cash, and from inside the government agencies trying to regulate this enormous economic opportunity. In all, I visited sixteen countries, representing just over half of the thirty that this book's data foundation rests on and nearly 70 percent of their population: I went to Tunisia, Morocco, and Egypt in North Africa; Saudi Arabia, Jordan, Iran, the United Arab Emirates, Kuwait, Qatar, and Bahrain in the Middle East; Turkey and Azerbaijan at the edges of Europe; Pakistan in South Asia; Kazakhstan in Central Asia; and Indonesia and Malaysia in East Asia.

The challenge that I had expected—that of gaining access to the homes and workplaces of these women, across a range of income levels—was almost never a problem. From my very first reporting trip

I came away surprised at not only the number of people, men and women alike, who were willing to help me get access to the women I wanted to profile but also the women's candor once I reached them. We discussed their new education and employment opportunities, the impact on their families, and their hopes for the future. Over the course of our conversations, we navigated a minefield of potential taboos—money, marriage, clothing, and religion—with unexpected frankness.[9]

Within the first few minutes of our encounters, my interviewees would often ask *me* questions, and three in particular: Where was I from originally? Was I from a Muslim family? And what was I writing about? After giving my answers—*I am from Pakistan, and yes, my family is Muslim, and I am trying to find out the realities behind the numbers about working women in your country*—I often felt like I had passed some kind of test. Many expressed frustration that even though they could *feel* the positive changes in their daily lives and see them reflected in the anecdotes of a growing number of women around them, the narrative about Muslim women remains largely negative in the West and largely unspoken within their own societies. Some stated outright that they were tired of seeing only negative stories about Muslim women coming out of the West and hoped their story could contribute to changing that portrayal. Others felt strongly that while women's growing educational and employment opportunities are indeed important, the traditional choices of motherhood and marriage should be respected too. But whatever their personal views, I often left receiving hugs, handshakes, or blessings from my interviewees, with appeals to "make sure you tell our story."

They had a point. When it comes to Muslim countries, the public conversation in the West often stalls on extremism and security. Surely, these are important, if not evocative, narratives. But they are far from the only narratives. When it comes to women in the Muslim world, there are major concerns, ranging from discriminatory laws to policing of their clothing to physical violence to honor killings carried out in the name of religion or culture. But there is also rising education and employment among them that has unfurled economic, social, and political power they have not had before. Both of these narratives can be true at the same time, in the same countries, in the same cities, in the same communities, and sometimes even within the same families. Women's economic empowerment opens up the path to other forms of agency. And the widening set of choices for one set of women slowly opens up choices for other women in their societies. Economics trumps culture—and then shapes culture.

One way to understand this book is to know what it is not. It is not the tired story of the downtrodden women of Islam. Neither is it an unrealistic and apologetic ode to the respectful place granted to women in Islamic societies. The reality is more complex. This book is about the new opportunities changing the everyday lives of millions of women in the Muslim world and the dynamism they are bringing to their communities and economies. It is written for these women but also for those men and women—policymakers, business leaders, civil society leaders, and individuals—who want to learn more about them, grow their numbers, and support them, rather than save or censure them.

As I was writing, I considered the potential reactions to a book that focuses on a segment of women in Muslim societies for whom a largely positive economic story is unfolding. My Western readers might wonder why I do not elaborate more on those women who have not been part of the education revolution, or those who face the overt discrimination and, at times, violence that have become almost synonymous with women's treatment in Muslim societies. And when I thought about my Muslim world readers, I also felt conflicted. These societies, just like any other in the world, are mosaics, and addressing just one part of the story, especially when there is a hunger among young Muslim women for narratives that reflect the diversity and complexity of their experience, could be construed as an oversimplification.

I understand—and anticipate—these points of view. I ultimately chose to keep the focus on the growing segment of working women across the vast section of humanity that makes up all Muslim women, because their story remains largely untold. Understanding more about their lives is imperative for understanding the rest of their modern societies, today and in the future. I start by laying out the shift in education over the last decades and how it created the foundation for the present-day trends in the labor force. I then dive deeper into the implications for women who have made the migration from home to work and the uncharted waters they often have to navigate in their societies as they do so, the unprecedented new opportunities offered to them by digital technologies, and the impact of their newly expanded set of options on the marriage market. Next, I explore the role of leaders—in both the economic and political space—in helping or hindering the change under way, and finally, what the future might hold for the working women of the Muslim world. I share the lives of about thirty women—and men—in depth in the pages that follow in addition to insights from scores of others. Some are low-skilled workers; others are intellectuals or business practitioners; still others are some of the richest or most powerful business and political leaders in the world. Through their stories, across their countries and regions, we can begin to understand how the sweeping changes in education and employment for women unfolded and how they are creating a new future.

The millions of individual decisions being made in households and families about education and employment for women eventually add up to a massive new segment of work and productivity, and subsequently an unprecedented rising—and very likely disruptive—*power*. If these women, Khadija's modern-day daughters, are successful in harnessing that power, they may well unleash a new golden age in the Muslim world.

one

Education Pioneers

ONE OF THE MOST POWERFUL FIGURES IN MY LIFE WAS MY maternal grandmother. Unlike most women of her generation in Pakistan, she was relatively well educated, having earned a bachelor's degree. The only girl among five siblings, she graduated from high school in 1932, a time when most girls simply never went to school. Then, while teaching at a high school in Punjab, she began to study for a teaching degree. Studying—and working—outside the home was rare among the female native Muslim population in British India at the time, and my grandmother donned a full burqa when heading to work to protect her modesty.

Her Kashmiri parents sent the boys to college but wouldn't agree to send her, as the nearest college was in another city and it would have been frowned upon in their rural community to send a young girl away alone. They did, however, allow her to continue independent studies toward the degree from home. When she was selected for a government scholarship to complete her bachelor's degree in teaching (now bachelor of education) from Lady Maclagan Training College in Lahore, her parents realized that she was gifted and they agreed to let her attend. She spent the two decades after her graduation teaching high school history, English, and physical education. Unexpectedly, at age thirty-nine, she married my grandfather, ten years her junior; theirs was a highly unconventional match in the early 1950s in the new independent nation of Pakistan.

My grandmother insisted that all four of her own children—all daughters—complete university education; overcoming her and her husband's initial cultural discomfort because her own parents had eventually agreed to do the same for her, she sent them to large public urban universities in the 1970s. Her eldest daughter, my mother, holds one of the first PhDs in environmental science in the country, and she retired last year after a thirty-year teaching career in Islamabad. Her other daughters, my aunts, are also professional women: one is a public health professional, one is a high-ranking government official, and the youngest is a food business owner. They are all part of the small but growing Pakistani middle class that provides a vital and stable economic backbone in an often volatile political environment.

The impact of education ripples across time, changing what people pass on to future generations. I grew up in the 1980s and 1990s between Lahore, the cultural heart of Pakistan, and Islamabad, the country's capital. It was common practice to spend weeks if not months during school holidays with paternal and maternal grandparents, so we often visited my maternal grandparents in their rural rice-farming town in central Punjab. I have fond memories of listening to my grandmother's stories about her daughters when they were children, but also of having her help me with my homework and forever imparting a love of languages as she tried to teach me some Farsi, her third language in addition to Urdu and English.

I might have thought this was quite normal were it not for the fact that my paternal grandmother, like the majority of women of her generation, was not as well educated. For a brief period after high school, she had started training as a nurse but was soon stopped by one of her brothers. She would often tell her children that had she been able to continue she would surely and rapidly have become a matron (chief nurse). Having traveled for a brief time on a path to economic independence and having believed in her own leadership abilities, she knew what might have been possible. But having been stopped, she also saw the roadblocks for women in her society. Unsurprisingly, she would often lament the fact that there were too many female grandchildren in her family. This sentiment echoed much of what I heard in the society around me, so I never found it shocking. She didn't love her granddaughters any less than she would have loved grandsons—she was constantly praying for us, cooking our favorite foods, and using her natural storytelling abilities to share old folk tales. But it was common to hear adults around me, both male and female, sometimes even other children, kindly wish for our family to have more sons. My maternal grandmother, however, never expressed this desire. Instead, she always encouraged us girls to study, to learn, and to expand our minds. I loved both my grandmothers of course, but at a very young age I started to realize that my maternal grandmother's life was rare for her time and that education, followed by economic opportunity, had been fundamental to creating a different mind-set and a different path for her.

My grandmother's, mother's, and aunts' stories used to be unusual. But today they are representative of the education revolution happening in millions of families in Pakistan—and more broadly across the Muslim world. The education revolution has created a virtuous cycle of vastly more education coupled with economic independence for a new generation. Its implications, for these countries and for the world at large, are profound.

A Revolution in the Muslim World

The billion and a quarter people who live in the thirty Muslim-majority economies this book covers are a relatively young population. Their countries' economic growth has been accompanied by a demographic transition in recent decades: mortality rates have declined faster than fertility rates, resulting in rapid population growth. Muslims are therefore younger, with a median age of twenty-three years, than the overall global population (median age of twenty-eight years).[1] For example, in Pakistan and Egypt, nearly one-third of each nation's population is between the ages of fifteen and twenty-nine. This youth bulge represents the Muslim world's own "baby boom"—a new generation that holds new attitudes, has acquired new knowledge, and uses new technologies that were never available to the generation before them.

This fifteen- to twenty-nine-year-old Muslim cohort is also the most educated generation ever seen in these countries, and the largest cohort to have entered the labor market in these economies at one time. Roughly half of them have a primary education, one-third have secondary education, and nearly one in ten have continued with college or additional schooling. And this advance in education levels has been rapid. For example, in Saudi Arabia under 2 percent of all young adults of college age in 1970 were in college.[2] By 1990, that figure had reached 9 percent. Today 57 percent of college-age Saudis are in college—roughly the same level as the United States in 1983.

This exponential growth in university education has not been limited to the wealthiest countries. In Turkey, for instance, the number of college-age people enrolled in college has gone up from 5 percent in 1970 and 13 percent in 1990 to 79 percent today—about the same as the United States in 2003. There are some exceptions. In Pakistan, Afghanistan, and the low-income economies of sub-Saharan Africa, the university enrollment rate is still under 10 percent. And in three former Soviet republics—Azerbaijan, Uzbekistan, and Turkmenistan—the rates have declined slightly since the high levels reached during the final years of the Soviet Union. Yet broadly speaking, not only are these economies growing, but they are poised for further growth because the younger members of their workforces are more educated than before.[3]

Most remarkable, however, is who receives this education. In 1947, when Pakistan was formed and when my grandmother was teaching at a girls' school, the literacy rate for women was only around 12 percent; by 1980, the year I was born, it had risen only to 15 percent.[4] Today it's around 46 percent. Although there is a long way to go before all girls and women in Pakistan attain basic literacy, the pace of change in the last thirty-five years far exceeds that of the preceding thirty-five years. What's more, the rate of change has sped up for girls in particular over the last decade or so, compared to boys, although there is still a persistent gender gap in education indicators. Primary enrollment in 2002 was at 48 percent for girls and 70 percent for boys. Today it's at 67 percent for girls and 78 percent for boys. Girls have enrolled at more than twice the rate that boys have over the last decade as access to education improves and more and more Pakistani families break with tradition and send their daughters to school for the first time. Secondary enrollment for girls was at 28 percent in 2006 while boys were at 36 percent. Today 36 percent of girls and 46 percent of boys are enrolled in secondary education. In university, only 2 percent of women and 3 percent of men enrolled a decade ago. Today there are more women than men enrolled in higher education, at just a little over 10 percent.

This unprecedented catch-up, which would have been unthinkable in my grandmother's generation or my mother's generation or even during my own college years in the early 2000s, has occurred in every single Muslim-majority country, leading to a complete reversal of the university gender gap in some cases. In some countries, the catch-up has been so pronounced that there are now more women than men in university. For example, in Indonesia, women's enrollment has gone up from under 2 percent in 1970 to nearly 33 percent today. By contrast, men's enrollment has gone up from slightly more than 4 percent in 1970 to 29 percent today. In those countries where the gaps between male and female university enrollments haven't yet closed, they soon will. In Turkey, both women and men enroll in university in much greater numbers than before, but women are enrolling at higher rates than men. Even in countries where the overall numbers in higher education have not made a leap, women's enrollment rates are going up faster than men's, bringing women closer to parity with men in university enrollment.[5]

As a result of these shifts, the education gender gap—in primary, secondary, and higher education—in the current working-age population in the Muslim world is already the narrowest it has ever been in history. Of the 240 million men who are twenty-five or older across the thirty countries studied here, 30 million have a university education. Of the 236 million women in these countries in the same age cohort, nearly 25 million hold university degrees. In the future workforces of these economies, this gap will disappear entirely if recent enrollment trends hold. Overall, of the 32 million young people currently enrolled in tertiary education across the Muslim world, half are women.[6]

These changes are even more significant because they represent very large proportions of the younger women in these countries' populations, numbers that are often higher than in many other emerging markets. For example, in Saudi Arabia ten years ago, about 30 percent of university-age women attended university. Today half of all university-age women attend university in Saudi Arabia—a higher figure than in Mexico, China, Brazil, or India.

The future of younger generations looks promising too. Of the thirty large Muslim-majority economies covered here, most now have either education parity or higher primary and secondary enrollment for girls compared to boys. In all, of the nearly ninety-two million young people enrolled in secondary school across the Muslim-majority countries, over fifty million—more than half—are now girls. Even in countries where there is still much to be done to improve overall enrollment ratios, parity indicates that those girls and boys who do get an education have equal opportunities to develop foundational skills.[7]

The paths taken by many of these countries to get to these education rates for women were not self-evident. Most Muslim-majority emerging markets of today were colonies of other nations in the recent past and became independent mainly in the second half of the twentieth century. For most of these newly independent nations, investment in education was a logical path to growth and development. However, investment in girls' education was not a given, owing in large part to the local customs. In some countries, change has taken decades and the equal inclusion of women in education is still not complete. External nudges tied to development aid have, in some instances, provided incentives for progress. But in most countries, the leadership of local pioneers blazed the trail for girls' access to education.

The United Arab Emirates is one such example. Soon after its founding in December 1971, Sheikh Zayed bin Sultan Al Nahyan, the ruler of Abu Dhabi and the first president of the young nation, let it be known that a strong emphasis would be placed on education for all, despite local traditions: "The real asset of any advanced nation is its people, especially the educated ones, and the prosperity and success of the people are measured by the standard of their education." One of his seven wives, Fatima, often called the "mother of the nation," joined these efforts. Sometimes this meant convincing their fellow ruling families to set the example by enrolling their own children in schools, while at other times it meant persuading low-income families that such a change was beneficial to them and to their nation. Sometimes cash transfers were given as incentives to enroll girls in order to overcome both conservative attitudes and financial constraints. Even though he lacked a formal education himself, Sheikh Zayed had the foresight to exercise leadership on this issue. A half century later, the UAE has more than twice as many women in university as men and full school enrollment for boys and girls. It is also regarded as a hub for talent in the region, attracting nearly 200 nationalities to live and work there, in no small part because the country has invested in building a culture of education for all.

Other countries, with fewer resources, have taken more circuitous paths to increasing girls' education. In the early days of the education revolution across the postcolonial Muslim world, education was often either considered an elite activity or provided through religious or charity institutions, through a combination of local and foreign educators, both secular and religious. My paternal grandmother went to secondary school at a convent run by nuns, a relic from the British era that continues to this day in some parts of Pakistan. But over time, elite schools and religious institutions—which also continue to grow, in the form of *madrassas*—were supplemented by both mass public education and private schooling designed for the emerging middle class. And as teaching became one of the most socially acceptable professions for educated women, a steady supply of new female educators became available. The education revolution grew exponentially as both the number of female teachers and the number of parents demanding their services for their daughters started expanding rapidly. This was particularly important because education remained—and remains to this day in many cases—sex-segregated in many Muslim countries, especially at the secondary level.[8]

A Virtuous Cycle

Research from various parts of the world shows that education, especially girls' education, multiplies across generations.[9] An educated woman is more likely to educate her children, both sons and daughters. In addition, better-educated women tend to be healthier, to participate more in the formal labor market, to earn more income, to have fewer and healthier children, and to provide better health care and education to their children, all of which can eventually improve the well-being of all individuals and lift entire households out of poverty. In the course of writing this book, I didn't meet a single parent, even among the most conservative households, who came to regret their decision to make that additional, difficult investment in their daughters' education, regardless of resource constraints. If anything, they soon realized how much their investment had paid off and took an enormous amount of pride in the accomplishments of their daughters. Indeed, because their expectations had been so low, some were even more proud of their daughters than their sons.

As the benefits of girls' education transmit across generations, entire communities begin to realize its value and reap its rewards. Development professionals consider girls' education a strategic development investment because it brings a wide range of benefits, not only for the girls themselves but also for their children, their communities, and society in terms of economic growth. Education for young women has been described by the World Bank as the single greatest investment a developing country can make. The reverse is also true. The exclusion of girls from education considerably hinders the productive potential of an economy and its overall development. In the Asia-Pacific region, it has been estimated that between US$16 billion and US$30 billion is lost annually as a result of gender gaps in education. The World Bank finds, based on a sample of a wide range of developing countries, that investing in girls so that they complete education at the same rate as boys would lead to lifetime earnings increases of today's cohort of girls of between 54 and 68 percent of countries' GDP, equivalent to an increase in annual GDP growth rates of about 1.5 percent.[10]

This recognition of the potential for a virtuous cycle is making its way across much of the Muslim world, changing underlying norms and behaviors. Although in the past girls' education may have been an elite activity, in most middle-income families across the Muslim world today, especially those in urban areas, it's now the accepted norm to educate girls at least up to secondary school and increasingly as far as university. Fathers and mothers, ministers and imams, have all been a part of the change in mind-set and the resulting education trends. The result is millions of young women equipped with degrees and diplomas.

I have long known that education changed my own prospects for economic independence and my hopes and dreams for the future. In the course of meeting hundreds of young women and speaking to many others, I saw how universal this pattern has been across the Muslim world. Girls' education has enhanced earning capacity and lifted women out of poverty. It has led to new professional ambitions for young women, often in fields that their mothers' generation would never have thought of entering. And it has empowered girls and young women within their families, strengthening their capacity to carve out their own path in society. These changes are nothing short of revolutionary.

A Taste of Meritocracy

One chilly winter morning in 2015 in Islamabad, the capital of Pakistan, I made my way to a local McDonald's to meet with its female staff. Passing through the metal detectors, I joked to the local branch manager that I had gone from the country with the most expensive Big Macs in the world—Switzerland—to the country with the most protected Big Macs in the world, given the extreme security at all Western-owned companies in Pakistan. The manager, Amir, gave me an overview of the patient experiment conducted by McDonald's in engaging female staff, something previously unheard of in customer-facing service roles in the food business. He then led me to a private room where a large group of young female staff members were sitting on neon-colored furniture, surrounded by walls covered in large photos of children's faces. Although all of them wore identical dark uniforms and black veils (*dupattas*), Saadia, a natural leader, stood out immediately. She seemed nearly as keen to ensure that I felt comfortable asking questions as I felt to ensure that they felt comfortable answering them.

Saadia is twenty-three years old and lives in the Chakklala neighborhood of Rawalpindi, Islamabad's nearby twin city. Chakklala used to be a rural area, but today it holds the main airport serving the two cities, an army and air force base, and several residential "housing schemes." As it rapidly urbanized, it became home to families like Saadia's who have made the transition in just one generation from a rural or semirural lifestyle to an urban one as the landscape around them changed. Her big extended family lives together in a typical *mohalla*—uncles, aunts, cousins, and grandparents all living together in the same house or in houses adjacent to each other. Meals are often eaten together, social life revolves around the extended family, and celebrations and sorrows are shared. Child care, elder care, household chores, and errands outside the home are also shared, as is income, often indirectly, across the family members. And older generations are intimately involved in all the decisions of the younger ones—whether to study, what to study, whether to work, where to work, who to marry, and when to marry. Saadia is the youngest of her siblings—one of three sisters and a brother, who is her parents' safety net. In her family, as in many others across Pakistan, girls are often considered temporary members of a family because they will one day join their husband's family. So parents often invest less in their daughters than in their sons. Boys become prized children, while girls are considered a burden; thus, boys often receive the lion's share of their parents' investment in education, with the expectations of a higher return compared to girls.

Saadia's parents made their choices a little differently. Although they invested less in the girls than in the one boy, they invested in them nonetheless. Saadia and her sisters are truly first-generation education revolutionaries. Their mother received no education at all, as their grandfather didn't believe girls should be educated. Their father, on the other hand, served, before retiring, as the vice principal of a coeducational homeopathic medical college, preparing students for practicing the traditional medicine that is still favored by many low-income families over Western medicine.

I assumed that it was Saadia's father, an educator, who chose to educate his girls, but Saadia credits her education to the insistence of her mother, who didn't want her daughters to suffer the same injustice she did. "My mother was never permitted to study, but she always supported us and always motivated us to study," Saadia explained. One of her sisters studied to become a nurse while the other became a schoolteacher, but both stopped working after their arranged marriages. Her brother is a medical doctor, lives at his parents' home with his wife and children, and gives his entire income to his parents, who head the household.

Saadia herself got a bachelor's of commerce from the Rawalpindi College of Commerce. A degree was change enough between her mother's generation and hers. With her elder sisters having carved out the path to the workplace already, the act of working was not revolutionary for Saadia, even though it was still somewhat new for women in the family. But then Saadia deviated from tradition even further. A friend of hers had started working at McDonald's and invited her to join the company. She told her mother that McDonald's is "such a safe and nice place to work, especially for girls," and that she wanted to join her friend there. Her mother's first question was about the uniform; she was familiar with the Westernized version of the local shalwar kameez that most McDonald's service staff wear. Saadia suggested that she would wear the hijab with the uniform. Satisfied, Saadia's mother went to persuade her father and succeeded. "To this day, he hasn't questioned me about my job," said Saadia.

In Pakistan, McDonald's is middle-class food; one meal costs much more than most families have for their weekly food budget. Saadia's own family would only rarely be able to afford eating there. So working in McDonald's holds very different connotations in Pakistan than it does in the United States and Europe. But working at McDonald's does have a specific stigma for young women in Pakistan, where traditionally women have rarely held roles in the service industry that require face-to-face contact with customers. Nearly all waiters, shopkeepers, bank tellers, and taxi drivers are men. The idea of their daughters serving customers—including male customers—in a mixed-gender work environment is usually the first concern of Pakistani parents, according to Amir, the branch manager. They are less concerned about the actual or perceived risks of such work and usually more concerned about the judgment from their extended families and others in their community. Saadia confirmed this, exclaiming: "Oh my God, so-called uncles and aunts were the main problem. They still are."

But after having seen her success and obvious devotion to her work, her parents, Saadia said, "feel not good but not too bad. Actually, they still have an issue about the uniform—trousers and a relatively short shirt. Otherwise, they don't have any problem." Saadia's "short shirt" goes down to the middle of her thigh but is still less modest—shorter and more fitted—than the traditional shalwar kameez. Her brother's support has helped—he has been a strong advocate, supporting her choice of work, her uniform, and her ambitions. And as for her aunts and uncles? "I'm used to it now. I don't care what they think or say," Saadia declared.

Saadia admitted that she started the part-time job just to "have some fun" and to mitigate the boredom she felt from being at home after her degree. But after joining, she said, "I really liked it and decided to make it a career." As she demonstrated her intelligence, skills, and ability to work hard, she was promoted three times in the two and a half years she had worked there. She went from a part-time crew position to a full-time crew member, then was promoted to crew trainer, and finally became a manager.

Meritocracy and clear pathways in the workplace are relatively new in Pakistan, where ways of working are traditionally shaped by nepotism and favoritism. For young women like Saadia, seeing their efforts rewarded in the workplace, just as they were in school and university, can be eye-opening and thrilling and lead them to become even more motivated to work. The independent income is an almost unexpected bonus. I asked Saadia how she spends her earnings and whether she saves. She gives 30 percent of her income to her parents, she said, and the rest she spends as she pleases: mostly on gifts to her parents, sisters, and friends as well as on lunches and dinners out with friends and gadgets like her cell phone—all new luxuries for her. She said that she has no interest in saving because her parents take care of housing and food, just as she expects her husband will do after she marries. So her disposable income is wholly hers to spend, allowing her to contribute to the household budget while also buying luxuries that were previously unimaginable for her parents, without adding a burden to them.

What about the perceived dangers of working with and serving men? Saadia and the other young women reiterated to me in private what the branch manager had said earlier. McDonald's enforces strict sexual harassment policies to encourage the recruitment and retention of female staff members. Saadia said that her "male coworkers are very supportive, and they all really respect all female workers. Maybe it's because of the strict rules of the company, but I think they really do." Saadia also said that "mostly the customers respect us." Even transport for her hourlong commute has been neutralized as an issue. McDonald's provides her and her female coworkers who work evening shifts with private transport. For day shifts she uses public transport, which is a concern, she said, only because of the possibility of petty crimes committed by pickpockets ("two boys tried to snatch my cell phone recently"). Sexual harassment is not a possibility because of the gender segregation on most public transport.

At twenty-three, Saadia has reached the average age of marriage for women in Pakistan. When I questioned her about marriage plans, she told me that she is currently under no pressure from her parents to marry. They expect her to enter an arranged marriage eventually; "I would like to choose," she said, "but my parents don't like love marriages." One condition she intends to put on any suitor's proposal is that she will continue to work after marriage, unlike her sisters. "I really love to work, but only with McDonald's. I would marry, but not now. I think I should make my career first, then I should marry." She recognizes that, even continuing to work, her role is likely to be seen as caregiving and homemaking, as it still is for most women around the world, so she wants to make more progress in her career before signing up for a double shift.

Saadia is not an anomaly. She said proudly: "You know what? I'm really happy that even from my neighborhood 40 percent of the girls are doing a job." This is remarkable for an area where just one generation ago girls rarely completed secondary school. She said things are truly changing for women, particularly in the last five years. The many women who have gone on to institutions of higher education in the past decade have begun to graduate and join labor markets. Among Saadia's bachelor's of commerce classmates, 60 percent were working, not only because of the awareness and ambitions created by educational opportunities, Saadia thinks, but also because of economic necessity. Even in marriage, she said, things are changing. "Fifty percent of men want their wives to be economically independent, and fifty percent think that wives only have to give birth to babies and look after them and their families."

A new generation of women and men like Saadia have grown up with different mind-sets and aspirations than those of their parents and their communities, shaped by newly acquired educations, new job prospects, and exposure to myriad views, information, and opportunities. Saadia may end up having a long career at McDonald's or elsewhere, or she may end up leaving her job when she marries. But either way, she feels like she has a choice that is hers to make about her future. That alone represents a remarkable shift.

Rational Choices

This isn't to say that there isn't much more work to be done, or that enough women have now had opportunities like Saadia's to go to university and begin working. In many parts of lower-income Muslim economies and also in the higher-income economies with vast regional disparities, education access is still limited—for both boys and girls. This neglect and, sometimes, incapacity by governments to deliver education to their entire populations have left many children and young adults without the opportunity to be educated and to climb out of poverty through higher-skilled work. It starts quite young. Of the sixty-one million children of primary school age across the world who are not in school today, fourteen million live in Muslim-majority economies. Out-of-school children are most common in the low-income and lower-middle-income countries of the Muslim world, and some of these gaps will hamper growth and prosperity for decades to come. For example, in Sudan nearly 45 percent of children who should be in primary school are not. In Pakistan, nearly 27 percent are not enrolled in primary school.

Although there is an ongoing education emergency for girls and boys alike in some regions of the Muslim world, girls are often more likely to lose out in areas with limited access and high poverty. Of the fourteen million children of primary school age who are not in school in the Muslim world, eight million are girls. The gender gaps in primary education are particularly marked in Iraq, Pakistan, and Yemen.[11] In addition to the access issues that apply to girls and boys alike, there continue to be pockets of resistance to girls' education specifically, particularly in poorer, rural areas. Resistance most frequently takes the form of passive discrimination and inertia about changing past practices, especially in areas where access to education is limited, employment opportunities are scarce, and families are large.

Boko Haram's kidnapping of girls in Nigeria's northwest, the Taliban's shutdown of girls' schools in Pakistan's north, and the education emergencies created by war in Syria and Iraq get most of the headlines, but the reality in many communities with low education levels for girls has nothing to do with guns and bombs. Resistance to girls' education is often subtle and more economically than ideologically based. Parents make trade-offs about which of their children they should invest in, if at all, and the traditional lack of economic opportunities for women combines with marriage customs—which are more costly for girls than boys—to maintain the view in many traditionally low-education communities that girls are the lower-return investment.

One of my greatest fears growing up was that one day I might have a brother. This fear was completely rational based on everything I saw around me. Female classmates in my middle-class private school would often switch to a lower-cost public school once their younger brothers started school or their older brothers started university. I knew that my family might make a similar choice faced with such a situation, despite their relatively progressive views. Resources are limited, and sons are culturally expected to support their parents in old age, while daughters are expected to get married and become part of their husband's household. So, unsurprisingly, when it comes to making a choice about whose school fees parents will pay, daughters often lose out. Saadia, for one, had been lucky that her parents invested in her and her sisters, even though she had a brother who was tasked with supporting their parents. Ironically, this lack of investment often creates a self-fulfilling prophecy. If parents don't invest in their girls, girls are certain to be dependent on them and unable to use their skills and talent or achieve their own hopes and dreams.

"Read in the Name of Your Lord"

It is not solely economic calculations holding women back. There are also cultural and ideological forces at play. In some parts of the Muslim world, the resistance to women's education is deeply engrained and traditional views about honor, marriage, and public exposure lead parents to hold girls back from formal education, even when they can afford it or when they have access to free schooling.

By and large these restrictions are cultural rather than religious. Most mainstream interpretations of Islam don't propose any prohibitions to women's education. Islam encourages its believers to seek knowledge and cultivate themselves. The very first Quranic revelation starts with the word "read": "Read: In the Name of your Lord who created. / Created man from a clot. / Read: And your Lord is the Most Generous. / He who taught by the pen. / Taught man what he never knew." Many scholars agree that the words "man" and "believer" when used in the Quran include both men and women and that Islam thus entitles women to the same rights of education as men. In fact, it is considered compulsory and beneficial for women to be educated—it is better for their understanding of religious and social obligations, and better for raising their children in accordance with Islam. And this education is wide-ranging. The concept of knowledge mentioned in the Quran is vast and embraces all types of knowledge; both religious and secular knowledge are considered productive for mankind. Therefore, for women to fully understand Islam, they cannot be withheld from an education that allows both types of learning. There is more debate on certain caveats to this argument. Some suggest that women ideally gain knowledge only from female teachers, to meet the requirements of gender segregation between unrelated men and women. And some cite the verses about the veil to argue against women leaving the house to pursue education, but even these passages state only that, when outside the home, a woman should wear a veil.[12]

Throughout the religion's history, Islam has had women scholars who taught judges and imams, issued fatwas, and toured distant cities, giving lectures across the Middle East. These include Umm al-Darda, a seventh-century jurist and scholar who taught jurisprudence in the mosques of Damascus and Jerusalem and whose students included men, women, and the Caliph. A fourteenth-century scholar, Syrian Fatimah al-Bataihiyyah, gave lectures that drew students from as far away as Fez. She taught both men and women in the Prophet's mosque in Medina. Mohammad Akram Nadwi, a scholar who uncovered the names and works of many of these women in a forty-volume study, said: "I thought I'd find maybe twenty or thirty women," but he ended up finding 8,000 of them. It is possible that these women scholars' names have been ignored—much as women scholars' achievements have been downplayed in Western history—because history has mostly been written by men, with women's contributions left unacknowledged until feminist scholars began to reclaim them. However, it is also plausible that women's lives and works were left largely unrecorded—or at least were never overtly publicized—because Muslim societies, most of which prize female modesty, sought to keep women shielded from public view. The Prophet's wives, while often extolled for their more traditionally feminine virtues, also provide a challenge to views about limiting women's roles. Khadija, to whom he was monogamously married for twenty-five years, was a successful businesswoman. Aisha, one of his subsequent wives, was an Islamic scholar, a military commander, and a jurist.[13]

In some communities where strict interpretations of religion have held women back, working within a religious narrative that highlights

Islam's promotion of women's education has been a powerful tool for overcoming barriers. For example, in Saudi Arabia, until 2002, girls' education was run out of the Department of Religious Guidance, while boys' education was managed by the Ministry of Education. But in most parts of the Muslim world, where it has been economics or tradition holding women back, perhaps more effective has been the direct impact of seeing the positive outcomes of education. In families, communities, villages, cities, and entire countries, as parents see that girls' education has led to benefits for others around them they have begun to take tentative steps toward change for their own daughters.

Dreaming of Fast Cars

Nearly two thousand miles away from where Saadia lives, in Isfahan, a central city in Iran, a similar story has played out. I met Fatima by chance as I tried to enter the Art University of Isfahan. Since the "Green Movement," the protest movement that swept the country after the 2009 Iranian presidential election, universities have become no-go zones for anyone but enrolled students—not even parents can enter the campus premises. I, as a curious visitor, was certainly not allowed to enter. Fatima and a friend spotted me being turned away and offered to try to persuade the security guard to let me in. They told him that they wanted to show me their latest design sketches, which were being kept in one of the classrooms, but he refused to budge. So Fatima and her enterprising friend Mina decided that they wanted to share their stories with me right there, in the beautiful rose-filled garden right outside the security guard's office.

Fatima is an industrial design student at the university. She comes from Mashhad, the second most populous city in all of Iran and the capital of Razavi Khorasan province, close to the border with Turkmenistan and Afghanistan. It is also one of the most deeply religious cities in Iran and attracts millions of pilgrims every year to its holy sites, including the tomb of Imam Reza, a Shia imam. At twenty years old, Fatima is only in the first year of her studies, but in some ways she is ahead of her contemporaries in terms of life experience because she is already married. Getting married was her family's prerequisite for being able to leave her hometown to attend university in Isfahan. The couple is now in a long-distance relationship as her husband, who is a few years older and an expert on water pipes, works for a company in Shiraz, a city farther to the south of Iran. The bus ride is nearly six hours each way, but they try to meet every few weekends.

Fatima is passionate about her choice of subject matter. She told me she wants to design cars—her dream is to work for BMW. I asked her how this dream came about, and she answered simply: "They are the best in the world, and I want to work for the best." Iran's Supreme Leader Ayatollah Ali Khamenei himself has been spotted in a BMW and is rumored to have indirect ownership in some of the dealerships selling foreign luxury cars in the country. But Fatima quickly added that her professor had told her that she was very unlikely to work there, as BMW doesn't manufacture in Iran and, as an Iranian, she would not be accepted for a job in Germany.

When I asked her what she thinks about her job prospects in Iran, both Fatima's and Mina's faces fell. They said that there is an ongoing jobs crisis in the country that is particularly hard for women. In their chosen field, the prospects are uncertain because the automotive sector is struggling under international sanctions.[14] Iran has a 20 percent unemployment rate for women nationally, compared to 9 percent for men. The statistics are even worse for young people—41 percent of young women and 26 percent of young men are unemployed. Both Fatima and Mina know the everyday reality of these statistics. Mina is twenty-four and in her senior year. She has seen some of her older friends graduate and then remain idle—not for lack of trying to find work but simply because of lack of opportunity.

Yet neither young woman doubts her ability to create her own opportunity. They both expect to find a way to work and earn a living—but know that it's unlikely to match their dreams of designing products the world will use. Mina told me she wants to be a student forever, to maintain for a little longer the hope for bright prospects in a distant future and delay the loss of a cherished dream. Saying good-bye to them, I too wished they could stay in their university bubble a little longer, until economic opportunities improved. Those opportunities may arise faster than any of us imagined. Just a few months later, as sanctions were lifted, sales of foreign cars shot up and several European car companies began to draw up plans for assembly and possibly manufacturing facilities in Iran.[15]

Making Hawazen Happy

On the other side of the Persian Gulf, over 1,500 kilometers or 900 miles away in Riyadh, I met Hawazen over lunch at the up-scale Al Faisaliah Hotel. At twenty-eight, she is a few years older than both Saadia and Fatima and further along in her education-to-employment journey. Although Hawazen lives in Saudi Arabia, one of the countries with the most restrictions on women's dress, she clearly enjoys fashion. Wearing expertly applied makeup and flamboyant jewelry, she had on an outfit underneath her richly de-tailed *abaya* that would not have been out of place in a high-end restaurant on a night out in any major metropolis in the world. So I was not surprised when she told me that she is a fashion design graduate. Hawazen studied at the Princess Nora bint Abdul Rah-man University, which, with sixty thousand students and nearly five thousand staff members, is the largest university for women in the world. King Abdullah bin Abdulaziz Al Saud, who died in January 2015, inaugurated the university's modern consolidated campus in 2011 to both promote women's economic role and recognize the dual burden they face. "Women take on the responsibility of more than one role," he said in a statement, "maintaining the stability of society, contributing to building the economy of the country, and representing both society and nation as best as they can."

Today, however, Hawazen does not work in fashion design but is a professional in one of the largest pharmaceutical companies in the country. Noting my surprise, she laughed and said, "I also never thought I would end up doing this, but I have succeeded." Hawazen's journey from studying fashion design to becoming a pharma professional has seen her through a lot of change in the six short years since she graduated. After graduating, Hawazen knew that she wanted to start her own business one day but needed to acquire some skills first. So she started to work at the Al-Nahda Philanthropic Society for Women, helping to bring low-income women's arts and crafts into the mainstream market for clothes, furniture, and decorative accessories. There, she said, she learned the basics of how to deal with people in a professional setting. After six short months, she became engaged to marry through an arrangement facilitated by her parents. Her future husband was living on the East Coast of the United States, and anticipating her upcoming move, Hawazen quit her job. During the short engagement, they talked by phone or Skype to get to know each other a little, but once married the relationship did not turn out to be what either of them was looking for. Hawazen came back after nearly two years abroad and got a divorce. She said, "Sometimes you learn, even from a rough experience. God is making this happen to get me to a better place."

While she was in the United States, she was a stay-at-home spouse, although she had been hoping to enroll in a master's degree program, funded by the Saudi government. Over the last ten years, the King Abdullah Scholarship Program has generously supported nearly 200,000 young Saudis to attend the world's best universities—both men and women, provided the women travel with the consent of their guardian, typically their father if they are single or their husband if they are married. At the time, under Saudi law, women required the permission of a male guardian to travel and marry and, in some cases, to be granted employment or access to health care or other government services. Since then, the laws have become more flexible. According to the Ministry of Higher Education, between one-quarter and one-third of the participants have been women since the program's inception.[16] The scholarship program aims to train youth for areas that are in line with the needs of the Saudi labor market, and it stipulates that beneficiaries return afterward to work in Saudi Arabia. However, Fashion Design and Society, the program Hawazen wanted to study, is not one of those areas, so she decided to put that dream on hold until one day it is approved or she finds another way to get there.

After her divorce and return to Riyadh, Hawazen took a position in a local pharmaceutical company, where, she said, everything was "like Greek," but her natural curiosity led her to learn quickly. She left within a year, though, because she felt that the local company directors and her male peers did not have any interest in advancing her as one of their first female workers.

That was when she was contacted by Glowork, a Saudi platform dedicated to matching skilled women with white-collar jobs through job fairs, support in developing CVs, interview training, and more. The executive at Glowork, herself a young woman, proposed to Hawazen that she try out for a coordinator role in the Regulatory Affairs and Quality Department at Janssen Pharmaceutical, a company started in Belgium and now owned by Johnson & Johnson. Hawazen got the job and has thrived in it ever since, in part, she said, because this subsidiary of a foreign company is far more interested in investing in female talent than the local company she worked for before.

Hawazen's sense of pride at being in charge of major projects is clearly visible—she is impressed with her own ability to develop a skill set in an area that she knew nothing about. She said she knew only that she had a job with one of the largest companies in pharma but didn't even understand what her title meant at first. But she thought, *Why not try? I am a person who likes to learn. If you try to learn, the company will fight for you.* She explained that she accepted a low salary at first because of her lack of experience, but after dedicating herself to learning on the job, she felt "a power in myself and I realized I can prove myself in any place." Now, as each of the company's products is registered with the Ministry of Health after arrival at the port and then transferred to the company's supply chain for distribution to hospitals, Hawazen transmits the distributor registration files, archives all the legal documents and coordinates travel arrangements and conference participation for the thirteen people in the department. Unlike many of her Western counterparts, Hawazen said, subsequent salary negotiations have been easy for her. Very aware of her own value to her employer, she knows that a gap would be left in the company if she were to leave.

This confident young woman is the granddaughter of an uneducated woman who was in a polygamous marriage. Her paternal grandfather married at least four times; Hawazen told me that she has forty-two uncles and twenty-five aunts. An early marriage and traditional role as a mother might have been expected of her too had it not been for her own parents' more liberal outlook. Her father, a civil engineer with his own business, not only believes in education for girls but also believes that education should be used for future employment. Her mother graduated from high school in the early 1980s at a time when only 30 percent of girls were enrolled in primary school. That number was even lower in the small town she grew up in. Although Hawazen's mother got married directly after her high school graduation, she wanted her children, including her daughter, to receive more education and have greater opportunities in the workforce.

I asked Hawazen what made her parents so open to change, despite their own upbringing. Her parents had an arranged marriage, and there is a ten-year age gap between them. She said of her father, who unlike his father is married to only her mother, "He saw the problems that my grandfather had. He wants a simple life, not a complicated life with many wives and many kids. He wanted everyone to have best education and have enough money for all. If he had more kids, he wouldn't be able to afford it." In part, she said, this attitude was the result of her father having gone to the United States to study and staying there for fifteen years before coming back home and getting married. Her mother too, she said, had to shift her mind-set when she moved from her small town to Riyadh, Saudi Arabia's capital and its largest city, after she got married. She believes that these transitions made her parents "accepting of our ideas and our thoughts—but also because we have proven ourselves with our parents." Socially, her father is more liberal than her mother. Her mother permits her to live her "own life" but is more conservative because of her concern, Hawazen believes, about the potential social repercussions of her daughter's relative independence.

I asked her if the social stigma traditionally associated with divorce had made her own divorce difficult. She said that it has in fact been a boon for her, making her much more optimistic than before and determined to "make Hawazen happy"—not anyone else. The atmosphere around her is changing too—Saudi Arabia's divorce rates have skyrocketed in recent years. With a rate estimated at just over 30 percent in Riyadh itself, it has become harder for people to point fingers when they are much more likely to have divorces within their own families.[17] Hawazen is making plans to reconnect with her passion for fashion design while continuing her work in the pharmaceutical industry. In parallel to her work, she wants to start developing a brand, a budget, and a business plan so that she can build the basics of her own business while still working. She wants to create denim-based clothing, using crystals and appliqués to personalize each item. "This is trendy right now. I need to see the market needs and add my sign on it." In particular, she wants to make clothing suitable to any culture, not just Saudi Arabia, and she's certain that her designs could have that appeal in the long term. I asked her if it wouldn't be easier to start her retail business in a neighboring Gulf country, where she would be close enough to family but would have more freedoms. It was my second trip to Saudi Arabia, and I had found it constricting to wear the abaya, to be so dependent on my driver, and to deal with the gender-segregated entrances to office buildings and restaurants. Hawazen dismissed my question right away. She told me that although, like many others in her socioeconomic class, she often takes trips to Bahrain, Kuwait, and Dubai for pleasure, she would never want to live alone abroad and instead prefers to live at home with her family.

So Riyadh is where she will base her future business, and despite her broader ambitions, for now she plans to start with what she knows best—the market in Saudi Arabia. "Anything anyone makes for women will sell here. Everyone wants to be unique. People are starting to realize they don't want the same old high-end brands anymore. Social media is big here, and people are seeing that there are more than those brands. They realize that not all the high-end brands have good finishing. And they want to support local designers." She added, "Who is my market? I think it is working women who have a disposable income. And there are a lot of them. Most ladies working in companies and government also have their own business on the side. They sell clothes, food, interior design, photography, drawings, accessories, abayas. For many it is an income, yes, but mainly they do it because they want to accomplish something in their lives. We don't have anything to do. Our routine is dying. Everyone is traveling, and they are seeing many things outside Saudi Arabia that entertain them. So we have to do something for ourselves to entertain ourselves. So if these women have a passion, they take it forward."

⁘

LISTENING TO SAADIA, Fatima, and Hawazen and so many others like them as they told me their stories, it became clear that these young women are shattering stereotypes about Muslim women—stereotypes that exist both in the West and in the societies around them. The strides they have made in just one generation are remarkable: Saadia's determination to climb the career ladder at McDonald's, Fatima's dreams to design for BMW, and Hawazen's resolve to teach herself professional skills in a field not her own while incubating the dream of having her own business—these are all unprecedented ambitions. The foundation for these ambitions has been their unprecedented access to education. To put this in context: none of them has a mother who studied beyond high school or worked outside the home.

I set out to write this book because the statistics show, on paper, that an extraordinary change is under way. However, speaking to these young women in person—in their classrooms, their homes, and their offices—revealed the true magnitude of this quiet revolution and its implications for the Muslim world's economic and social fabric. Saadia is one of the millions who are the first women in their families to obtain higher education and, at a time when labor markets are more open than before, are creating a virtuous economic cycle and upending their place within their family hierarchies. Fatima represents those who may not be the first woman in their family to receive an education but who are certainly the first to think about it as preparation for a career in a field previously unexplored by women. And Hawazen is one of the many young women whose growing educational and economic opportunities have been matched by newfound confidence and social freedoms that were previously unimaginable.

As girls' education has become normalized in the family structures of those who pioneered it, the resulting wider cultural acceptance has led more and more families to make the decision to educate their daughters. And as some of these young women take tentative steps into the formal workforce, more positive feedback loops are created. Muslim families begin to see that women can be breadwinners with little significant impact on the type of honor and propriety they hold dear. Seeing these examples, more families begin to consider a similar future for their own daughters and a virtuous cycle is launched. This economic agency creates, in turn, further social empowerment.

The emerging and developing markets that make up the Muslim world have more educated youth today than at any point in their history—and half this talent is female. Parents, companies, governments—and of course these young women themselves—want returns on their education investments. Even as some families struggle to adjust to their daughters' new ambitions—such as Saadia's parents' discomfort with her McDonald's uniform—the growing economic power of these young women is unmistakable. Rapid urbanization, the rising cost of living, and growing consumerism have made the single breadwinner model no longer workable.

Most importantly, these young women are hungry for opportunity themselves. From Dushanbe to Marrakech, they are a new powerful segment of the economy, politics, and society—and have more ambition, and the means to achieve their ambitions, than at any other point in history.

two

Workforce Trailblazers

S AMIRA NEGM GRADUATED FROM AIN SHAMS UNIVERSITY IN Cairo with a degree in computer engineering in 2009. She is one of the 110,000 women enrolled in science, technology, engineering, and mathematics (STEM) disciplines across universities in Egypt. "At school, I loved math and science. Math was my passion. If there was a Mathematics Olympics, I would have won gold. And it was clear for me that I would choose the faculty of engineering in university. There I discovered software specifically, and I was very attracted to it, as it was writing code to solve problems," she said.

There are currently 340,000 STEM students enrolled in universities in Egypt. The most recent graduating classes were nearly 34 percent women—a rate higher than in the United States in the same time period. And these women are going on to careers in STEM fields. Egypt, like many countries in the Muslim world, has a higher percentage of women going into STEM fields than in the United

States or Europe. As industries requiring STEM skills take off, the local war for talent escalates. With women making up over one-third of that talent across the Muslim world—and nearly half in places like Oman, Qatar, Kuwait, and Tunisia—most companies cannot afford to miss out on their talent, and this demand has in part driven millions of young women to the economic frontlines.[1]

For Samira, and many others like her, early professional opportunities combined with the challenges around her opened up her mind to new possibilities for her own professional trajectory. I asked one up-and-coming male Internet entrepreneur—men in the local start-up scene are the majority and often more visible—if he knew of women entrepreneurs trying to solve everyday problems like he was. He quickly came up with several names, but Samira's story stood out because she was choosing to tackle one of the most challenging problems: transport.

Soon after graduating from university, Samira joined a multinational company as an engineer, designing software for smartphones. A few years later she moved over to another multinational, this time writing software for intelligent cars. Smartphones and automated cars might have originated in the West, but the many eager consumers in countries like Egypt were leading to innovation and production, by both multinationals and local companies.

In her job at her second employer, Samira was one of two engineers selected to work on an autonomous parking project for BMW in Germany. It was her first trip outside the Middle East and North Africa region. She told me she had a "strange feeling" that everything is organized in Germany. Laughing at her previous naïveté, she added, "Egypt is . . . I would say, spontaneous? Or maybe that's just chaos? Because I am an engineer, I liked the organized nature of Germany and it was opposite of Egypt. While I was there, I tried a carpooling service between Stuttgart and Cologne. I thought, *Here is a way to solve everyday problems like commuting*. In Egypt I was adding luxurious things to cars—auto-parking—a feature we don't even use much in Egypt. Germany integrates technology into public services to solve daily life problems, for example, to control traffic lights and trains. We don't do that enough."

Inspired, Samira returned home after a few months to a new house. Her parents, with whom she lives, as is the norm for most young people, had moved. What used to be a three-hour daily commute with the company's own pickup-and-drop-off service turned into a five-hour commute, from the east to the west of Cairo and back. The company bus didn't go as far east as her family's new house, so Samira had to take public transport first and then connect to the company bus. On the crowded public transport, she was always concerned about the rampant sexual harassment, but taxis were too expensive. She soon started losing energy and felt that her performance at work was slipping too with the grueling commute. Frustrated, she started looking for some other solution to her problem. She thought back to her car-sharing moment in Germany and wondered if that might work for her. Soon enough, she thought beyond her own needs and wondered if there might be a way to solve the issue for many of Cairo's frustrated commuters by bringing together colleagues driving the same route to work and sharing costs.

Samira quickly realized that even if there were a way to match people commuting to the same places, a bigger obstacle was the culture around money. "People wouldn't want to pay each other. They don't want to look like needy, lower-class people. So any solution would need to be tailored to our culture." There was a second constraint—safety, particularly for women. So she set about doing some market research and found that carpooling was already going on but on a very limited scale and only within people's own networks—among university friends, work colleagues, or, at the furthest remove, friends of friends. She decided to create a network around relationships that already existed on Facebook and scale up from there, rather than begin by trying to create a mass platform. Thus was Raye7 born, bringing the sharing economy and social networks together.

Soon enough, the idea attracted prizes in competitions and even recognition from the Ministry of Communication, which was trying to support an ecosystem of tech entrepreneurship. Samira quit her job and started working on the venture nearly full-time; along her journey from employee to entrepreneur she also started a part-time master's degree in technology management at the Nile University. Her parents, worried about the risks associated with a start-up, encouraged her to work at the ministry and choose a more comfortable path in the public sector. But Samira was convinced of the viability of her idea. So instead, she pushed ahead and turned Raye7 into a family enterprise with her brother. While she handles the technology, Ahmad, who is four years younger, manages the sales and communication aspects of the business, building partnerships with companies and universities. In just a few short months after they started operating, Raye7 had eleven thousand users. Their aim is to reach a million users by mid-2018 and build beyond Cairo after that. On their target list of cities are others with traffic congestion and large, digital-savvy workforces, including Khobar in Saudi Arabia, Lagos in Nigeria, Mexico City, and several places in India.

Samira found a smart solution for the payment problem. "We created a virtual currency so that people wouldn't have to feel like they are paying each other. So if I 'spend' fifty kilometers [thirty-two miles] to take you somewhere, tomorrow you 'spend' fifty kilometers. If I don't have a car, I have to buy points—transforming actual currency into a points system—and if I have a car, I collect points, and then they get it converted back to cash. Currently this is done manually, for example, gas stations will transfer the points to vouchers for fuel, as we don't have two-way payment systems, but we can also deliver cash." Recalling her own concerns about harassment on public transport, Samira knows that some women would share that concern and avoid a ride-sharing service to get to work. So she also designed a feature that would entice women specifically: using the app to ask for a women-only ride. Today 70 percent of their users are men, but they want to educate more women about the solutions they are designing just for them.

Samira gets incredibly excited describing her innovations, "geeking out" like other technology entrepreneurs around the world. If the stereotypical image of a tech entrepreneur is a guy in a hoodie in Silicon Valley, Samira defies that stereotype completely with her small frame and headscarf. But her passion, energy, and desire to solve a problem are the same as what drives entrepreneurs anywhere in the world.

Fifty Million Migrants

Of the 1.25 billion people in the thirty Muslim-majority countries studied in this book, just over 808 million are of working age (fifteen to sixty-four years old), while the rest are dependents—children or people over age sixty-five. Of this group, nearly half a billion are in the labor force, both employed and unemployed, while the rest are not in the paid workforce at all—they are neither at work nor looking for work.[2]

Among the half billion in the labor force, 342 million are men and 155 million are women—just over 30 percent of the overall workforce in these economies. These numbers are unprecedented. At the turn of the millennium, only a little over 100 million women were in the workforce. The 50 million women who have migrated from home to the workforce in the last decade and a half represent nearly a 50 percent increase in the female labor force of the Muslim world. In the same time period, the male labor force has increased more slowly—by 37 percent.[3]

The percentage of adult women who work varies between countries.[4] In Azerbaijan, Bangladesh, Indonesia, Kazakhstan, Kyrgyzstan, Qatar, Tajikistan, and Uzbekistan, the labor force participation rate among women ages fifteen to sixty-four is already well over 50 percent. In other words, the majority of working-age women in these countries are already working or searching for employment. In Kazakhstan, the female labor force participation rate, at 75 percent, is higher than anywhere else in the Muslim world, closer to the rates in Nordic countries like Norway (76 percent) and Sweden (79 percent), and higher than in either the United States (66 percent) or China (70 percent). In Indonesia, the most populous Muslim economy, nearly 54 percent of working-age women are in the workforce, a rate higher than in South Africa (49 percent) or India (29 percent). Many of these women are the second generation of working women in Indonesia. In Bahrain, Kuwait, Malaysia, Turkmenistan, and the United Arab Emirates, the share of adult women who work outside the home is over 40 percent, while in Oman, Sudan, and Turkey it is over 30 percent.

Diversity research suggests that 30 percent is the proportion at which critical mass is reached—in a group setting, the voices of the minority group become heard in their own right, rather than simply representing the minority. Additionally, the positive returns of diversity become visible with a 30 percent critical mass.[5] Eighteen of the thirty Muslim-majority economies in this book are now well beyond this threshold. In Egypt, Morocco, Pakistan, Saudi Arabia, Tunisia, and Yemen, the numbers are lower, ranging between 20 and 30 percent, but the pace of change has rapidly accelerated. In Algeria, Syria, Jordan, Iraq, and Iran the numbers are between 15 and 20 percent, but also growing.

It's not just the quantity that has changed but, thanks to the education revolution, also the quality—or education level—of these workers, which is markedly different from the past, even in some of the lower-income economies. In 1998, when the first of the millennials were about to enter college, women made up 13 percent of the total workforce in Jordan, and of these working women, one-third had a university education. Today the total percentage of women in the workforce has increased to 17 percent, but among them the share of those with a university education has nearly doubled, to 57 percent.[6] This is not surprising. At the turn of the millennium, around 73,000 women were enrolled in university in Jordan. By 2012, this number had more than doubled, to 162,000 women. As they have graduated these women have sought paid work, and as a consequence, the overall share of college-educated women in the workforce has dramatically increased. In fact, while the number of working women may still be low, the share of college-educated women among them is now higher in Jordan than in Brazil, India, Norway, or the United Kingdom. Meet a working woman on the streets of Rio and there's a one-in-five chance she holds a university degree. On the streets of Amman, two out of every three working women hold a degree.

Similar patterns can be found in other economies. In Algeria, the percentage of university-educated women has gone up from 20 to 40 percent during the same time period. In Iran, it is up from 24 percent to 40 percent today. In Kyrgyzstan, one of the poorest of the ex-Soviet states, it's up from 2 percent to over 20 percent today. In Turkey, this number is up from 14 percent at the turn of the millennium to 25 percent today. Even seemingly smaller shifts can be dramatic. In Indonesia, the number is up from 2 percent in 1996, when the first cohort of millennials was still in high school, to 10 percent today. So, even though on average only one in ten working women in Indonesia today holds a college degree, this still represents *millions* of women who are changing the character of the Indonesian workforce and the talent available to its businesses.

In some countries the relative proportion of women with a university education is partly bumped up, even if the overall size of the female workforce remains small (as in Jordan), by the fact that many low-skilled women stay out of the workforce completely because of limited economic and social opportunities. The numbers also reflect the relatively higher level of opportunity and expectations for less educated men to be breadwinners. But mainly they signal the virtuous cycle that college education offers to women in making the leap from home to economic independence.

Most of the fifty million new female entrants to workforces across the Muslim world are women in their twenties and thirties—university-educated millennials. Many are new migrants to the economic frontlines whose mothers never worked outside the home—like Saadia, the young woman working at McDonald's, or Hawazen, the aspiring denim entrepreneur. They are "first-generation" participants. Others represent the second or third generation of women in their families to enter the workforce, and building on the experiences of their mothers, and even some grandmothers, they often define a new path.

In most cases, these women are capitalizing on their newly acquired higher education and the doors it opens to engage in remunerated work of some form. Like Nazia, the field engineer who worked with my father, or Fatima, the aspiring industrial design student, these women sometimes venture into fields that have rarely, if ever, employed women in their communities and countries. Others, like Samira, eschew "safe" roles in the public sector in order to carve out a path of their own, one that may generate jobs and services for others in the long term. Some are older women who had dropped out of the workforce, or never entered, despite having a higher education and are now taking their first steps into the workforce. Yet others are low-skilled women, young and old alike, who are joining the workforce for the first time as working outside the family becomes a possibility—and a necessity—for the first time. Some are in the workforce out of necessity, and others are in the workforce seeking fulfillment. For all of these women, work is opportunity.

Wife, Widow—and Worker

It was late in the summer one warm evening in Cairo when I made my way up four flights of stairs in a dilapidated building to the apartment of fifty-three-year-old Mozah. We were in Ard El Lewa, a sprawling, informal working-class settlement bordering Cairo's Ring Road. Mozah's street is next to a crowded bazaar. After having spent most of my day in public spaces meeting mainly veiled women—as were many in this bazaar—I was slightly taken aback to see Mozah in a spaghetti-strap top and skirt. I shared my surprise with her, and she explained that when she is at home with family she dresses the way she wants. Since she knew I was a woman and had a female translator, she had decided not to cover up. But, she told me quickly, she would certainly not step out of her house that way. She would be fully covered, including a hijab, which most women in Egypt wear. These days, Mozah often dons her hijab because, after decades, she has started to work outside the home again.

When Mozah was a child, child labor was more common than adult women working outside the home. Mozah first started working at the age of seven, starting with sewing in a clothing factory. For her parents, sending a daughter to school was unheard of in their very low-income community, but it was acceptable, even normal, for children to work at an early age to supplement the family income and help make ends meet. Mozah's three sisters, too, were uneducated. Their one brother started school but dropped out quickly and started working too. Their mother informally helped their father in his bird shop, but her main role was in the home.

After a decade at work, Mozah stopped at seventeen to get married. Once married, housework and child care became her primary role. Three children came in quick succession: a boy, Ahmed, and two girls, nicknamed Sherri and Riri. As the kids got older, Mozah began to hone her cooking skills. Cooking was never a chore to her, but something she enjoyed. As she became a better chef, her neighbors and friends started asking her to cook for them, for small celebrations, often for free. Once in a while she would sell the food to those who wanted large orders, but it was mostly just a hobby.

All three of Mozah's children finished high school, a remarkable achievement with two uneducated parents. None, however, went to university; instead, all three of them married young. Her son, she said, was not interested in studying, although she had hoped he would go to college and thus become the family's skilled breadwinner. Today he is a driver and has two children of his own. One of her daughters—Riri—didn't have grades high enough to gain admission into college, although she badly wanted to go. She is now married with two children and doesn't work outside her home. Sherri, Mozah's other daughter, had stellar grades but encountered a different roadblock: she was "too pretty." As a teenager, Mozah said, Sherri was often harassed in the street. She was engaged to a young man while still in high school, and to prevent her fiancé from meeting her outside school, her father stopped her from pursuing her education any further. Soon after graduating, Sherri got married and had one child.

Mozah herself might well have lived out the rest of her life from her home, with children and grandchildren close by, selling some of her cooking to her community now and then for some extra cash. But two events changed the course of Mozah's life—her husband's untimely death from a heart attack and her daughter's divorce. When Sherri separated from her husband soon after the marriage, she moved back to her home.

Suddenly economic necessity pushed Mozah from thinking about cooking as her hobby to developing it as her new—and only—source of income. Mother and daughter now run the business together, joining the three million additional women who have entered Egypt's workforce since the turn of the millennium.[7] Sherri takes orders at their home by telephone, while Mozah cooks outside the home, for four different families in disparate parts of Cairo. Although Mozah often spends hours commuting through chaotic Cairo streets to get to the homes of her employers, this is not enough to occupy her full-time, and both mother and daughter are hoping to get more clients, mainly through word-of-mouth communications about their products. Mozah would consider expanding her business to take orders exclusively from home, thus avoiding the long, exhausting commutes and employing someone else for deliveries instead, but she doesn't yet have enough clients to do so. Needing to grow her market, she is hoping to gain new clients through her existing ones, relying on traditional word of mouth. Wistfully, Mozah recalled once turning down an opportunity to present her cooking on a TV show, an opportunity she would now accept in a heartbeat, given the exposure it would give her and its potential for expanding the client base of her small business.

White-Collar Women

Opportunities to work have shifted for women like Samira and Mozah not just in Egypt but in nearly all the countries in the MENA region.[8] In the United Arab Emirates, which since independence has relied heavily on both skilled and unskilled foreign labor for its development, the government has recently tried harder to bring more of its highly educated local talent into the white-collar workforce. And these efforts have paid off. The workforce participation of both local women and local men has increased over the last decade. But the relative change has been greater for women and so, in turn, has been the impact of entering the workforce on their lives and opportunities.

One such woman is Amal Al Mutawa. She describes herself as a "third culture kid." Her father was a diplomat, and she went to ten different schools in Syria, Morocco, and the United Arab Emirates, building a strong arsenal of social skills and cultural dexterity along the way. After earning a degree in computer science in the UAE, she began working as a network and security engineer in the early 2000s—the only woman in the entire company. "The guy I was reporting to said I don't want a girl working for me and especially not a girl engineer. I decided to prove them wrong—that I can do all this. Walk around with large cables and do everything anyone else in my role would do," Amal said.

From there she switched to the security department of a telecom firm, but left eventually to get married. Within a year she was divorced. "We have high divorce rate, and it's becoming the norm, so the social stigma is going down. It was the best decision I made in my life . . . made me much happier. It also triggered a lot of other stuff on what I want."

Rethinking her values and interests affected her professional life too, and in 2009 Amal began working for the government. "Social media was just becoming the buzz in the government world. I was one of the team putting together the social media strategy for His Highness [Sheikh Mohammad bin Rashid Al Maktoum, the vice president and prime minister of the UAE and the ruler of Dubai]. I was privileged to work on one of the e-sessions with His Highness: he asks people to send in questions and then publishes them and his responses on his website." Amal's experience took her eventually from the government communications department to Sheikh

Mohammad bin Rashid's innovation office. In the government's bid to make the country more innovative and more focused on the future, the cabinet appointments in 2016 took some bold steps. Seven of the twenty-nine ministers appointed were women—or over 27 percent. This number is higher than in the United States—and higher than the global average. There is a minister of state for happiness, who is responsible for taking a strategic and proactive approach to happiness in the government and the private sector, happiness as a lifestyle, and the measurement of happiness. And there is a minister of state for youth affairs who, at twenty-two, is a youth herself.

With the public sector being one of the largest employers in the country, particularly for women, these appointments also signaled that broader changes are under way to instill gender equality across the public-sector workforce. For Amal, it has meant a new job, chief happiness officer, which she describes as an "awesome role" that "comes from the direction of the government to embed happiness in our culture"; in this role, she believes that she can help "create the right environment for people to choose happiness." Although the details were still being worked out when we spoke, Amal explained that new chief happiness officers have been appointed across different government entities, with each one holding a different role. "My 'clients' are all the staff within the Prime Minister's office. But at Ministry of Education, the 'clients' are the employees of the ministry—and students and teachers across the country."

Amal knows that, even without the new titles and new strategies employed by the government, the very fact that she is a working, professional woman today is part of a major shift in her society. Her mother was married at fourteen and gave birth to Amal when she was fifteen. "When we were in Morocco, my mother went back to school—my mom and I graduated from high school together. Back in the '70s, the UAE's founder's wife, Sheikha Fatima, opened a school for married women to continue their learning because they weren't accepted into regular schools. Today universities accept all women." This delicate balance of education, culture, and employment has paid off for women in the workforce. "I have two brothers and two sisters, and each has their own success story. The changes in our country have been both strategic and organic. The next five to ten years will be even more transformational. In our office, for example, the majority of the workforce are ladies, and I think women are paid even more than men. They have changing aspirations and want to show that we can make a change in society."

A Dual-Income Life

The influx of women into the workforce goes well beyond the Middle East region and has unfolded broadly across the Muslim world. On the other side of the Muslim world, a new breed of "Asian Tigresses" zip through the streets of Jakarta and Kuala Lumpur on their scooters and motorcycles. Like women in Brazil, China, and South Africa, they have leveraged the dynamism of their economies to fill a vacuum for talent and entrepreneurship, particularly in manufacturing and services. Since as early as 1990, Indonesia and Malaysia have seen women's labor force participation grow to more than 50 percent and over 45 percent, respectively.

Early investments in successful family planning campaigns and education have led to more economic freedoms for women coupled with employment opportunities that emerged through new industries in this steadily growing new market region. Although older and married women in Indonesia and Malaysia are still more likely to be found in informal enterprises that enable them to combine household work and paid work, younger women tend to work as wage employees in services and trading enterprises and have a wholly new outlook on career and family. As parents see these young women in the work place, they have a stronger incentive to educate and motivate their own daughters. The growing awareness of the economic sense of gender equality thus creates a contagion effect.

Gita, a corporate lawyer by training, is one such "second-generation" professional woman. Gita's parents, who met in university, trained as architects, and both went on to have careers—her mother as a researcher in the Public Works Ministry and her father running a private architecture firm. They came from families of five and seven children each, but they chose to have only one child, Gita, reflecting the overall decline in birth rates that often accompanies a rise in prosperity. She said that they always expected her to get higher education degrees and to work, but it was equally expected that she would meet and marry a similarly educated and affluent man. The longer Gita delayed marriage, the more concerned her immediate and extended family became.

Today, she said, they are satisfied because she is finally married, even if she did wait until age thirty, far above the average age of marriage (twenty-two) for Indonesian women. She also has a thriving and challenging career, working with companies to change their sustainability policies. As Indonesia grows, so too does the consciousness that its unique environment and biodiversity must be preserved. The other side of growth, however, is the desire for new luxuries that are now within the reach of middle-income households but require two incomes, particularly in urban households. Gita said that life in Jakarta is simply unaffordable without the two middle-class incomes she and her husband bring in. This trend is further bolstered as improved health care, including family planning awareness and access, leads to longer, healthier lives and fewer children. The old model of one male breadwinner supporting a wife, parents, children, and other dependents is no longer adequate and has begun to give way to the dual-income household. As women's new earnings expand the range of spending options, slowly turning past luxuries into today's necessities, there is impetus for yet more women to go to work in order to fulfill the new standards of a middle-class life.

Gita has one child, and while her role as wife and mother may have been the sole marker of success in the past, today it is still one of her most important roles. High-skilled women like her need to combine new economic opportunities with the traditional expectations of marriage and family. When both economic and family pressures are high, these women face a dual burden, one that men usually don't face. Many of the women at the economic frontlines in the Muslim world face the same trade-offs between work and family that women in developed countries face. As we will see later, in the absence of supportive policies for working parents, women like Gita who can afford it pay other, lower-income women or rely on family to help them manage these trade-offs.

By Women, for Women

The influx of educated, urban women into the workforces of large emerging markets is not limited to traditional white-collar work. It is also driven by a boom in the services that working women need to manage their new lives, including, for example, professional clothing, food delivery, and transport services.

Parveen lives in Islamabad, the capital of Pakistan, which is home to one-eighth of the eight hundred million women in the Muslim world. Although Pakistan, along with Bangladesh, has the largest share of people who live on less than a dollar a day, it also has a newly emerging middle class that is both the cause and effect of more women entering the workforce. Parveen is evidence of this new middle class.

In the early 1990s, she was a housewife. Most of her friends and acquaintances—the wives of her husband's friends—were women who worked outside the home, at least part-time. Some had taken positions as teachers in the booming new private school industry catering to the middle-class families who wanted to offer their children more than the low standards of public school education but couldn't afford the few elite schools in the country. Others practiced medicine part-time or worked in civil society organizations engaged in social development. Parveen had a college education but little interest in one of these typical roles for women of her background.

Instead, she spotted an opportunity for a new entrepreneurial venture. Her friends' work called for new wardrobes: neither the simple

clothing they had previously worn at home nor the elaborate outfits needed for family gatherings, weddings, and other celebrations
were appropriate for the workplace. Concurrently, a new style icon
had emerged for working women's professional wardrobes: Pakistan's
newly elected, thirty-six-year-old, female prime minister, Benazir Bhutto, who combined traditional shalwar kameez and a loose
headscarf with Western-style blazers and jackets in her day-to-day
activities.

So Parveen started a tailoring business from a spare room at the
back of her house. She asked her husband for a loan of 10,000 rupees
as seed capital to create her first collection. This was equal to his entire monthly income at the time. Some months later, her collection of
moderately priced shalwar kameez sold out in just three days, filling
a niche for both professional women and housewives who could not
afford the custom designs of local tailors but wanted the luxury of
fashionable, unique garments.

Today Parveen's business is booming: she brings in nearly as much
income as her husband. She now applies her entrepreneurial zeal to
politics too, bringing in funds and votes from her large network of
middle-income female consumers for the local candidate of the political party she supports. The party is led by Imran Khan, who as a
"born-again Muslim" has a checkered past when it comes to views on
women and women's work, but has a strong base among many urban
middle-class voters, women and men alike, who are inspired by his
self-made-man image and his message of hard work and bootstrap-
ping, a message that his fellow politicians, products of dynasties and
vast feudal and industrial wealth, are unable to convey. Parveen and
her network of working women identify with that message.

The Trillion-Dollar Club

Using the current average earnings of working women for the twenty-
three Muslim-majority countries for which data are available, I estimate that total annual earnings of the 150 million working women

in the Muslim world is just under US$1 trillion. To understand the magnitude of this figure, consider this: only fifteen economies in the world cross the trillion-dollar mark. And as more and more women make it into the workforce, their earning and spending power is set to grow further.

Women's influence goes beyond the capital they earn—and usually control—directly. A US-focused study found that "women make the decision in the purchases of 94% of home furnishings, 92% of vacations, 91% of homes, 60% of automobiles and 51% of consumer electronics." According to one consulting firm, women drive as much as 80 percent of all consumption decisions. In the Muslim world, while working women are likely to have greater influence on household spending than nonworking women, as they contribute to the household income, even women who are not working have significant say in domains that are considered most pertinent to women.[9]

Because women tend to make different spending choices than men, their increased earnings will change the nature of consumption and thereby which businesses grow in the coming years. Women tend to spend money on their households and for their families. One study found that the "sectors likely to benefit from women's expanding buying power include food, healthcare, education, childcare, apparel, consumer durables and financial services."[10]

Gyms, swimming pools, and yoga centers are popping up across urban areas in Muslim-majority emerging markets. Many are female-only, while others offer specialized hours for women. In tapping into the growing consciousness among women of their health and bodies, this is a business that goes beyond vanity. Changes in diet and lifestyle have sent obesity rates skyrocketing among men and women in many Muslim countries, especially the rich states of the Gulf and especially for women, who often lead more constricted and sedentary lifestyles and are bound to the home. Governments are even beginning to subsidize some fitness businesses as a public health investment. The mobility industry is also racing to offer women-focused options. Uber's service in the Middle East has options for women, as does the more popular Dubai-based company Careem. For busy women who want to navigate a delicate "third way" combining work and family, there are a range of time-saving services. Young women and men in Almaty, Kazakhstan, for instance, talked about a "mother-in-law gift basket"—an elaborate collection of gifts for married working women to offer their mothers-in-law for specific holidays, saving them time while meeting the need to maintain social norms.

The growing spending power of the 150 million women currently in the labor force of the Muslim world has not just helped these new niche markets flourish. It has also created new opportunities for women to create and run their own businesses. All businesses, whether led by women or men, stand to gain from the rise of the female workforce—and their earnings—but women have a particular comparative advantage because they know these new markets so well.

One such market aims to help women—who traditionally have not managed their own income and wealth—manage their money better. Ozlem Denizem, an executive at the Dogus Group in Turkey, has started a TV program for promoting financial literacy to Turkish women so they can better manage their hard-earned cash. There are also new ventures that bet on the growing financial awareness of high-net-worth women and help them redirect more of their spending from consumption to investment. Elissa Freiha is the twenty-six-year-old cofounder of WOMENA, which facilitates the investment process from start to finish for high-net-worth women and seasoned investors. WOMENA is also a platform for entrepreneurs, giving them support in understanding and executing fund-raising. Although the investors have to be female, the entrepreneurs are both women and men. Freiha sees that, while women entrepreneurs—and investors—are occupying stereotypical "women's business" niches, a change is under way as high-net-worth women begin to support nontraditional ventures. "One trend we see is that a lot of the younger women in wealthy families are being trained to join the family offices—and join the decision-making," she said. "The average age in our group is thirty-three. As they learn more about managing their wealth, they will diversify where they invest. The next wave of investors—in any field—will be women with wealth."

A Perfect Storm

A confluence of factors has created a "perfect storm" that has brought this new generation of women—even two generations—into the workforce in a highly compressed period of time. For Samira, Mozah, Amal, Gita, and Parveen, the starting points and the specific critical factors may have been very different, but the broader forces at play—the wider context within which they make their decisions—are the same.

Most Muslim economies have been growing. Since the turn of the millennium, half of the thirty countries covered in this book have had average growth rates of 5 percent or more.[11] This rate compares favorably with growth rates during the same period of 2 percent for the United States and 3 percent for Brazil, although it is lower than the 9 percent growth in China and 7 percent in India. This growth, though not evenly distributed, has nevertheless lifted millions of people out of poverty and contributed to an emergent middle class.

This combined economic growth and social mobility has raised the demand for new goods and services. Prices have risen too, and single incomes in households are no longer enough. In the dual-income households that are becoming increasingly common, the second income has usually come from a woman. Sometimes a husband and a wife are both earning an income outside the home, like Parveen and her husband or indeed my own parents. In other cases, the dual earners are a father and daughter, or a mother and son. There has also been a modest rise in the number of women who are solo breadwinners. Decades ago, male relatives might have supported a widowed woman, but today they are already stretched in meeting the needs of their own immediate families. For women such as Mozah, then, work becomes a necessity.

Economic growth has created new opportunities for women—and men—to work and to earn, but it has also raised new problems to solve and new demands to be met. Cairo's burgeoning population and growing middle class have led to gridlocked traffic. For women like Samira, however, that's a problem to solve—and a business opportunity.

The concurrent expansion of girls' education over the last decades has ensured that millions of women have already built up a base of the skills required to leverage these new opportunities and create new ones. For women like Amal—or Saadia, Fatima, Hawazen, Gita, and Samira—increasing educational opportunity has opened up exciting new pathways for professional development, earning, and self-actualization. Governments in some places, like the United Arab Emirates, have recently made deliberate efforts to bring educated women into the workforce, but by and large the change has been organic and unprecedented.

A decline in fertility in the Muslim world, mirroring the decline in many other emerging markets, has also contributed to the ascendance of women in the workforce. As the time spent by women in being pregnant and taking care of infants has been reduced, their potential time for engaging in paid work has increased. In 1990, none of the thirty Muslim countries covered here was below the global replacement fertility rate of 2.33 children per woman. By 2000, four countries had reached this threshold, and today twelve countries are at or just below this rate.[12]

As more women have gone to work, serving their needs has opened up new pathways for yet more women to work. For Parveen, for instance, selling tailored clothing to professional women with their own money to spend for the first time in their lives provided the base for what is now a high-performing, medium-size business.

Technology has also offered new ways to work—both for low-income, low-skilled women running small businesses with mobile phones and for white-collar women, who can now work more flexibly through their smartphones. This is a global trend for high-skilled women and men around the world, but women in Muslim-majority countries, whose entry into the workforce coincided with the new availability of these technologies, have at times been in a stronger position than their Western counterparts to change organizational cultures as they adopt these technologies.

These trends are compounded by the modern world's interconnectivity and globalization. What they see in their own families or communities is no longer the only influence on women's social aspirations, although the influence of these factors remains significant. Today even some of the lowest-income women are exposed to the lives of their more privileged compatriots and beyond through television and the Internet. Educated women from middle-income or high-income households with digital access have the world at their fingertips—and along with it, exposure to the aspirations of women around the world. This changes their dreams and ambitions, both professional and personal. Their husbands and fathers, who are often still the gatekeepers of their access to the working world, are changing too.

The results of all these changes are most visible in the ambitions and aspirations of the fifty million Muslim women, young and old alike, who have entered the workforce. They don't have a road map to follow, but they have access to information that no feminist movement before them did. They compare themselves not only to their classmates and neighbors—all of whom are more likely than ever to be educated and economically active themselves—but to high-profile professional women in their own countries as well as in other Muslim countries.

Exposed to the lives of other Muslim women in other countries through entertainment and information flows, many of these women begin to see that it is education access, income, and cultural barriers that stand in their way, not religious ones. Turkey, which is second only to the United States in churning out soap operas, is sending intriguing, addictive stories about young female Turkish protagonists across the Middle East, Iran, Pakistan, and beyond.[13] Young women with access to television and web streaming in these countries see portrayals of women who are relatively more empowered than women in their immediate milieu, and these fictional characters become inspiration for renegotiating authority over education, marriage, and professions with their parents and husbands. Through tourism and online exploration, women in Saudi Arabia look to the more socially empowered women of the Emirates as role models for what could be as their own country opens up. There is competition too. Modern, urban women in Kazakhstan look down on the "backward" ways of women in neighboring Kyrgyzstan. Women in Pakistan lament the fact that despite having more apparent social freedoms than women in Saudi Arabia, far fewer women in Pakistan are educated.

Women's access to information does not end at the borders of Muslim countries, of course. Exposed to women around the world by online news and entertainment, they find that the struggles of other women are not so different from their own. At the very least, seeing how other women balance work and family has some lessons to offer, both to emulate and to avoid.

This exposure, which is most evident among educated working women, brings deep familiarity with how feminism and womenomics are unfolding elsewhere. At a women's leadership training at the headquarters of Saudi Aramco in the Eastern Province of Saudi Arabia, I heard impassioned views on Sheryl Sandberg's book, *Lean In*. Although there was consensus in the room that the tips in the book didn't work in the context of these women's work lives, they nonetheless found inspiration in hearing an American perspective as they sought to carve out their own path to leadership. At a gathering of women leaders in Istanbul, I heard women admire Japanese prime minister Shinzō Abe's "Abenomics" plans, which include addressing demographic and growth challenges by integrating women into the economy. In Islamabad, I heard female entrepreneurs express appreciation for the Korean focus on female education and suggest that it was one of the reasons why South Korea had stopped female infanticide relatively quickly and elected a female president. In Almaty, I heard several women and men, business leaders and their high-skilled workers alike, quote the words of International Monetary Fund chief Christine Lagarde about how economies can grow faster by including women in the workforce. Women are using narratives from elsewhere to push for local change, while also discarding the narratives they do not want or need.

This wealth of ideas is the result of unprecedented access to information for many women across the Muslim world—images and commentary that have changed how they view their own potential. Their mothers never had this information, and it has changed their own aspirations in just a few short years. While the inspiration from around the world has been an important impetus for them, these women have lacked accessible role models within their families and communities. With no preexisting paths to follow, millions of courageous women have created their own, becoming their own role models and quietly changing the society around them.

Latent Talent

This is not to suggest that the work of gender equality in employment is complete or that all educated women are able to overcome the norms, biases, and lack of role models around them. The gaps between women's and men's labor force participation and earnings remain large. Even as more women than ever before have joined the workforce in Muslim-majority economies, millions remain outside it. For example, out of all the women over the age of fifteen who could work in the United Arab Emirates, only 44 percent are employed or seeking employment, while out of all the men in this pool, 90 percent work or are looking for work.[14] The gap is 19 percent versus 77 percent in Saudi Arabia, 27 percent versus 75 percent in Tunisia, 53 percent versus 86 percent in Indonesia, and 25 percent versus 86 percent in Pakistan. Despite the rapid recent progress of the fifty million Muslim women who have joined the workforce since the turn of the millennium, there remains a vast underutilization of women in economic growth and development.

These women's recent gains in education, including advanced degrees, are squandered when they do not join the workforce. Even simple comparisons between the overall labor force participation numbers and the overall university-educated or high school–educated stock can reveal some striking gaps in talent use.[15] For example, in Iran, more women hold university degrees—6.8 million—than are active in the workforce—5.0 million. Thus, at least 1.8 million Iranian women with college degrees are not part of the workforce. In Saudi Arabia, this "higher education surplus" (more women with secondary education than total women in the workforce) is nearly a quarter million. The surplus of high school–educated women outside the labor market is even bigger—4.3 million in Algeria, 1.1 million in Jordan, 1.3 million in Kazakhstan, 1.2 million in Kuwait, 1.1 million in Mauritania, 4.2 million in Saudi Arabia, nearly 1.0 million in Tunisia, and 8.9 million in Turkey. In reality, these rough calculations underestimate the wasted potential because not all educated women work and not all working women are educated. The true size of the wasted potential is even larger.

Even these rough comparisons make it clear that educated women in Muslim-majority countries may represent the world's greatest waste of skilled talent—and human potential. They could be employers, employees, entrepreneurs, executives, and taxpayers. Instead, they are often performing unpaid domestic labor—cooking, cleaning, child care, and elder care—as stay-at-home daughters or wives. While these tasks are valuable too in any society, they come with a trade-off for those who have the desire and skills to do otherwise.

Sabah is one of these women. She lives in Pakistan's Balochistan province and is the only woman in her village with a college education. This in itself is an extremely rare accomplishment for a young woman in a province where literacy rates for women are below 20 percent.[16] Sabah earned a degree in math at the university in Quetta, the provincial capital. She wants to teach at the local school for girls—a sort of "ghost school" that is housed in a shack because it was never properly built when the local corrupt politician channeled the building materials for a girls' school to his personal residence. The girls sit at ramshackle desks, and the one teacher, an older woman with health troubles and close to retirement, teaches nearly one hundred girls a day, covering all basic subjects. The school desperately needs a new teacher, and the older woman has tried to convince Sabah to take over the position—in the absence of any other women in the village qualified to do so.

But despite having put his own children through the school and allowing Sabah to go to university, her father won't let her work outside the home, preferring that she observe the strictest rules of female seclusion. At twenty-two, Sabah may already be considered too old by any of the local respectable families for making a good match in marriage. In his community, her father believes, an employed daughter will have fewer, not more, marriage prospects. Yet, without Sabah, the school will close and a hundred girls will lose their chance at an education. Although her father took one step forward in granting Sabah an education, the entire community will take one hundred steps back if he will not permit her to become the teacher in the girls' school, possibly crushing the entire community's economic development for generations to come. And for Sabah herself, to not take the position is to live an unfulfilled life, a prospect that saddens her but to which she is resigned. "This is the way things are," she said.

For other Muslim women who may seem to live under no constraints at all, the roadblocks are more subtle. Take Jawaher, a thirty-two-year-old with a PhD degree in child psychology and five years of teaching experience at a private school in Dubai. She is now a stay-at-home mother and wife and expected to feel completely fulfilled, with her immaculate home, busy social life, holidays abroad, and multiple employees who take care of cooking, cleaning, gardening, and driving. No one would overtly stop her from working should she start again, but there might be tacit disapproval from her parents, husband, parents-in-law, and broader social milieu. She thinks the emotional price she would pay for pursuing her career would not be worthwhile, but she is conflicted. She said that she hopes to work again after both her kids start school, but has no practical plan for doing so. She admits that it will be hard to go against the grain of expectations.

There are many more like Sabah and Jawaher—women who simply never start working outside the home or those who drop out quickly owing to lack of opportunity, discrimination, family responsibilities, and cultural pressures. Some are simply swept away by culture and duty, some make a conscious choice, and still others are deeply frustrated at home. Some aim to work after their children grow older but struggle with being out of the workforce or never having joined it to begin with. Given the millions of Muslim women who have acquired an education but not employment, governments and businesses have an opportunity. Bringing more of them and their talents into the workforce will only help their communities, cities, companies, and countries to grow, develop, and prosper.

A Woman's Worth

Economists around the world have long argued that educating girls is one of the highest-return investments a country can make. In part, the returns of this investment are generated through the multiplier effects on the health and education of the next generation. But they are also the result of the expanded earning potential of women who are educated. Economists have also shown that one of the largest forces shaping the growth of Western economies in the last half century was the steady rise of women in the workforce and that these economies stand to benefit further if they increase the participation of women. If women's paid employment rates were raised to the same level as men's, US GDP would be an estimated 9 percent higher, the GDP for countries in the European Union would climb by 13 percent, and Japan's would be boosted by 16 percent. In fifteen major developing economies, per capita income would rise 14 percent by 2020, and 20 percent by 2030.[17]

The Muslim world is no different. In fact, the returns to women's economic participation may be even greater there than elsewhere.

For example, if female labor force participation in the Muslim world rose to current Western levels of around 60 percent in the next fifteen years, the GDP of the MENA region alone would spike by 20 to 25 percent.

When women work, their families go through a profound shift, as do their communities and economies. The economic pathways through which these positive effects work are relatively obvious. Multiple studies have found that, at a macro level, women's economic empowerment helps the economy through the expanded labor force, the broader pool of skills, and the added potential for innovation and new ideas. This positive effect also plays out at a micro level. An analysis of Fortune 500 companies found that those with the greatest representation of women in management positions delivered a total return to shareholders that was 34 percent higher than the return delivered by companies with the lowest representation.

The reverse is also true: gender gaps are a permanent drag on the growth of economies. For example, gender inequality in labor force participation (as a proxy for gender gaps in employment) has a sizable negative impact on economic growth in the Middle East, North Africa, and South Asia when compared with other regions.[18]

So what potential gains are we talking about? The consulting firm McKinsey & Company has calculated that women's equal economic participation could add US$12 trillion to the global economy. Applying the methodology behind those forecasts to the thirty Muslim-majority countries, nearly half of that amount—US$5.7 trillion—would be added in the Muslim world alone.[19] The gains for individual countries are enormous too—US$1.6 trillion in Indonesia, US$1.3 trillion in Saudi Arabia, US$1.3 trillion in Turkey, US$500 billion in Iran and Pakistan, and US$333 billion in Kazakhstan.

The potential economic gains are reason enough for further expansion of women's economic participation in the Muslim world. But the societal benefits may be even greater.

Decent work gives people value, self-worth, and a sense of contribution to and participation in their society that is very different from the satisfaction derived from being a mother—or father—to children and raising the next generation. In fact, work combined with parenthood can set off a more virtuous cycle for the next generation. Study after study shows the value of work in balance with family and relationships, and the value of children observing working parents, both mothers and fathers. For example, research on maternal employment in Denmark found a positive effect on children's academic performance. A report on gender equality in the United Kingdom outlined the role of increases in women's wages in reducing child poverty and crimes of violence. Evidence from a range of countries shows that increasing the share of household income controlled by women, through either their own earnings or cash transfers, changes spending in ways that benefit children. Female employment and earning have also been found to exert an equalizing force on the distribution of income—when women work, the gap between the rich and the poor narrows.[20]

The positive effects of women's work play out in the developing world too. A study in India has shown that child mortality—and female child mortality in particular—is inversely related to both maternal education and female labor force participation. A strong son preference has led to excess female child mortality in certain parts of India, but girls are likely to be valued more when women and their communities directly note that women can be productive, earning members of their community.[21]

Even in regions that have seen military conflict and civil unrest, women's participation in the labor force can have a transformative effect. A report by UN Women points out that increases in the labor force participation of women in conflict-affected areas are in some cases associated with increases in overall household and community welfare. Remarkably, positive household and/or community benefits in some case studies were observed despite the low-status jobs performed by women who were affected by conflict, and despite the fact women earn on average less than men.[22]

The combined impact of the economic and societal gains from women's economic participation could revitalize the Muslim world, including those countries most affected by conflicts. That even the more conservative assumptions show tremendous gains is hardly surprising.

Imagine a situation in which every educated woman like Sabah and Jawaher could make different decisions. They would change more than their own self-fulfillment, income, and the financial prospects of their families. Beyond their economic contributions, there would be a multiplier effect on those around them, both materially and socially. Their children would see better role models. Their families would have more disposable income. Their employers would have a more highly skilled workforce, opening the path for further growth. And working women's communities would benefit from their expertise, their agency, and their empowerment.

three

Uncharted Waters

G ENDER GAPS IN LABOR FORCE PARTICIPATION ARE SOMETIMES interpreted as evidence that women don't want to work outside the home, but the experience in most countries shows this is not the case. Although some women—and some men—would truly prefer not to work outside the home, for many work is a matter of incentives and opportunity. When new conditions arise, their decisions about working outside the home also change. In much of the Muslim world, these new conditions have already come about— economic growth, rising prices, increased education, declining fertility, and globalized aspirations have already led many women to enter the workforce.

Social acceptance of working women, however, is still in flux, creating uncharted waters for women—and men—to navigate. Many of today's young women feel privileged for having more access to education and labor markets than their mothers ever did. And they expect to pass on an even more expanded set of options—better education and better job opportunities—to their daughters. Having seen the benefits of women's economic contribution and independence first-hand, today's young fathers also plan to encourage their daughters to "have it all." This powerful change in beliefs and expectations bodes well for the future. As women become ever more integrated into the workforces of the Muslim world, this transformation becomes more normalized and more deeply rooted in society.

In spite of the new norms, however, traditional attitudes persist. A recent Gallup and International Labour Organization poll asked people around the world, both women and men, if they preferred for women to work at a paid job, to stay at home to take care of family and housework, or to do both. In the Middle East and North Africa, 45 percent of men and 36 percent of women believed that women should stay at home.[1] An equal 17 percent of women and 17 percent of men believed that women should be engaged in paid work, and 35 percent of men and 45 percent of women believed that women should do both. In all, then, over 50 percent of men and over 60 percent of women believed that women should work or manage both work and home. With the current average labor force participation of adult women in the MENA region at 23 percent, this implies that there is room for more women to come into the workforce, even with the current attitudes, provided they still bear the burden of responsibilities in the home. The expectation that women should manage a double shift isn't unique to the Muslim world. In Western Europe, 51 percent of men and 60 percent of women believed that women should manage both work and home, while in North America, 46 percent of men and 59 percent of women thought they should do both. But attitudes can also shift over time. In both Europe and North America, women's labor force participation has hovered around or above 60 percent for two decades. Yet in Western Europe, only 12 percent of men and 13 percent of women believed that women should be exclusively in the home, while nearly twice that number—21 percent of men and 23 percent of women—believed women should only be in the home in North America. Whether traditional attitudes toward women's roles evolve relatively quickly in the Muslim world, including the MENA region, remains to be seen.

For now, as Muslim women start working, they are met with a new challenge: how to combine work with traditional notions of marriage, motherhood, and femininity. Many Muslim women who work neutralize the potential conflict between economic empowerment and cultural norms by finding a "third way": taking responsibility for both home and work, but outsourcing some domestic tasks to others, both hired help and other family members.

The Third Way

Women in most societies around the world are primarily responsible for unpaid housework and caregiving and perform the bulk of the unpaid labor at home: cooking, cleaning, child care, elder care, and laundry. These critical tasks, while unrecognized in GDP statistics, must be performed in any family or household. Almost invariably, regardless of income or geography, the division of household labor is largely skewed toward women, while men perform the greater share of paid work. This is true across the Muslim world too.

In urban Iranian families, housewives are commonly the ones who drive to the supermarket to buy groceries for the week. In rural Mauritania, groups of girls walk long distances together to fetch water. In other parts of the Muslim world, women's unpaid work is done "out of sight." For example, in rural Pakistan, it is the men of the family— sons, brothers, or husbands—who go out to buy food, and it is the women who then cook it and feed the family. And almost universally in agriculture-dependent parts of the Muslim world, women provide the backbone of labor in small family farms, but their unpaid work doesn't show up in national data because the property is allocated to the head of the household, usually a male.[2]

Unpaid work imposes a time constraint on women who work already—and those who might. For many Muslim women, who until very recently were mainly in the home, the expectation of this traditional division of labor has stayed firmly in place even as they take on more paid work. Therefore, like women in developed economies, they face a "second shift"—performing unpaid labor at home in addition to paid labor at work.[3]

There is an opportunity cost to this unpaid work—it reduces the time that could be spent on remunerated work. Unsurprisingly, in most countries gender gaps in labor force participation mirror the gender gaps in unpaid work. On average, men do about half the unpaid work that women do in the Organization for Economic Cooperation and Development (OECD) countries. In Norway, Sweden, and Denmark, men perform more than 40 percent of the unpaid work, but even in these egalitarian cultures men and women have not reached full parity when it comes to unpaid work. In India, men perform only 13 percent of the unpaid work, and in Japan and Korea only around 17 percent. In Mexico, men do 19 percent of the unpaid work. Comparable data are available for only one Muslim-majority country: in Turkey, men take on about 24 percent of the unpaid work in the home.

Trying to have it all, then, becomes a matter of redistributing the tasks traditionally accomplished by women. Data from the OECD show that when the time women spend on unpaid work shrinks from five hours to three hours a day, their labor force participation increases by 10 percent. The same pattern plays out in many Muslim households.

The hours spent on unpaid work chores such as washing and cleaning have been partly reduced by technology and better infrastructure. As more and more middle-class homes acquire gadgets—often bought with the second incomes that women bring into the household—some minutes or even hours are shaved off the daily unpaid work that is still the primary responsibility of women. These hours become available for paid work or other pursuits, but by and large, full oversight for the home continues to lie with women. Moreover, much of this household work, such as cooking and child care, is time intensive and not amenable to automation.

Many educated working women have thus turned to unskilled or low-skilled working women to do this household work for wages, using their own newly acquired salaries to offset the cost. The supply of such predominantly female, low-skilled labor has been abundant thus far, and their wages low enough that it has been an easy trade-off for most higher-paid working women. The care services economy has thus become a massive but unregulated sector, employing hundreds of thousands of women and freeing up others to be employed in return. Cheap labor for care work is often complemented by family support, especially for child care—provided, once again, by women.

Hawazen, the Saudi woman working in a logistics firm and aspiring to be a denim clothing designer, sees a close friend taking this third way—combining a new work-related identity with traditional roles based around marriage and motherhood. "My best friend manages to go to the gym, run an independent event planning company, raise three kids, and do her actual day job at King Saud University. She does have a very supportive husband, and he has a good income—more than middle-income level. But still, I don't know how she finds the time! I can barely manage myself!"

A supportive husband in this case means someone who is willing to encourage his wife to play a role outside the home, but it does not mean an equal division of labor in the home. To balance the household chores—for which they are still primarily responsible—along with their work responsibilities, some women hire help if they can afford to, as many middle-class Saudis can. Drivers, cooks, and nannies, nearly all foreign workers, are inexpensive and easy to hire.

In addition, proximity to grandparents—particularly grandmothers—and other extended family helps working mothers seeking help with child care. Despite urbanization and migration, the extended family unit has remained largely intact in most Muslim societies. Working couples often have both sets of parents close by, and given the early age of marriage across most Muslim societies, their parents are often young enough to be active, in good health, and able to provide child care support.

Sara Khurram, a doctor turned entrepreneur, has this advantage in Karachi. She told me, "My work and family balance is still something I have to shape every day. There are some day care centers and crèches, but I would not use them. I would not leave my child with anyone but my mother and my mother-in-law." The older generation of women may never have worked outside the home themselves, but they are willing to subsidize the work of a younger, more educated generation.

This is true for women regardless of their economic status, including those low-income women who are working as domestic help for others. Mari, who works as a housemaid and nanny in Jakarta for a middle-class family, brokered through an online platform for care work, would not be able to work if not for the combined child care support she receives from family and neighbors in looking after her own three-year-old. She wakes up at 5:00 a.m. every day to cook, clean, and play with her daughter. At 7:00 a.m., she and her husband, who works in construction installing window frames, set off from home. Mari drops off her daughter with either her elderly neighbor, a woman who looks after a few of the young children in the neighborhood for a small fee, or her sister, who works from home. As rural migrants, neither she nor her husband have their parents in the city. After an hourlong commute to work, she spends the day washing, cooking, cleaning, and looking after her employer's four-year-old daughter, whom she said she loves like her own. On her way home by 7:00 p.m., she picks up her daughter from the neighbor or her sister, even though her husband gets home earlier. However, he looks after their daughter while she makes dinner.

Even though Mari's neighbor looks after her daughter more for the company than to earn money, and even though her sister takes care of her daughter half the time, the fee she pays her neighbor nevertheless takes up around 10 percent of her income. If she had to pay her neighbor full-time or at the going rate, she would probably not find the trade-off worthwhile. For middle- and high-income working women, the combined commercial and family help for child care is an integral part of the balance; for low-income working women, including those who work as nannies themselves, family and community support is indispensable.

This compact—mothers, sisters, and grandmothers agreeing to care for the children while their daughters, siblings, and granddaughters venture out into the world of work—may not be possible in another generation or two as the age of marriage rises and proximity to parents may present a dual care burden for both aging parents and young children. But for now and the foreseeable future, many Muslim working women are reaping this cultural dividend, which helps them strike a delicate balance between work and family and makes it culturally acceptable for them to take on roles outside the home.

As new economic opportunities create new social terrain, millions of women—and the men around them—will have to learn to navigate it rapidly. For men, the task is to "allow" women to venture into education and work, something they too have no road map for. For women, the challenge is to take the economic opportunities while finding ways to maintain their role in the home. Many are managing to do so very successfully.

The third way is built around keeping the social aspects of patriarchy intact even as women gain ground in education and employment. Like the men of previous generations, today's Muslim men can maintain relative power in the household, knowing that at the same time they have made a step beyond what their fathers would have accepted in terms of women's roles outside the home. Women, meanwhile, get to venture into new fields to which they would not have had access in the past and are able to broaden their identities, provided they don't upset the balance in the home.

When I spoke to women about the third way, I struggled at first with the concept. It didn't seem fair. If unpaid work continued to be the primary responsibility of women, the inevitable time constraints would reduce their chances of thriving in the workforce, contribute to salary gaps, and increase their incentive to drop out of the workforce. And in many instances it does. But the truth is that men have held most of the economic, intellectual, and social capital in the Muslim world for a long time and many of these men are still in a position to deny women education and employment opportunities outright. So women who gain an education and a job, or who want to work, have to find ways to make it culturally acceptable for the men and women around them—and even for themselves. When I thought about it in those terms, I began to see these women as smart and success-ful, if overburdened, negotiators. In other words, it is more than the megatrends of growth and education and more than the availability of family support and low-cost care services that have brought a large female cohort into the workforce in the Muslim world so rapidly. It is also the extraordinary deftness of these women in negotiating wholly uncharted waters and slowly but decidedly shifting cultural norms.

A Bridge to a Different Future

The longer-term impact of this short-term trade-off to create a third way cannot be overstated. Although women's influx into the work-force has largely happened because of economic necessity and new opportunities, once women's work takes root, it transforms culture. Nowhere is this more apparent than in the homes of low-income, ru-ral women who are accessing economic opportunity for the first time in their communities and attempting to maintain a balance between their old and new identities as they do so. Their communities begin to change from within. The third way, then, is the most sustainable path toward gender equality, unleashing change at a pace that society can absorb and laying the groundwork for a bolder stance by the next generation of women.

In a small village in the Governate of Fayoum, a couple of hours' drive out of Cairo, in an area that voted overwhelmingly in favor of the Muslim Brotherhood in the last elections, I went to the women's wing of the local mosque. The women's prayer room doubles as a com-munity center. I was there to meet four women: Emaan, Rania, Salma, and Naglaa. We sat down in a circle on the floor on a green carpet, trying to remain cool under a ceiling fan. All four of the women had their preschool children with them and the kids watched me curiously, once in a while offering me a shy smile. None of the four women had completed more than a primary school education, but now, under the tutelage of the nongovernmental organization (NGO) Alashanek Ya Balady (the Association for Sustainable Development), they are receiving short-term vocational training to enhance their business skills in order to support them in setting up their own small businesses. In addition to this kind of capacity building, the association offers them microloans to launch their businesses. As these four women chatted with me, other women and their toddlers came in and out of the room with their training materials—books teaching them the basics of accounting, pencils, and exercise mats—and sat down to work.

Emaan, Rania, Salma, and Naglaa all agree that women have always played a role in breadwinning for their families by providing informal, unpaid labor on the farms in their rural community. But the small-scale farming of their parents' generation no longer offers a viable livelihood. Their husbands work either in local factories or in places with more economic opportunity, like Sharm El Sheikh and Cairo. But this work is also not enough to sustain the family. And so these women have taken on a part of the breadwinning duties, independently rather than as part of existing family enterprises like farms. The training and loans from Alashanek Ya Balady have transformed their families' lives by creating new revenue streams for their household income.

They admitted that their husbands were at first hesitant, but the use of the local mosque as the training center reassures them, as does the all-female team from the NGO. Most importantly, all four of the women fully maintain their "primary" roles as housewives and homemakers in addition to their new responsibilities. This gives their husbands time and reason to adjust their thinking. It's a win-win for their husbands: they get both their wives' contribution to the household income and a continued division of labor and hierarchy in the home.

But it's clear that the implications are more than economic and that a deeper social change is under way. Emaan told me that her negotiating power with her husband over financial decisions has changed, without her even being aware of it until recently, and she thinks it's the same for the other women. There are also implications for the next generation. Salma insisted that I see her business up close, so we walked over to her house. In the front part of her tiny apartment, occupying more than half the room, was a small incubator for unhatched eggs. As we stepped back out, her teenage son proudly showed me a small cart he had attached to the back of his motorbike. Salma told me that he now goes around the village selling her eggs and chickens to others. In the past, a son would only have become involved in his father's business, but now Salma's son is eagerly helping with hers, seeing his mother as an economic contributor—and a woman with greater authority and agency than ever before.

The impact may be even more pronounced for the mind-set of the women's daughters. Rania, who has five children—two daughters and three sons—said that one of her daughters wants to be a doctor and practices on her dolls, while the other wants to be an airline stewardess and travel the world in order to see everything that she sees on TV. Although Rania's own parents put limits on her aspirations, she wants her daughters to have the autonomy and freedom she didn't have while still maintaining the conservative values that she holds dear.

In most Muslim economies, husbands have more authority than wives, and fathers hold greater authority over children than mothers in the social structure in the household.[4] Women like Emaan, Salma, Naglaa, and Rania are negotiating this traditional authority structure carefully, not challenging it overtly but making determined change that creates a win-win for the entire family. And as fathers, husbands, and brothers begin to see the overall positive change, their view of the economic engagement of their wives and daughters changes and they influence other men to see women's economic contributions differently too. This domino effect leads to a fundamental reevaluation of the value of women in society. Despite the occasional resistance, the forces set in motion are too potent to be stopped or reversed. Values and traditions are beginning to catch up with the new realities, as are products and services across the economies of the Muslim world.

An Angry Young Man

Many women entering the workforce manage to quietly balance work along with their responsibilities in the home that has given them a license to operate, but not all men are comfortable with the changes taking place in their households. As Mozah, the cook, and I were talking, all three of Mozah's grown children—Ahmed, Sherri, and Riri—were present, as were two of her young grandchildren. Sherri and Riri sat with us and talked mainly to each other, but they also interrupted their mother with a few extra details to add to her story. And as happened with all my conversations in Cairo, although I tried politely to decline an offer of tea, the young women soon brought out a small feast with some tea and I got to sample some of Mozah's excellent cooking. I noticed then that Ahmed appeared to be brooding on one side of the room, despite having been the one to welcome us out in the street and lead us up to his mother's apartment. He seemed unable to smile at any of the humor passing between mother and daughters or with me and the journalist who was helping me translate.

Mozah offered a part-apology, part-explanation. She told me that Ahmed is deeply unhappy about his mother's work outside the home. He feels a sense of shame that his work as a driver is insufficient to sustain his own young family—his wife and two children—as well as his mother and divorced sister. In a previous time, his income might have been enough, but in today's Cairo it is not. Mozah said, "He has been able to stop his own wife from working, but he cannot stop me." Like many women of Mozah's generation, discovering economic independence late in life has opened her eyes to her own power, especially after having spent first her childhood working to supplement her parents' income and then her adulthood dependent on her husband. Along with the responsibility has come a change in her views about cultural norms. Recalling again her invitation to demonstrate her cooking on television, Mozah was defiant. At the time she had said she was "too conservative" and didn't want to appear on TV, even with her headscarf on. Today, she said, she would jump at the opportunity for the exposure it might bring to her talent and her home-based business.

Although low-skilled women in low-income households have often supported male breadwinners in an ad-hoc way with supplementary economic activity, in addition to doing unpaid care work in the home, today more and more of them are joining the workforce as equal rather than supplementary players, even among Mozah's generation. The rising cost of living, high unemployment for unskilled—and even skilled—youth, and changing consumption patterns have leveled the playing field for women and men in millions of families. In Mozah's case, economic necessity following the death of her husband drove her to become the main breadwinner for herself and her divorced daughter.

Such disruption upends the social order, and women like Mozah can feel awakened and empowered for the first time in their lives. Mozah said that she certainly needs the money but also loves her work—and wants more of it. I asked her how her work is accepted in her community. She said that it has become "normal that women help out" because "men can't do it alone." But for her son, Ahmed, this is still a difficult transition to accept in adulthood, having seen something quite different in his childhood. Ahmed and many other men like him feel a loss of power and pride. Mozah said that her daughter-in-law, Ahmed's wife, used to work as a saleswoman in a shop. "Ahmed has now stopped her from working because of the ideas he has from his father. But he can't stop me because he can't afford to take care of us on his own," she added. Ahmed looked even gloomier as she spoke.

But Mozah is trying to maintain a delicate balance. Even though he is socially the head of the household, Ahmed is still her son and thus more obliged to deal with her late-in-life bid for independence and professional fulfillment than her husband or father would have been. For her daughters, however, she is more circumspect. Mozah quickly pointed out that work cannot be everything to a woman. "It is important for women to maintain their femininity. They have to take care of themselves. They have to dress up and wear tops, leggings, and heels," she said, pointing to her daughters. "I raised them this way. Even if times are tough financially, they have to maintain a balance."

Her daughters' manicures, makeup, and clothing made it clear that they have taken their mother's lessons to heart. But this attempt at "balance" to resolve what Mozah sees as the dichotomy between work and femininity has not been enough to convince her son-in-law. Riri used to work in an NGO, but after her first child was born, her husband stopped her from working. "He was always worried when she was on the street. Now he is reassured that she is safe at home."

Muna Abu Sulayman, a TV personality and entrepreneur in Saudi Arabia, believes that some young men are resentful because they now hear about women's empowerment from the government and "even though most policies are still designed largely for men, they think all the resources are going to women. That resentment could spill over into personal relationships or lead to men thinking the government treats them badly."

Nada, a young woman in Tunis, referred to another challenge, one she called the ambition gender gap. "Women should determine the future of our country because men have been left behind not only in learning and education—but also in ambition. They are lost and they want things to go back to the way they were. We want things to move forward."

For the vast majority of working women and the men around them, the benefits of women's economic participation outweigh the discomforts, and the potential backlash is limited. But understanding where it does occur is important to facilitating change. The reactions of Riri's husband and Ahmed are partly due to tradition but also stem in part from their own sense of current and impending loss. Although women are not overtly challenging traditional norms, and in spite of the vast economic benefits both at the family level and for national economies, in some subsections of society men resist women's rise in the workforce. Some young men who were brought up to believe that it is their primary role to be the breadwinner, but have found themselves unable to fulfill this role on their own, feel a loss of pride and identity when they see their mothers, wives, and sisters working. For others, a lack of economic opportunity outside the home leads to a desire for more control in the home, where men have traditionally exercised complete control, including over women. And especially for men in traditional trades and blue-collar work, which are disappearing in some urban areas, economic disruption has arrived too quickly. Seeing their better-educated sisters and classmates sometimes finding more job opportunities than they do, some of these men begin to perceive women's gains as men's losses. Idle young men without economic prospects are a potentially disruptive political force, turning to violence and radicalism in the most extreme cases. More often, however, they are simply one more barrier for young women seeking opportunity outside the home.

A Double-Edged Sword

In a TED talk titled "Three Lessons on Success from an Arab Businesswoman," Leila Hoteit, a consultant based in Dubai, talks about how professional Arab women manage to be successful despite juggling more responsibilities than their male counterparts and facing more cultural rigidity than Western women.[5] She explains that dual-earner families like hers with a comfortable income can afford to hire care workers and that they recruit and manage these personnel as they would their teams at work. Explaining her relationship with her nanny Cristina, Hoteit says, "She makes sure that the house is running smoothly while I'm at work, and I make sure to empower her in the most optimal conditions for her and my children, just like I would my best talent at work. This lesson applies whatever your child care situation, whether an au pair, nursery, part-time nanny that you share with someone else. Choose very carefully, and empower."

The services of low-income, low-skilled women have been a boon to white-collar Muslim women, who thus receive the support they need to be able to concentrate on their professions while maintaining their overall responsibility as chief homemaker. The outcomes for low-income women themselves, however, are varied. For many low-skilled women, care work is a new paid work opportunity that they would not otherwise have had. The extra income they gain from it often enables them to contribute to household income for the first time, which changes the power dynamic and income levels in these poorer families. For those lucky enough to work for an employer who empowers them, as Hoteit does, work offers dignity and learning too. For others, the reality is more complex. These new employment opportunities can be precarious, and because the economic need is more urgent in their families, those opportunities can create unintended incentives for women to remain trapped in low-income work.

Jamila is the twenty-year-old middle child among five siblings, with two older sisters and two younger brothers. Her parents migrated to Islamabad when she was an infant, in search of opportunity. Her father found work as a guard at a government-owned building. Her mother began to provide domestic help on a part-time basis in several homes in a high-income neighborhood, one of the thousands of rural migrant women who began to provide support to middle-income professional women in Islamabad in the last couple of decades. When Jamila's two older sisters finished primary school, they too were brought along to their mother's various workplaces and little by little began to learn the tasks and chores required of domestic help. As teenagers, they began to acquire their own clients. These women faced a second shift too. Jamila's mother and elder sisters had to do their own housework, getting up earlier than the men and boys to cook and clean.

By the age of fourteen, Jamila had been in school longer than either of her sisters, and she wanted to stay long enough to complete high school. But after her older sisters got married—both through arrangements facilitated by their parents—their chores became Jamila's responsibility as the only daughter left in the household. Her parents made their main investments in her two younger brothers. With earnings too meager to allow for any savings, and with no government-funded benefits, their sons were their future safety net.

When they decided to send the boys to a private school they could barely afford in order to improve their future employment prospects, Jamila's income became a vital cash flow for the family.

Sharing the hopes of her parents, Jamila is proud of her brothers. She told me that the elder brother is a "computer science genius." But she also admitted wistfully that she would do anything to return to school and learn to become a skilled child care worker, because she loves children. Although she is largely resigned to her likely fate—an early marriage, children of her own, and life as domestic help—she still keeps some dreams of a different future. At twenty, Jamila is starting to become older than the typical age of marriage for young women in her community. Her parents have arranged her engagement to a man in a nearby community similar to hers—also rural migrants living on the fringes of the city—but the wedding is on hold because her parents still need her income to continue to pay the school fees for her brothers.

For young women like Jamila, growing economic opportunity is a double-edged sword. Her work is essentially a short-term subsidy for the family unit, with her wages stimulating long-term returns for her parents and brothers through the investment in their education, but she herself does not stand to benefit from the investment and has little say in her destiny. It is not the life she might have had back in her rural community—no education, child marriage, and several teenage pregnancies—but it is also not a life that enables her to complete her education, exercise agency over her marital choice, and carve out her own economic path. And she cannot outsource her unpaid care work to someone else as her own employers have done; instead, she has to complete both shifts fully, at home and at work. At best, she can share some of the care burden at home with her mother.

Not all stories, however, are like Jamila's. Gita, the Indonesian lawyer, worries about her future prospects in finding household help because of the new opportunities arising for low-skilled women. "Girls from the villages don't want to be maids anymore. They have usually completed some basic education. They want to work in factories.

There they can have fixed hours, they can earn more and have more independence."

This competition for young low-skilled rural women expands choices for them and increases their access to more formal work, often with relatively better conditions. This change has forced the care sector to become better organized and, by consequence, safer and higher-paid. Online platforms and off-line agencies have sprung up that make the transaction between employer and employee a little more transparent—and safer—for both. Young rural women use these sites from Internet cafés—and for some, from hard-won smartphones—to create profiles, listing the tasks they can perform, from cooking and cleaning to child care. Some register themselves with domestic staff agencies. White-collar women like Gita pick out those best suited to the roles they have to offer. Many of these platforms are created by working women themselves, because they understand the needs of professional women but also want to help empower low-skilled domestic workers by creating a fairer trade between them. For both sides, then, these platforms create a more efficient marketplace. Some social enterprises combine work with other services, such as financial management and education, ensuring that domestic work serves as a stepping-stone for low-income women to higher-value-added work in the future.[6] In the absence of public infrastructure and regulation of care services, this subeconomy built by women for women provides a solution for care consumers and workers alike and makes the third way a little easier for both sides. For these patchwork solutions to endure, however, governments will need to do much more to incentivize and regulate them—to ensure fair pay and security not just for the women who are fortunate enough to have employers who wish to empower them but for all service workers.

A Clash of Civilizations

The context within which working women are negotiating a new space for themselves is not static. Economic growth, technology, and globalization have brought different demographic groups into closer contact—and at times into conflict—along income, age, and religious lines.

As more people are lifted out of poverty and as the middle class grows, owing in part to women's new incomes, they buy an ever larger range of experiences, products, and services. In Egypt, small groups of young women and men from poorer neighborhoods of Cairo pool money to jointly buy good cameras and then walk through upper-class neighborhoods to take high-resolution selfies for their large followings on social media. In Isfahan, young lower-middle-class couples go out for dates to local versions of Western fast-food restaurants. In Dhaka, lower-middle-class families travel within the country for holidays, a luxury experience limited to the upper-middle and upper classes until recently. Consumption and culture are intertwining to change how different income groups and classes relate to each other.

As millions are exposed to education and employment opportunities that their parents never knew, stark generational differences emerge. Today young people are trying to create a new identity for themselves, one different from the identity handed down from their parents. Samira, the ride-sharing entrepreneur, told me: "The older generation is everything I want to change about this culture. Mainly I want to change the resistance to change. We need to be free to make our own choices. It's not about wearing hijab or not. It's about taking risks, like I did when starting a company. My parents didn't stop me, but also didn't like it. Their generation is afraid, and they resist change. We are bringing new trends, but they want things to be as they have been always. This is not only in Egypt. If you look at Brexit [the British electorate's 2016 vote to leave the European Union], it was the same—the older generation against the new generation. Technology is changing our generation very fast, but our parents didn't have this rate of change so they don't understand."

There is flux around religion too. As extremist agendas grow louder, they hold an outsized influence in the public imagination, even as they are rejected by the majority. And with news from the West usually conveying negative views of Islam, the sense of defensiveness against these stereotypes is growing in Muslim-majority countries, even among people who are not regular practitioners of Islam.

Within this internal clash of civilizations among generations, classes, and degrees of religiosity, women are reexamining what it means to be liberal or traditional—in essence, they are redefining what it means to be a "good" woman. This is nowhere more starkly visible than among middle-class millennial women, who now have more spending power than their parents had and more exposure and access to global trends than any generation before them. But being connected with the world has not necessarily "Westernized" them. That term is often interpreted to mean wholesale acceptance and adoption of the Western worldview. Instead, these young women are clearing a unique path for themselves. Influenced by their class, their values, their religiosity, their upbringing, their education, and their exposure, that path is neither wholly "Western" nor "traditional." To Westerners, these women may appear traditional, and to their compatriots, they may appear Westernized, but they are in fact espousing something new.

Clothing is a flashpoint across the Muslim world. In Egypt, with security fears keeping tourists largely away, hotels and resorts have lowered their prices and let in a very different kind of customer— the lower-middle class. Young women in burqinis—a combination of a bikini and a burqa that provides full body coverage to modest female swimmers—now go swimming in resort pools and beaches in Sharm El Sheikh, which customarily hosted foreigners or upper-class Egyptians. On social media, upper-class Egyptians complain about the "unhygienic" practices of lower-class women who go into pools clothed in burqinis.[7] At those same beaches, men from conservative, usually lower-income backgrounds both deride and take photos of higher-income women in bikinis, without permission. Both sides judge each other. The opening up of the traditional realm of the rich and upper-middle classes to lower-middle-income and middle-income women has led at times not so much to a battle of the sexes as a battle of the classes.

In Indonesia, the headscarf is locally known as a *jilbab*. Over dinner, several young men and young women, both those who wear the headscarf and those who do not, told me, with plenty of snickering and eye rolls, about the colloquial term "jilboobs" (a combination of "jilbab" and "boobs") to refer to hijab-wearing women whose clothing is otherwise tight or revealing. Although the Indonesian Council of Ulema (religious body) issued a fatwa against the style, Hidayat Nur Wahid, a previous head of the Prosperous Justice Party, an Islamic party, was more tempered in his response: lauding the fact that young women wear hijabs to begin with, he suggested that over time they should "have a commitment to fully cover the body."[8]

There are other versions of this new mix of modesty and sexuality among young women in other Muslim countries. In Riyadh, I spent nearly an hour dissecting with a group of young women how far one could push the limits of color and design on an abaya and the different color codes for different cities, with more color being acceptable in Jeddah than the traditional black in Riyadh. In Islamabad, with the latest designs of traditional shalwar kameez switching between long and short, teenagers and twenty-something women try to push the boundary as far as they can. They often post their latest outfits on social media, with the less bold among them cropping out their heads to remain unrecognizable.

For a generation that grew up in the long shadow of the post-9/11 world, one where Islam is associated with violence and terror, some young women deliberately reclaim what they see as pure Islam. Their rebellion, unlike that of their fellow millennials who want to expose more of themselves, is to more fully cover themselves. A subculture of young women who choose large, elaborate headscarves and loose-fitting clothing is growing in parallel with the "jilboobs" phenomenon. Some adopt the *niqab*, which covers most of the face. Their parents, having never asked their daughters to be covered, are often surprised.

In some parts of the Muslim world, dressing more conservatively than the local historical norm is viewed with suspicion. In Kyrgyzstan, the only one of the Central Asian republics to have had a female head of government, massive billboards began to appear on the streets of Bishkek in mid-summer 2016, showing three sets of women: some in traditional Kyrgyz clothing, some in a burqa, and some in a niqab; the burqa and niqab are traditionally most popular in the Gulf states.[9] Below the pictures is a single question: "Oh poor nation, where are we headed?" President Almazbek Atambayev soon spoke out in support of the posters: "Let us not confuse Arabian, Pakistani, and I don't know, Bangladeshi culture with Kyrgyz culture. This is an imposition of foreign culture. A foreign culture of dress. We have our own clothes."[10] Ironically, many in Pakistan and Bangladesh worry about the same infiltration of their local culture, just as others celebrate it. A few days after Atambayev's statement, a new billboard appeared, this time juxtaposing the traditional Kyrgyz costumes with revealing Western clothing and posing the very same question.

Pushing the "Western" way too much also has a price, especially for women from low-income backgrounds in conservative cultures. In Pakistan, the singer, model, and actress Qandeel Baloch used a unique combination of overt sexuality and "girl power" to become an overnight social media celebrity, one who was both loved and derided. As young women increasingly follow the route of education and employment, a woman with a degree and a job no longer shocks, but a woman who tries the route taken by Baloch to earning a living does. That level of boldness, particularly for a "lower-class" woman, attracts both admiration and ire. Baloch was strangled to death by her brother, who said he was proud of killing her for having destroyed his family's honor. Such incidents—and protagonists—remain rare, but they send a warning to other women on where the boundaries must be drawn—for now.

In sum, the labels traditionally used to describe societies in the Muslim world, by both Westerners and locals, simply no longer apply. A wealthy, working woman can be socially conservative. A socially conservative, low-income millennial man can be a champion for women's economic empowerment. These new combinations of behaviors, values, and beliefs transcend conventionally recognized divisions of conservative or liberal, religious or Westernized, traditional or modern, and other distinctions. The new boundaries are still undefined and still being tested, but the rise of new subcultures and values that traverse income and class boundaries has expanded the set of options about what women's empowerment and gender equality mean in the Muslim world.

Mona Lisa Smile

For many young women, the traditional roles and tasks of wife, mother, and sister are precious and important to preserve, along with their new identities.

Kazakhstan, with its Soviet history, is one of the most "liberal" Muslim-majority countries in the world, at least in outward appearances. There are nightclubs where young people mingle with the same ease they would feel in London, New York, or Moscow. Few women wear the hijab. Alcohol is available. Religion is tightly moderated and controlled by the government. Over 70 percent of all working-age women participate in the workforce, the highest percentage in the Muslim world.

At a young entrepreneurs' club in Almaty, I met Togzhan, a twenty-one-year-old IT graduate. Around 36 percent of computer science graduates are women in Kazakhstan, compared to 30 percent in the United States. Togzhan is idealistic and cheerful. She talks energetically about her experiences meeting other young people from Asia through travel in India and the United Arab Emirates. She said that money is not important to her, that she simply wants to help the world come a little closer together. She has been a serial entrepreneur thus far in her young life, launching platforms for everything from guitar lessons to test preparation. She said that she falls naturally into the role of leader in group projects and often directs the work of the groups she joins. She talked excitedly about her strong performance in math and her plan to get her next degree abroad. Her parents are high school teachers, both now retired. Togzhan is the youngest and has two older brothers and one older sister. One brother and one sister are married and live with families of their own. She and her twenty-four-year-old brother live at home. Whatever she earns, she aims to give at least half to her parents.

Togzhan is, by all standards, an educated, empowered, highly ambitious twenty-one-year-old. And yet she is also highly traditional when it comes to gender roles in her family. She always does all the dishwashing and the laundry because, she said, she would never want her brother to have to do it. "It would be wrong." Such adherence to traditional gender norms in the home for young women who otherwise break gender norms in school and work is not uncommon. It is one more piece in the mosaic of values, religion, and norms that has emerged across the educated, millennial generation in the Muslim world.

While equality of outcomes tends to be the goal among women's movements in the West, the women I spoke to often argued for equality of opportunity rather than equality of outcomes and for the coexistence of traditional and modern values. This approach also extended to the choices they made about marriage and family: after being exposed to family models from around the world, they wanted to make choices that were wholly their own.

Diajeng, the CEO of Hijup.com, an Indonesia-based online platform selling modest fashion, is married, with one daughter. She said that her husband, himself an entrepreneur, has been one of her greatest supporters from the very start, both for the business and for the overall concept of the personal development of Muslim women. In her personal Instagram feed, which has nearly 42,000 followers, Diajeng often posts about her husband and daughter. But she said that the equal division of labor in their home is not necessarily the norm and different couples must make different choices depending on their situation.

In 2015, the *New York Times* reported that American "millennial men aren't the dads they thought they'd be," and a 2017 study showed that American millennial men had more traditional attitudes than those of their fathers after having seen the generation ahead of them struggle without public support for parents.[11] Even young men who planned to share responsibilities in the home have found themselves in traditional arrangements a few years down the line. "Young men today have aspirations of being hands-on fathers as well as breadwinners—supportive husbands who also do dishes. But as they enter that more responsibility-filled stage of life, something changes: Their roles often become much more traditional." This trend appears to be playing out across the Muslim world too. While many young women plan to manage both home and work to start with, some single women and men told me they aspire to share responsibilities equally in the home once married. Their married friends who are just a few years older, however, generally told a different story. Often the men have fallen into the traditional role of breadwinner, while the women have taken on the dual role of breadwinner and caregiver.

However, Diajeng is hopeful about a different, more balanced future. "More and more women will join the workforce. In our information age, people can get inspired by each other. And we have to compete economically. If 50 percent of the population doesn't play a role, we won't succeed. Even if they choose to be at home, they can do it in a positive way. In our religion, everyone has to be the best version of themselves."

While she and her husband take a shared approach to parenting and have hired a nanny to support them, Diajeng thinks that more investment is needed in the care infrastructure to free up more women. But she also believes that companies need to take on the core responsibility rather than the government. "They need the talent, and if they don't give day care, they will lose women employees because most women can't find good nannies—and it is still the job of women to find a solution."

She added that there is no religious restriction on getting support with child care and no obligation for women to prioritize home over work. "I think we see an example. The Prophet Muhammad, peace be upon him, was taken care of by Halima Al-Sa'diyah, a nanny, very much like a modern family. Just Google it. And his wife Khadija was an entrepreneur." To some, both in Indonesia and across the Muslim world, such a statement would be surprising, because it may not be part of the traditional narrative they learned. But this is what those in Diajeng's generation have been able to learn—by themselves—about the freedom and choice offered by their own religion, unfiltered by textbooks, religious leaders, or parental beliefs.

Minutes later Diajeng told me that for her another model for balance comes from "the *Mona Lisa Smile*." Confused, I asked her what she meant, and she explained that the film of that name inspires her because it reminds her that "whatever you choose, it's your own decision." The film, which stars Julia Roberts, Kirsten Dunst, Julia Stiles, and Maggie Gyllenhaal, is set at Wellesley College in the early 1950s and tells the story of a young professor who tries to inspire her students to want more than marriage. The student who is the most outspoken and ardent supporter of traditional values marries, but leaves her husband when she finds out he is having an affair—despite family pressure to stay with him—and considers law school instead. Another student, who at first is far more interested in going to law school, eventually chooses to focus on being a wife and mother instead, despite the professor's disappointment. The professor herself chooses to stay single and eventually leaves the college, unwilling to compromise her values to follow the curriculum.

When the movie first came out, I remember seeing it with friends simply because it's set in an all-female college campus similar to Smith College, our alma mater. I remember some friends admiring the professor for choosing to stay single. Some were disappointed with the student who chooses marriage over professional growth. Others praised the one who chooses further education. And yet others thought the story had little resonance in the modern world. For Diajeng, the fact that these characters from an America of half a century ago could make these very different choices was an inspiration—and the model she wants to see emerging in society.

For other young women, gender equality cannot be defined as simply expanded choice. Instead, they believe that women should be strongly encouraged to make new and different choices. Samira Negm from Cairo said: "I want to change the clichés about women. If I look at my high school class, I wouldn't see potential in most of the class. The other girls chose to be a reflection of their moms and marry and stay at home. The cliché is not forced. It's accepted. And this is what we need to change. What would be the way to change? Role models mainly, focusing on the areas where women are not usually seen, like STEM. When I look back at school, the girls were talking about boys or fashion. I see the change happening, but this has to be encouraged and deliberate. Sometimes the exposure through the Internet is having a bad effect, reinforcing stereotypes, but we are also using the Internet in a good way. For example, Egypt consumes a lot of pornography, but we also have high shares of people taking educational courses online, especially women. It's a strange contradiction, but we can encourage the good side."

Diajeng wants equality of opportunities and expanded choices, while Samira wants equality of outcomes and deliberate efforts to nudge young women to make more progressive choices. What they have in common, however, is that, like other young women, they are forming their own visions of gender equality based on local and global influences, tapping into everything from self-acquired knowledge about Islamic history to Hollywood to their own experiences and everything in between. Like millennials everywhere who have access to the Internet, they are armed with knowledge and information they have found themselves rather than been given. Their knowledge base from which they make choices and decisions is vastly wider than their mothers'. Their marriages, fertility choices, and decisions on how to divide roles in the home are evolving along with the shifts they have already experienced in education and employment. Cautiously but determinedly, these women are navigating uncharted waters toward a future with greater choice for all.

∾ four ∾

A Digital Opportunity

Amira Azzouz, the thirty-something founder and editor in chief of Fustany, based out of Cairo, is one of the many digital-savvy Muslim millennials who recognized early the rapid rise of the female workforce and turned it into a business opportunity. Fustany is a "fashion & lifestyle portal by Arab women for Arab women to inspire them to live a life full of creativity." The team itself, as curators of the content, is critical to building the audience. To understand their customers—Arab women in their twenties and thirties—they simply have to understand their own desires and needs.

On their site, they describe their brand's origins: "It all started from our love for fashion, that je ne sais quoi that happens when you try a designer item, when you watch a movie for Audrey Hepburn, or when you see that first look from a Chanel runway. Fustany.com is a fashion and lifestyle portal that stems from our love for just that! 'Everything fashion, art and style.' Everything that made us fall in love with fashion over and over again." But they are also clear about what they are not: "We are not trying to reinvent the wheel. It's just us flirting with fashion, giving perspective, helping you curate items, and aiding you in satisfying your addiction 'and secretly' our addiction to everything glamorous." In other words, they don't want to be seen as an authority. They are having fun and keeping it light, and so should you.

Amira and her colleagues understand Arab millennial women well. The sleek and well-designed site easily rivals any large fashion and lifestyle magazine in the West, but the content and tone are entirely local. Amira told me that her aim is to make the content timeless for the issues that matter to the region's twenty-five- to thirty-five-year-old women rather than focus on short-term events and celebrity news. They cover health, beauty, nutrition, and fashion but also discuss careers, relationships, infants, and children. "We want to empower women through little things. When they look good, they feel good—a lot depends on them," said Amira.

Fustany covers a wide range of options for middle-class millennial women, including those who are liberal in their clothing choices as well as those who may be more traditional. One article notes, "Long-sleeved wedding dresses are not only great for modest brides. They're also a great bridal look for anyone who's seeking an elegant look." There's an article on "twenty stunning Ramadan iftar outfits," featuring both women in headscarves and those without. There's an in-depth interview on maternity style with Rita Lamah, a Lebanese stylist and blogger expecting her third child and "walking around with one of the most stylish baby bumps out there!" But there's also an article on the maternity style of Blake Lively, a Hollywood actress. This seamless mixing of regional and Western content reflects the seamless mixing in the lives of many women in Fustany's audience: Arab, millennial, middle- and high-income women who blend liberal and traditional values to create a mix wholly their own. Language is blended here too: the site is in both English and Arabic. "English is more for the niche, while Arabic is for the mass," said Amira.

Amira knows that the entire basis of her business is about engaging others like her. She is a part of the product and must have an image to match. Her online profile says: "A little princess—not! The first thing you notice about Amira is her smile. She warms any place up. Her attention to detail is evident in everything she does, even picking her daily statement accessories—cat-ears headband anyone? Or maybe avant-garde funky glasses? Everything about Amira oozes style and quirkiness. Amira is Fustany's Founder and Editor-in-Chief. Her favourite items are statement jewellery like funky headbands, sunglasses, or a hand full of rings. She won't be seen dead in Uggs or high thigh leather boots."

When I walked into her offices, I expected someone as effusive as the tone of her profile and potentially wearing a cat-ears headband. Instead, Amira turned out to be fashionable, certainly, but also reserved and serious. While she clearly loves fashion and her image is carefully cultivated to match her product, she is also as much at ease talking about the bottom line of her business and the breadth of her customer base as she is in talking and writing about fashion and lifestyle.

As I peeked behind the sleek website, the start-up nature of Fustany also became a little more transparent. I was reminded of the nondescript offices of small and medium-sized enterprises (SMEs) across the emerging world, from Latin America to South Asia to Africa. Fustany is housed in a small apartment turned into an office, with one coworking space for five staff members and a private office for Amira. The air conditioning, a small luxury, is a relief after the heat and dust of the Cairo streets, but otherwise the office is unremarkable. A couple of feather boas and hats indicate a link to fashion.

Amira's journey with entrepreneurship started when she studied communication engineering at the German University of Cairo. She took on an online freelance project based in the United Kingdom and managed to get a big client. Soon realizing she was a natural at pitching and deal making, she reassessed her choices. *I'm good at this, so I should build my own thing,* she thought. With an early success under her belt, she started Fustany in 2009, her last year of university. The first version was scraped together with help from friends. The site has come a long way since then. When Amira started, the site had around five thousand visitors a month. Today it has nearly two and a half million a month, from both Egypt and the broader Arab world.

Women, she told me, have traditionally been told, "You need to marry and make your happy home." She said that women her age and younger are trying to do this differently, focusing on both careers and family life. She estimated that about 70 percent of her friends manage both. Amira is not married, so she has not yet had to strike this balance herself. She thinks it would be challenging but doable. As with everything else in life, she said, she is a "fighter," so she will "do it" when the time comes. She also believes that "strong men can handle it." Amira recognizes that her circle of friends who manage to cater to home and work represent only a subset of Egyptian society. But this group of women is growing, and their expanding choices, changing social cues, and emerging norms around empowerment, including the constant search for ways to balance work and social obligations, are at the heart of Fustany's mission.

"Whether staying at home or at work, she wants to feel empowered," she said of the typical woman reading Fustany. For Amira, her work is not just a lifestyle business but a social mission. "Women should have a responsibility to empower other women, if you actually have the mind-set to help other people." But her work is also profitable. Fustany has managed to attract some big labels and receives revenue from advertising, subscriptions, and affiliations from others for a share. Before working on Fustany, Amira said, she didn't know there were investors who targeted women-related companies, but she soon found that she was able to pitch convincingly on the high potential for rapid growth and returns.

Amira lives with her parents. "My dad is a power engineer, he started his own company focused on elevators and escalators. My mother is an architect, and joined my dad when I was four years old." Her sister, too, is an architect, who works at a solar energy company, now in Canada. When her father started the company, Amira said, he had a hard time, but "he made it happen." She has brought a similar determination to her own business. Having a supportive family has helped her, and as a female entrepreneur in Egypt's start-up scene, Amira said, she has "never faced a problem" with discrimination.

She did think, however, that there could be many more thriving ventures like hers if there were a broader culture of women's economic empowerment and the infrastructure to support it. The day before we met, Egyptian president Abdel Fattah el-Sisi had announced a pending cabinet change. Amira told me that she hopes there will be more women in the new cabinet because she believes that success stories and role models are critical if women are to feel they can "take a step too," especially in the absence of supportive families like hers. Additionally, she wants to see better funding for SMEs and a greater focus on education so that young women can develop the skills for the future, including entrepreneurship. Looking at the situation as it stands today across the broader Arab world, she thinks that Egyptian women are beginning to get more opportunity through their own efforts and notes that the Emirati government is proactively supporting women's entrepreneurship, but she sees the greatest potential in Saudi Arabia. "People are controlled, but they are exposed too. So, at some point, change will happen," she said.

An Entrepreneurial Spirit

The greatest migration from home to work has been enabled by digital technologies, which have redefined both home and work. If the narrative of the American westward expansion was "Go west, young man," the new narrative for up-and-coming Muslim women may well be "Go digital, young woman." Much like Fustany, a new range of digital bazaars has emerged, led by women who are monetizing technological, economic, and social change—and building new products and services around it. Like Amira, these women reflect the core attributes of Muslim, urban, middle-class millennial women: they are worldly, digitally connected, and determined.

If the stereotype of the Western millennial is a young person with a sense of entitlement, Muslim millennials defy it. These women are new to opportunity and hungry for its potential rewards. The most likely comparison for millennial working women of the Muslim world is the postwar, college-educated boomer generation in the United States, who carried with them the memory of war but marched onward in the quest for economic prosperity. But young Muslim women are also similar to Western millennials in their quest for a cause and for meaning. They are also the mostly globally connected generation in the Muslim world, aware of events, trends, and concepts not only in their own communities and neighborhoods but also in their broader regions and most certainly in the West.

This unique combination of traits—passion for making a difference, determination, and a strong work ethic—makes many of these women the perfect entrepreneurs. Many of their generation choose employment in the private sector or in government, but a significant number choose self-employment or supplement their work with "side hustles."[1] Some women are self-employed by necessity—other forms of employment may be scarce, or may not provide a sufficient income—but for many it is their preference. Some, like Amira, succeed in creating their own viable businesses.

As their generational cohort becomes the largest in the female workforce, these women's entrepreneurial creativity will determine what many middle-class families, especially the women in them, will consume. They will shape the new products and services that connect, power, serve, feed, and entertain their economies. They know their audience well. They understand women who have a desire to balance career ambitions with family. They understand women who want to balance tradition and modernity in their clothing and lifestyles. And they see no conflict in these dualities. Instead, they see a business opportunity, one that helps meet the needs of such women and generates a social impact while turning a profit.

The Modesty Market

One rising source of consumer demand comes from the desire of some women to combine professional ambitions with sartorial preferences in a way that merges modesty and modernity. This new market for "modest fashion" has exploded in the last five years as some young women sell products that match the new tastes to other young women with spending power—often in digital bazaars.

Hijup—a play on the words "hijab," or headscarf, and "up"—claims to be "the world's first Islamic fashion ecommerce" site and caters to devout women with disposable income and new tastes. Diajeng Lestari, whom we met in the last chapter, is the thirty-five-year-old founder and CEO. She represents the essence of the women she sells to: millennial women with earning power and cash to spend who are constantly striving to balance their professional roles with their roles as mothers and wives. In other words, they are very busy people. I first tried to meet Diajeng when I was in Jakarta, hoping to speak directly about her unique brand of products for fashionable, covered women. She was out of the country promoting her company in London, so we didn't manage to meet in person. Instead, we set up a Skype date for a time when she would be back in Jakarta. When I called her at the appointed time, Diajeng answered from a hospital bed with an intravenous drip in her arm and her family sitting around her bed. She had been taken in a few hours earlier, after fainting from exhaustion. Alarmed, I told her she should rest and we would reschedule. And yet her dedication and professionalism, which I am sure contributed to her exhaustion, got the better of her and she followed up with an apology and a video about the company so I could continue with at least part of my research while she recovered.

When we finally connected on our third try, Diajeng was restored to her fully energetic self and mildly embarrassed about her brush with exhaustion. "I didn't realize. Maybe I was doing too much." This was an understatement for the founder of this thriving start-up.

Hijup now has half a million followers on Instagram and a quarter million on Facebook, as well as its own mobile app. The site has around one and a half million visitors a month. There are 200 client designers on the platform, and all are women. Most are under thirty. On average, each brand has between 20 and 100 employees; the largest has more than 500 workers. Hijup directly employs 120 workers, and 80 percent are women. Diajeng said that Hijup has been turning a profit since it launched during Ramadan of 2011.

The site says: "Hijup stands for Hijab Up (just like in Make Up or Dress Up). Because we believe that we can bring something Up to all Moslem women around the world. That while wearing Hijab, they are not limited to do anything worthwhile, create something wonderful, and earn a lot of respect from others. They deserve to be happy and looking great in pretty but syar'i [Islamic-compliant] outfit and fashionable hijab."

Diajeng came up with this message of combined empowerment and modesty out of professional necessity. In 2007, after graduating with a degree in political science from the University of Indonesia, she was working for a market research company when her boss told her, "You are a hijaber, but you need to present yourself in a good way." Implied in her boss's statement was the assumption that women who wear the hijab cannot look good. Diajeng admitted that there may have been some truth to this, because "there was no hijab fashion at that time." Instead, she and others had to waste their precious time searching far and wide to collect items they liked. She thought to herself, *Can I solve this problem for other professional Muslim women?*

She had joined a group called the Hijabers Community, the brainchild of the modest fashion designer and blogger Ria Miranda, who has over half a million Instagram followers of her own. The community brings together women who wear the hijab and provides a platform for them to discuss their values, religion, jobs, and more. There Diajeng met one of her best friends, Hanna Faridl, who also happens to be the daughter of the president of the Indonesian Council of Ulema in Bandung. She also met various fashion designers who were beginning to design and sell to groups of women who wanted exciting but modest fashion choices. She estimates that at that time nearly 50 percent of the community was made up of fashion designers, running small or medium-sized businesses as something they "loved" and selling fashion for fun. So she suggested designing a platform that would help the designers grow their market and provide them with better marketing. For the consumers, it would be a one-stop shop for all their modest fashion needs.

Hijup states that it provides "a wide range of the best products from Indonesian Islamic fashion designers. The products we provide are for Moslem women in particular, from clothing, hijab/headscarf, accessories and more. Since its establishment, HIJUP.com functions as an agent between designers and their prospective buyers around the world. With HIJUP.com, designers can increase their profits more efficiently while making it easier for buyers to find the products they want."

But Diajeng sees the company as more than a fashion and beauty business. For her, Hijup is a cause and a community, not just a market. "It's not about the type of fashion where people want a beauty contest. For us, fashion must be great but also serve as an inspiration. It's okay to look beautiful, but character is more important. It's about spirituality. I don't want to be seen as just a fashion business. *Muslimah* need specific clothing to cover themselves and look good. I like makeup and clothes but also simply to be in this community with others and discuss spiritual issues." For some, including women who live secular lifestyles, modesty and fashion are simply incompatible.[2] But the success of modest fashion businesses proves that for many other Muslim women there is no contradiction.

Diajeng comes from a line of entrepreneurs. "My parents, several of my eight siblings, and even my grandmother was an entrepreneur," she told me. So spotting opportunity and turning it into a business was a natural next step for her. And her ambitions are big. "There are

1.6 billion Muslims in the world, and the majority are under thirty. They are the next middle class. By 2030, over 100 million Indonesians alone will be part of this middle class. Their buying behavior is driven by values. They want ethical Muslim fashion." Currently, 90 percent of Hijup's business is in Indonesia, but it is expanding in other parts of the world and attracting strong interest elsewhere, particularly in Southeast Asia.

Diajeng is among the older millennials or the youngest of Generation X, depending on how you look at it. Comfortably straddling these two generations, she is able to observe both. I asked her how the younger generation differs from those who came before them. "I think this millennial generation is very open for innovation," she replied. "They are already influenced by Western culture, but they adapt and create their own mix. For example, a woman can aim to be covered, but she can still wear many things, mixing her hijab with capes and shawls. They are sophisticated. Their behavior is different because they have lots of information. Nearly eighty million people in Indonesia are on the Internet already, and while they are very open to global culture, they also have their own values."

Millennials are more sophisticated, she thinks, in part because professional Muslim women now have access to a larger set of role models from around the world, Muslim and non-Muslim alike. "The UAE has just appointed several female ministers, and Indonesia's very popular finance minister, Sri Mulyani, is also a woman. Nowadays women have their own position in economic and political areas. We see that Muslim women have no barrier as long as they are good at what they do."

Sharia-compliant finance is already a multitrillion-dollar global industry. The global halal industry, encompassing food, clothing, tourism, and health care, is expected to double between 2012 and 2018 to US$6.4 trillion.[3] Investors are now starting to notice the business potential of newly educated, connected, and empowered Muslim millennial female consumers and entrepreneurs in particular, including online modest fashion and lifestyle platforms.

In 2015, Hijup closed its second round of investment. In 2016, Diajeng participated in the Twelfth World Islamic Economic Forum, held in Jakarta. At the forum, a prime slot was dedicated to a session on the topic "Can Islamic Fashion Become Haute Couture?" Modest fashion alone is estimated to be worth about US$96 billion, according to the organizers. But the opportunity is even greater. In 2013, Muslims spent US$266 billion on fashion broadly, more than the spending of Japan and Italy combined, and this figure is expected to increase to US$484 billion in 2019.

As modest fashion itself becomes more fashionable, it is also expanding in the high-end side of the market, and as its potential for profits becomes clearer Western brands are taking notice of it too. Modest fashion brands have recently been showcased at London Fashion Week, and there is now a wholly dedicated London Modest Fashion Week. Condé Nast, the parent company for publications like *Vogue*, launched *Vogue Arabia*, supplementing its existing presence in the Muslim world through *Vogue Turkey*. Deena Aljuhani Abdulaziz, a member of the Saudi royal family who was briefly its first editor in chief, is well-known for her sophisticated taste that incorporates Western brands into fairly conservative looks. "There's not just one formula to follow when it comes to a fashion publication, and I perceive *Vogue Arabia* as an opportunity to create innovative editorials that celebrate Arab women in our own way," Abdulaziz said soon after her appointment. "It's true that our region is conservative by nature, but Arab women are no different than their counterparts around the globe in that we want to feel empowered and look beautiful."[4]

"No More Cupcakes!"

At a Saudi women's empowerment conference, a European woman with Arab origins was invited to give a talk on scaling entrepreneurship. In a rousing speech, she covered funding, scale, team building, and more. When it came to the product, though, she was openly disapproving of, even derisive about, the vast majority of women's entrepreneurship in Saudi Arabia: "No more cupcakes, please! All the ladies want to open up online businesses for cakes or bags or other small things. We need new ideas, we need innovation!" Several local women on the panel agreed with her, saying with equal parts admiration and exasperation that while the entrepreneurship of Muslim millennial women has really taken off, these businesses are too focused on food and beverage, clothing, or small personal care products, limiting their opportunity.

To some extent I sympathized with these views. I, too, often found myself gravitating toward the ecommerce businesses that sought to solve "real world" problems or created wholly new markets rather than those that sold food or consumer products, which seemed like frivolous luxuries. But for many women across the Muslim world, particularly in the wealthy states of the Gulf, consumer and retail products are their comparative advantage. Although they may not have much exposure or access to broader markets, they know other female millennials well: their tastes, their preferences, their spending habits—and their newly available incomes.

The young women in this income class have many of their most fundamental needs—housing, transport, food—taken care of by their fathers or husbands, so they can spend their own earnings on more lighthearted matters—cupcakes for birthday parties, fashionably adorned abayas, and unique handbags. Many of the young women I spoke to feel embarrassed about their consumption patterns, and often prefaced their words with "unfortunately" and apologetically suggested that when they are older they will spend money on nobler causes like their children's education or charity—or make smart investments with returns or simply save. Being economically dependent on men has been the norm thus far, and as the first generation of women to have their own earned income, it may take time for them to acquire the skills and the desire to become better money managers. But in the meantime, they are creating a new consumer class. Thus, budding female entrepreneurs who create products specialized to the tastes of these consumers are not making the frivolous or lazy choice but the most strategic one.

Online entrepreneurship by women for women has become near-ubiquitous across the Muslim world. Some women are selling specifically to other women of faith, whether it's Hijup's modest clothing or the halal-compliant cosmetics of Wardah, which has quickly become one of the largest brands in its industry. Although these are now big businesses, some of this entrepreneurship has not been scaled up and remains a side gig. In Kuala Lumpur, a young journalist told me that she supplements her meager income by selling hijabs online. She makes a lot more from selling hijabs than from reporting, but journalism remains her first love.

And it's not just tradition that sells. In Turkey, sisters Merve and Beste Manastir's Manu Atelier handbags, started from their father's workshop in Istanbul, have a cult following globally and are regularly featured in Western magazines. They have taken their father's traditional craftsmanship not only global but digital, with Instagram being one of their most popular platforms. In Riyadh, multiple women told me about running cupcake businesses that allow them to be economically active without having to leave their home. Moreover, digital entrepreneurship is not limited to middle- and high-income women. In Kuwait, an activist told me that connectivity has transformed the lives of low-income women in the poorer parts of the country; she cited the example of a woman who uses Instagram to make her homemade pickles popular in the homes of high-income women. In Egypt, the website SuperMama provides Arabic and English content about health, especially maternal health.

But not all Muslim millennial women entrepreneurs are focused on women's fashion, food, and other consumption primarily targeted at women. Samira Negm's carpooling service in Cairo has a specific line of business aimed at women looking for safety and familiarity by traveling with their friends and colleagues, but it also aims to serve everyone who is trying to beat Cairo's notorious traffic. In Bangladesh, Maliha Malik Qader has created Shohoz, a pioneer in the country's budding online travel industry that offers bus tickets, hotel reservations, and ferry tickets in one consolidated spot, saving women—and men—time they would have spent lining up in multiple locations. In Saudi Arabia, Emkaan Education, the brainchild of three women, Mounira Jamjoum, Basma Bushnak, and Sarah Zaini, is bringing a variety of educational services to schools and parents alike. In Jakarta, younger and tech-savvy low-income women get to pocket a small cut of the profits when they use ecommerce platforms to sell products created by older women who are unable or unwilling to use ecommerce sites themselves.

Digital access and smartphones have given millions of women across the Muslim world the opportunity to create businesses and reach new markets rapidly. As a growing number of them take advantage of these new opportunities to become CEOs of their own businesses or to use digital platforms to sell their wares, they have been freed up from traditional constraints like concerns about culture and safety and, if they wish, can work from their homes. The definition of who works and who stays at home has also been changed. Sometimes women who describe themselves as housewives turn out to be running ecommerce businesses or using ecommerce platforms to sell all manner of products and services. They have not yet recognized that they are working women.

Platforms for Parity

Some digital pioneers are specifically designing their platforms to lower the implicit and explicit transaction costs that women face in accessing work, such as limited and unsafe transport, discrimination, social censure, and child care costs. These new online marketplaces open up wholly new avenues for accelerating gender parity and helping women generate returns for themselves, their families, and their societies.

Later during the same evening that I met Mozah, the woman cooking from her home, I met Waleed Abd El Rahman, a young entrepreneur. A graduate of the American University in Cairo, Waleed worked at Procter & Gamble in Lebanon, then at Red Sea World—a food and beverage company—back in Cairo, started up his own restaurant, and then managed the Arabic edition of the *MIT Technology Review*. Over dinner in the elite Zamalek neighborhood, overlooking the Nile River, Waleed and a number of other young professionals told me about the opportunities and barriers for all working women—old and young, poor and rich, skilled and unskilled. Only toward the end of the evening, while giving me a tour of Old Cairo, did Waleed start to talk about his latest idea: an online marketplace for home-cooked food that would enable women to cook and sell from their own homes. The customers for this fresh home-made food—delivered by a fleet of drivers on motorbikes—would be the young professionals who live and work in the sprawling city and want to avoid Cairo's traffic and high restaurant prices.

Waleed said that he wants to give Egyptian women with culinary talent the opportunity to have others try their food and maybe someday open their own restaurants. "There are so many moms, housewives, and freelance female chefs who would take the opportunity to cook and sell their food from the home." Over the next year, I followed Waleed's progress as he grew his idea into reality. Today his company, Mumm, is thriving, with nearly seventy cooks—all women—and six hundred customers. He has started with middle-class women as his suppliers—those who have good Internet access and enough education to manage the rapid growth in orders as well as his stringent hygiene and packing requirements. Some of these women are under economic pressure to contribute an income to their family—some are divorced, and others have husbands who are retired or out of work. For others, Mumm is simply an opportunity to test the skills that they use every day as their family's primary caregiver and that they can now bring to a business opportunity they never previously had.

Thinking of how someone like Mozah might benefit from the model—with the Internet giving her the market access that her previously missed opportunity on television didn't—I asked Waleed if he could expand his platform to lower-income women. Waleed said that he could do it if he had a broker—someone to ensure that the cooks receive the orders, follow the hygiene instructions, and are able to hire support when needed. Essentially, he needs someone who can provide the training and absorb the extra risk. Later he found such a broker to work with one particular set of lower-income women: Mumm partnered with a local NGO to employ Syrian refugee women with a talent for cooking. The NGO provides them with a large shared kitchen, and they in turn diversify the range of foods available on Mumm by bringing in Syrian delicacies, often considered one of the best cuisines in the MENA region. Waleed is adamant, however, that the sustainability of such an approach lies in tying it to the business model, not to charity. "This is not just corporate social responsibility. It certainly helps these women and our customers feel good. But we are doing it because it is both profitable and generates social returns."

Waleed's business model is based on two major trends that are obvious: the power of technology to create online marketplaces and the consumer culture in large urban areas—the desire for fast, healthy food delivered to the office doorstep. But there are two underlying gender trends supporting his business model too. First, as women have received more university education, living costs have gone up and social norms around women's work have changed. Women in middle-class households are no longer packing up homemade meals for their professional husbands and sons but instead are increasingly likely to be professionals themselves. And second, women who are staying at home no longer want to perform unpaid care work—they are also looking for ways to turn their existing skills into opportunities to earn a living. Mumm taps into both sets of changes and fills a new demand. For the women selling their food, Mumm provides an earning opportunity. For Waleed, Mumm has been an opportunity not only to create a new business but to have a social impact.

Platform models for connecting women to work are not limited to manual or service work. They are also being applied to more technical, traditionally white-collar knowledge work. Sara Khurram is a medical doctor from Karachi. She studied medicine at the Dow Medical College, and like many young women in Pakistan, she agreed to an arranged marriage directly afterward. Her husband had been supportive of her continuing to work, but a year into her two-year residency in radiology, she got pregnant. The hospital would not allow a pregnant woman to be present around radiation, and so Sara left. After having her baby, she began to think about her future. She realized that she was one of many female doctors with children whose talent went to waste even though doctors were scarce in Pakistan.

According to official statistics, in Pakistan, a country of over 180 million people, there are only about 160,000 doctors—a shortage that is central to the overall acute shortage of health care infrastructure and services.[5] The lack of access to primary health care is particularly severe for women, who, as the lowest-valued member of many households, are often the last ones in their families to receive any form of health care. This can hold true even if they are pregnant and even if access is not a problem—in part owing to cultural restrictions and in part because fertility rates are so high that the value placed on each pregnancy is low. Only about half of all births are attended by skilled health professionals. Cultural norms combined with poverty and poor health services take a heavy toll on health care for women and children, who remain a large and underserved market.

Two major factors add to the dearth of doctors in the country. Although nearly 70 percent of medical college graduates have been female in recent years, fewer than half of the annual graduates go on to practice because many of the female graduates either never join the labor market or leave relatively quickly.[6] Currently, only 23 percent of registered doctors in Pakistan are female. Sara puts the number of those who practice medicine regularly even lower, at 14 percent. A second factor relates to men. More and more male graduates seek opportunities for residencies and practices abroad, and the resulting brain drain contributes to the lack of doctors in the country. There are nearly 17,000 doctors of Pakistani origin—mostly men—in the United States alone. Many others go to the Middle East or Europe.

Another reason female doctors do not practice is that the marriage market puts a particular premium on women with medical degrees. Many middle-class families aspire to having a *doctor bahu*—a doctor daughter-in-law—and women with medical degrees often find especially good matches. For the most part, however, their husbands and in-laws discourage them from practicing medicine after marriage because the work of a young doctor often involves long shifts, including night shifts, and mixed working environments where women and men work alongside each other; both of these conditions go against the grain of many families' traditions and values. In addition, it is often a source of pride for many families that their daughters or daughters-in-law do not *need* to work.

For Sara, a potential solution lay in telemedicine. She thought a telemedicine practice focused specifically on hiring stay-at-home mothers who are qualified doctors would help them balance work and family. Knowing her own experience and that of others like her, she was certain that while the cultural restrictions around formal work in a hospital or private practice are barriers, time is not. Despite their duties as caregivers, most young women like her are not solely responsible for homemaking and caregiving. In extended family living arrangements, women share many of these roles, particularly taking care of children. And the low-cost services of uneducated women to perform domestic chores like cooking and cleaning would enable stay-at-home female physicians to take on at least part-time virtual work.

Sara was also certain that there was hidden demand from underserved patients, particularly women. For one, a telemedicine practice could significantly cut transaction costs in rural areas where travel is difficult and costly. In addition, few qualified doctors, having been trained and usually raised in urban areas, had the desire to set up practices in rural areas. The few who did were usually men returning to their towns or villages, but cultural restrictions still often prevented rural women from visiting them. Sara thought that these women— and their families—might be willing to go to female doctors on a video link.

Sara said that many people immediately discouraged her because they thought that "people who don't accept going to doctors at all certainly would not accept going to a doctor on video." Many also felt that "lady doctors" who had stopped practicing after marriage would not choose to return to work. But Sara was convinced the idea would work, and with this conviction, doctHERS was born. This telemedicine business now connects several remote rural and low-income urban communities with female doctors located in other parts of the country. Sara is one of three cofounders who together bring both business and medical experience to doctHERS.[7]

It has not been an easy journey. The female physicians who use this platform have sometimes spent years out of the workforce, while their medical degrees gathered dust. They also sometimes struggle to balance work and family. Of the sixty women whom Sara and her colleagues began to train at the start, only ten now work with them. Many couldn't make the radical shift in the skills required for an online practice. Others were unable to balance their family obligations with the strict demands of showing up on time for online appointments, despite the relative flexibility of virtual work, because their first duty was still to their role at home. But as the venture has grown, it has begun to fill a vital gap—working within the culture to connect female doctors with female patients in a country where there is an extreme shortage of doctors. Although still in its early days, doctHERS is being hailed as a unique new social enterprise with strong potential in Pakistan and possibly elsewhere.

Other platforms try to broker between employers and female job seekers in a wide range of fields. Glowork in Saudi Arabia provides a range of services to connect female talent to jobs and is one of a range of government-backed initiatives to open up the labor market to women while reducing reliance on foreign professionals. The nonprofit arm of Glowork provides career advice, support in crafting CVs, interview tips, and matchmaking with employers, using a range of online tools, including an app, and off-line support. The for-profit arm has created Glofit, a network of gyms across Riyadh that taps into the increasing mobility and health consciousness of women. Both are a vital service in a country with both a growing workforce and a growing female consumer base.

Platforms such as Mumm, doctHERS, and Glowork that seek to connect a supply of female talent with potential demand are successful because they combine appealing economic incentives with concessions to local cultural requirements, thus bypassing some of the transaction costs that women face in accessing work. They provide the delicate balance that most working women in the Muslim world have to strike in their daily lives.

The Future of Work

There are mixed views on the long-term future of work, in both developed and developing economies. Techno-optimists believe that technological change will be good for people, leading to more meaningful and creative work, shorter hours, and greater safety—and maybe even a utopia where we do not have to work at all. Techno-pessimists generally believe that machines will displace people en masse, especially those in low-skilled jobs, disrupt even those in white-collar jobs, and lead to fewer new roles. Some academics predict a dark future on the basis of these changes.[8] But whether experts believe that machines will automate large numbers of jobs without creating new ones or that machines will augment and complement humans and create new opportunities, almost everyone agrees that jobs of the future will require more and different skills than the stock of skills prevalent in today's workforce and that there is a short window of opportunity within which today's workers and today's school-children—tomorrow's workers—can learn to adapt to the changing world of work. If they do so, the longer-term future looks bright, however challenging the short term may be.

Some studies suggest that emerging and developing economies, with their large numbers of low-skilled workers, are going to be particularly vulnerable to the risks of automation and particularly ill prepared to adapt adequately because of their underfunded and stale education and training systems. Predictions about Uzbekistan, Kyrgyzstan, Tajikistan, Malaysia, and Bangladesh put the share of jobs at risk of computerization well above 50 percent. A study I coauthored at the World Economic Forum found modest job losses in the short term but predicted a high level of "skills instability" across most occupations. On the other hand, because the price of labor is low enough to make large-scale automation prohibitively expensive in the short term, there is a longer window for adaptation in many developing countries. Some contend that the shift to the digital economy may in fact allow developing countries to "leapfrog" and bypass the period of industrialization that many developed economies went through, while others are concerned about "premature deindustrialization."[9]

These forecasts and predictions are based on a set of current data and assumptions about the future. What matters most in shaping the future are the actions of governments, businesses, and workers today to handle this transition. It is up to us to create the new world we want—rather than simply the one we will get if we let inertia take its course.

Economies in the Muslim world are at vastly different starting points when it comes to technology and work. Countries with large low-skilled populations, like Pakistan and Bangladesh, are a long way from replacing large parts of their populations working in agriculture and manufacturing with robots. Countries like Indonesia, Malaysia, and Turkey are more susceptible to automation in their manufacturing sectors but also have thriving service sectors where technology is largely a boon. The small, rich states of the Gulf are rapidly adopting the latest technologies, from passenger drones in Dubai to investments in artificial intelligence to the use of the latest petroleum technologies in Saudi Arabia, but these nations also have young and highly educated populations who are relatively adept in the use of new technologies. How various Muslim-majority economies handle the transformation that is under way, whether it occurs rapidly or slowly, will determine the future livelihood of the half-billion people in their current workforces—and the millions more who will join them in the future.

Researchers at the Oxford Martin School suggest that "while the potential labour market disruption associated with the expanding scope of automation is likely to affect the developing world later than advanced economies, it may be potentially more disruptive in countries with little consumer demand and limited social safety nets. Developing countries would thus do well to plan ahead of such an event. This means investing more in education and boosting domestic demand. Because skilled jobs are substantially less susceptible to automation, the best hope for developing and emerging economies alike is to upskill their workforce."[10]

Political leaders around the world must determine how to navigate the disruption to labor markets by reforming education, expanding lifelong learning, updating labor laws, designing better social protection measures, enhancing digital access, and supporting entrepreneurship. Business leaders too will need to strike a balance between adopting new technologies and remaining competitive, on the one hand, and helping to upskill their own workforces and supporting the adaptation of the communities around them, on the other. Muslim economies will be no different: their leaders need to tackle these challenges and harness the new opportunities. But the transformation will also be shaped by people, especially youth. The current stock of knowledge, agility, curiosity, attitude, capacity to upskill or reskill, and entrepreneurial mind-set among today's young women and men will determine how well they adapt to the changes under way—and how effectively and proactively they can begin to shape the future.

There will be gender differences in the disruptions across labor markets because of the gender differences by sector in today's employment. The World Economic Forum's *Future of Jobs* report found that not only is blue-collar work in manufacturing, which largely employs men, at risk across major developed and developing economies, but jobs in the lower- to medium-skilled end of white-collar work, such as administrative and salesperson roles, which have provided employment to large numbers of women in recent years, are also at risk.[11]

Job growth is expected in the health, green, education, industrial, and IT sectors. Overall, the growth of high-skilled roles will help create a more level playing field for women and men as brain becomes more valued than brawn, but there are gender differences in specific areas. Growth in, broadly speaking, care-related professions—such as nursing, child care, elder care, and therapy—or in education could enhance opportunities for women because of their traditional comparative advantage in these areas. However, the picture is more mixed for IT and STEM-related professions. High demand is predicted in the IT sector, especially for security analysts, data scientists, cloud architects, and those skilled in implementing and analyzing the "Internet of Things."[12] Professions in other sectors that use IT skills will also grow. However, women and men are currently present in—and training for—these areas in different numbers. For example, the number of women in Muslim-majority economies who are studying STEM subjects is larger than the number in the United States, but there is still a gender gap; thus, the pipeline of female talent for roles that use these skills is going to be smaller than the pipeline of male talent.

On the other hand, in comparison to the West, there are relatively high numbers of women in tech entrepreneurship in some parts of the Muslim world already. As this chapter has shown, digital technologies offer a new avenue for growth to SMEs, including businesses focused on women as workers and consumers, as well as to individual workers on digital platforms. "First, they make it easier to learn about available jobs and requirements; second, they reduce the cost of recruiting; and third, they allow individuals to market themselves to a wider audience," says a recent Brookings Institution report on the future of work in the developing world. Individuals can sell their products or their skills to others well beyond their own community, beyond their own city, and sometimes well beyond their own national borders. In comparison to the West, where platform work may be relatively precarious compared to standard forms of employment, many new workers in developing economies—including own-account or independent women workers in many Muslim economies—find that platform work offers an opportunity for more work and more stable work than they had before.[13]

A final area for potential gender differences in the future of work relates to adaptive capacity. Research has shown that reskilling and upskilling, even when support is available, is hard for workers whose identities are deeply tied to their work. For example, blue-collar men—such as coal miners, rig workers, or woodworkers—do not want to reskill to professions they consider less masculine in the United States.[14] Similar patterns, or even more pronounced identity gaps, are likely to hold in many other parts of the world. Women, as newer entrants to the labor market in most Muslim economies, have a largely blank slate to work with when it comes to work and identity and are likely to be relatively more flexible.

This has been the experience of Fareeha, a young woman from an industrial town in southern Punjab in Pakistan. Her father worked in the local surgical goods factory, a job her brother was expected to move into alongside his father before replacing him when he retired. This was the norm in their small community, with roles passed from father to son. When the factory moved away, in part because of technological upgrades that required a slightly more skilled workforce than they could find locally, the community was devastated, as was Fareeha's family. Her brother, after being certain about his future for most of his life, is still struggling to adapt. But for Fareeha the factory's departure was an opening, a crisis that created a new opportunity. Moving in with an aunt in a larger city, she began training as a gym instructor, helping to train a few women from her aunt's home three times a week. "I went into this with no expectations. I just had to try something." A year later, a local textile company advertised a competition for aspiring fitness instructors, offering both training and placement, and Fareeha won. Now she works in one of the top gyms in Karachi, training wealthy women in an upscale neighborhood. It is a very different life from anything she or her family imagined for her.

While it may be impossible to predict who will be more affected and who will be better prepared—men or women—to handle the changes under way, or indeed if there will be any differences at all, one thing is certain. Given that women make up the larger share of high-skilled talent in the younger cohorts of the population, as governments in the Muslim world build strategies to prepare for the future of work, they would be wise to ensure that they tap into this talent and use this moment of transition to accelerate parity.

∽ five ∾

A New Marriage Market

DAMMAM IS SAUDI ARABIA'S THIRD-LARGEST METROPOLITAN area and home to Saudi Aramco, the world's most valuable company.[1] Saif, a business development executive at Aramco, had invited me and nearly twenty young women and men for dinner. All friends and acquaintances, some were in couples and others were single.

I was surprised when, as I walked into their home, Saif's wife, Yasmine, kindly told me that I could dress as I wished in their house and offered to take my abaya. I had expected to keep it on. It was not the first time that night that I found my expectations challenged. Over a spectacular meal in their garden that could easily have fed three times the number of people who were there, I heard the views of these young Saudis on marriage, work, and parenthood and learned how their generation of well-educated, middle-class, white-collar professionals in their twenties and thirties have redefined in just a few short years the social patterns that have been in place for decades, if not centuries.

They all had higher education degrees, including bachelor's, master's, and in some cases PhD degrees, from both Saudi universities and universities abroad. Most of those who had studied abroad benefited from the King Abdullah Scholarship Program for Saudis to study at foreign universities and were among the earliest of the two hundred thousand graduates of the program thus far. Even those who had not studied abroad had been exposed to a globalized culture through their connection to Saudi Aramco. Nearly all the guests had been associated with Aramco at one point or another; while some still worked there, others had started their own businesses.

Saif had a PhD from Stanford and worked in business development for Aramco. Yasmine had a master's degree in interior design and was a stay-at-home mother. Yousuf was an entrepreneur in the coffee business, and his wife Leena was a consultant. Hana worked on talent acquisition at a holding company, and her husband, Abdulaziz, had his own investment fund. The single women—Salma, Noor, Awtha, and Feda—worked in various fields, from finance to petroleum engineering to coordinating youth groups. The single men—Amr, Muhammad, Ahmad, Hamad, Haitham, Majid, and Bandar—were in equally diverse professions, both at Aramco and elsewhere.

Nearly all of the young couples had chosen to have dual-career families, balancing two career ambitions with their lives as couples and parents. Those who were single were certain that they wanted a dual working career model for their future families too. The only exception was Yasmine, the interior designer, who had stopped working after the birth of her two children. But this didn't necessarily mean that Saif and Yasmine had a traditional division of labor in the home. As their kids ran shrieking up and down the stairs, they both went to put their children to bed. Multiple times they took turns following up with their cook on the progress of our dinner. This kind of partnership would not have been the norm even in well-to-do households of their parents' generation. In this they were closer to the young millennial couples in New York, San Francisco, and London than to their parents.

These couples are children of working fathers and stay-at-home mothers, but they have chosen a new way for their own marriages, diverging from the cultural, political, and social forces at play in Saudi life. The model they have adopted keeps many elements of the traditional division of labor—women in the home and men outside at work—but is at the same time based on much more involvement from women in work and from men in the home. The women blend traditional notions of motherhood and marriage with workplace ambitions, choosing the third way as described earlier. But the men too have changed their values. Much like their Western counterparts, these Saudi men express the desire to be more involved in their children's lives than their own fathers ever were. They may not be stay-at-home dads or even equal partners in the home, but they are also not the distant, detached husbands and fathers of generations past.

The shift is due to the very same factors that drew women into the workforce, starting with the broader economic conditions. When I met this group in the midst of the oil price decrease, they did not yet expect the major restructuring of the Saudi economy that was to come with the government's new "Vision 2030" plan, released a few months later. That plan makes diversification away from oil one of its central tenets, a strategy built on the human capital investments the country has already made. The group gathered that night was among the vanguard benefiting from the talent development policies the prescient King Abdullah had already put in place, in anticipation of the start of efforts to wean the economy off oil. In fact, this particular group mirrored the changes to come in the entire economy. The children of fathers who worked for Aramco, some had chosen new paths after short stints at Aramco themselves. Fueled by the talent and skills they gained there, they were now diversifying their own professional futures, whether it was to sell coffee, like Yousuf, or tackling human resources in industries other than oil, like Hana.

Other economic factors have also played a part in shifting values. Middle-class, white-collar life is often accompanied by aspirations for more consumer goods, better health, better housing, and better education for children, but in contemporary Saudi Arabia a single income is often no longer enough to achieve these aspirations. The dual-income model has quickly become an acceptable norm for the upwardly mobile millennial generation, who strive not just to survive the demands of modern life but to fully enjoy the pleasures of their chosen life. And all this has happened in an era when cheap household labor from foreign countries has become abundant. Women's traditional roles in the home can now be handed over to someone else: cooking to a maid, child care to a nanny, and cleaning to a housekeeper. Many of these women hail from Southeast Asia—some of them are Muslim women from Bangladesh or Indonesia, and others are Catholic women from the Philippines. With the Saudi driving ban for women still in place until mid-2018, foreign drivers, men from Pakistan or Bangladesh, are often hired as well.

Exposure to the West—through foreign scholarships, TV, and the Internet—had also partly changed local values around gender roles. The group at Saif and Yasmine's house, as well as young people in nearly all my interviews in Saudi Arabia and elsewhere in the Muslim world, thought this exposure has provided a lens, even if a sometimes fictional one, into a world not their own, both its perceived positives and negatives. At the very least, they felt, this exposure has increased their ability to make more informed choices about the type of marriages and professional lives they want, but it has also done more than that. Values about the roles of husband and wife in a marriage have also changed because of the increased education and employment of women. In particular, the fact that women now work has changed marriage itself as men—and other women—begin to see the positive impact on their lives of their wives' work.

Arranged Love

In 2003, the Saudi government began an educational campaign to inform first cousins who planned to marry about the risk of genetic defects. Since then, the government has offered genetic testing in centers across the country for prospective first-cousin marriages to test for the risk of disease before they go ahead and marry. The authorities in Saudi Arabia and other Gulf countries have had to do this because of the high rates of consanguineous marriage—marriage between people who are second cousins or closer. Islam allows such marriages, and they are common in many parts of the Muslim world, as they were in Europe and North America for several centuries. In Saudi Arabia and Iran, the rates are just under 40 percent, in Pakistan over 60 percent, in Turkey over 21 percent, and in Sudan 50 percent. As health concerns become more evident, some are beginning to point to religious as well as scientific grounds for change, referring, for example, to a hadith, or saying, of the Prophet Muhammad: "Marry those who are unrelated to you, so your children do not become weak."[2]

But things are changing for other reasons too. Consanguineous marriages were often the outcome of economic and social factors: they allowed for wealth to stay within family units—marriage was as much a financial merger as a social one—and when personal choice was involved, they were the natural step for young people involved in cousin romances because they rarely got to mingle with the opposite sex apart from their own near and distant relations. Now young educated people are getting to meet each other in new ways, outside of their families. The economic fundamentals of marriage remain the same—like still marries like—but the circle has widened from primarily family to those within the same socioeconomic class, making the options markedly more expansive than they were just a generation ago, particularly as the educated middle class itself has grown rapidly in recent years.

This subtle shift in the decision-making behind the marriage, from parents to their children, comes in many forms. Majid, a millennial who comes from a conservative family and had his mother pick his bride, said that a choice like his is increasingly rare. Young people are starting to meet directly in some workplaces, online, at malls, and through friends. In between these two models is a range of other ways in which marriages come about. Often parents serve as an initial gateway, providing a set of options and naming certain tribes or types of families who will have a similar mind-set. Majid told me that it is mainly women in the family who present these options because "they meet young women in women-only circles outside of the immediate family and understand whether she is a suitable match." Often this means a man's mother, aunt, or sister will spot a young woman at a wedding or another female-only event and inquire discreetly about her education, family, and values. If the young woman is suitable to their family's background, she may make a recommendation to the man. Once the young people are put in touch, they may talk by phone and, at times, in person to learn more about each other. If they move ahead, they will have a brief engagement and then marry.

Majid believes that today only 1 percent of marriages among educated millennials are wholly decided by parents. From his perspective, 80 percent of marriages seem to be the result of some form of family introduction, followed by varying levels of interaction between the couple before marriage, and the remainder (nearly one-fifth) are decided by young people themselves—although these are also nearly always brokered by the parents. There is little recent research on the matter, but anecdotally, most people I spoke to agreed that nearly all marriages are given the appearance of a family arrangement regardless of how the union came about.

In the past, character, income, and other signals of compatibility were transparent to both sides in the marriage market, because it was all in the family. You knew what you were signing up for—or at least your parents did. Now, for marriages that are brokered by parents through circles that go beyond the immediate family, there is a need for new signaling mechanisms. In this new marriage market, there are new markers of desirability. Educated millennial men want to marry educated millennial women, and vice versa. The side making the more overt search—the groom and his family—often look for a "girl from a good family, with good education, who went to good schools and did well at school," said Majid. With little or limited previous relationship experience, they are unlikely at this stage to decline, on either side, but this expanded choice already represents more agency than young people have had before.

I asked scores of young women and men how they felt about these arrangements. Most gave some version of the sentiment: "Who better to know who I will be happy with than the people who raised me?" Majid provided a slightly different explanation. "Being able to get along with each other's families is a large part of what will make for a happy marriage." In a collectivist, family-centric culture, some middle ground in the continuum of parental authority and individual choice becomes necessary for a sustainable, happy union.

Men and women still do not mix in many public places, and yet values have changed as young people are exposed to new mind-sets. Increasingly, young working women are looking for partners with whom they can maintain their professional lives—and many young men are starting to share this point of view. Sometimes young people stipulate this as a requirement to their parents, who then search for a suitable spouse. But more than ever before, young people are also doing their own matchmaking. More and more of them want love and commitment in a marriage, not just the functional arrangements of the past. The change is reminiscent of what happened for upper-class men and women in the West as marriage went from being an economic arrangement between two wealthy families to one based on love, attraction, and partnership. That change unfolded over the course of a century in the West—for this generation of Saudis, it has happened in the space of a decade or two.

Young people in Riyadh or Jeddah are now meeting each other online—and at work, much as happens in any large metropolis in the West. Nearly all the couples at Saif and Yasmine's house had met through work. However, they had all then asked their parents to "broker" the arrangement. This type of arranged love is becoming more common than ever before with the influx of women into higher education and white-collar work. Young people get more say now, but social norms require that families align to create a family-sanctioned union. Once again, most young people I spoke to felt that this is only fair: you don't just marry your partner, but also must recognize that two extended families are coming together. It remains extremely rare for a young person in the Muslim world to wholly break away from family in pursuit of love.

Old Taboos, New Taboos

The changing dynamics between education, work, marriage, and new norms have all but eliminated polygamy—one of the most archaic marriage practices in the Muslim world—from the young, educated urban middle class in Saudi Arabia. At our dinner, several people in the group told me that they had grandparents who had been in polygamous marriages, and some even had fathers with a second wife. They felt certain, however, that these were the last generations, in their own families at least, to engage in the practice. They didn't know anyone in their cohort who had done so or even wanted to.

The statistics on polygamous marriages are murky, but the young people in the room—particularly the young men—confirmed that a change is under way in this particular segment of society. One of the single young men explained, "It is economics—most middle-class men simply cannot afford to maintain a second wife." One of the married men said, "But it is also because of the new values held by men—and women." Men who now want love and commitment that goes beyond the functional arrangements of the past are less likely to opt for polygamy a few years down the line. Another added, "And if a man wanted to do it today like they used to, it wouldn't be a polygamous marriage for long because women won't put up with it. They prefer divorce to a marriage where they would have to share a husband." With some visible distaste, they also suggested that while their urban, educated, middle-class millennial generation has largely given up polygamy, two groups are still maintaining it: the very poor, who still engage in the practice out of tradition, and some of the very rich royal family, who do it, despite their education, "simply because they can."

The generational shift is striking. The father of Rawya, a Saudi woman in her midthirties, is in a polygamous marriage. He got married for a second time to a woman nearly Rawya's age and announced it as a fait accompli to his first wife and children. "I almost understand," Rawya said. "He did it because he can. It is acceptable in our society for a man to do this even if in our family it was a shock." Women of her grandmother's generation might even have found ways to work together with other wives, sharing the responsibilities for unpaid work and forging strong alliances between women within the household that might prove helpful against male dominance. In her mother's generation—and class—each wife maintains a separate household, with the first sometimes accepting the arrangement only if the two wives are in different countries. It is not unusual for men to have their "original" family in Saudi Arabia with a more traditional wife and to have a more "public" second wife in Dubai, London, or New York. But this practice is dying out. "The difference today is that while my mother is forced to accept it, women of my generation will not. We would rather get a divorce than be among multiple wives. We have other options now," said Rawya.

For the educated middle class, the old taboo of marrying for love is now increasingly accepted. And practices like polygamy are starting to become the new taboos for them, even as they remain accepted in the wider society—and by law. Like a preference for monogamy, staying single and getting divorced are also starting to become more common and, by consequence, more accepted.

Single Ladies

For many women, new education and employment opportunities as well as new expectations of marriage have made staying unmarried a viable, though not preferred, option. Hafsa, a high-ranking executive at a conglomerate in Saudi Arabia, has chosen to remain single into her forties. Her father was a deeply conservative man who had two wives and two families, but he was willing to support the educational, professional, and marital ambitions of his daughter. Her career has always been extremely important to her. On the personal front, Hafsa has not been willing to settle for anything less than a man who would be her intellectual equal and who believes in equality. That man hasn't come along yet.

Hafsa thinks she may have been a generation too early for the type of man she would be willing to marry. She is a female Gen-Xer whose professional and personal ambitions put her well ahead of her cohort. She now sees in millennial men some of the traits that might make them more adapted to the ambitions of young women today. She never came across such a man in her own cohort. But she has no regrets about remaining single. She is happy to have lived up to her own ideals and is glad that she didn't marry simply because of the pressure women in her society feel. That pressure is by no means limited to women in Muslim-majority countries. Many women in America feel that they may have to "settle" as they approach an age when they begin to worry about the biological clock. But to withstand that pressure in Saudi Arabia requires an iron will—and supreme confidence in one's own abilities and choices. "The main reason that I'm still single, in addition to not finding my intellectual equal, is holding on to the blessing of my freedom," said Hafsa. "Married women in our society have huge responsibilities towards their own and extended families. The cultural expectations of a married woman are huge! It's a burden on her progress, especially professionally. Being single means more freedom!"

A new generation of Saudi women are making similar choices. Estimates suggesting that nearly half of women over thirty are single are disturbing to conservatives, who worry about their "spinsterhood."[3] For many women, remaining single is a combination of choice and circumstance, including a desire for greater professional freedom and a sense that this would be incompatible with a traditional marriage. This desire leads to a search for a more equal marriage. It often turns out that highly ambitious women and highly ambitious men do not have the same preferences in the marriage market.

At twenty-nine, Samira Negm, the ride-sharing entrepreneur in Cairo, is expected to turn her attention to marriage. "My parents would like to convince me to leave what I am doing and focus on marriage. I am too engaged in my start-up and career, and that's keeping my focus away from marrying. Most of my friends are married, but some are not. Marriage is still very traditional for us even if it is not arranged anymore. For women like me in Egypt who are excelling in knowledge or business, the problem is either that men would feel offended that you are successful or they won't feel offended but you don't feel satisfied about not finding someone as competent as you are. Men who are ambitious prefer women who are not ambitious. Men who are not ambitious prefer women who are—maybe they think you complete them, but it's not in a healthy way."

Professionally ambitious women like Samira are in a bind similar to what Hafsa and women of her generation have experienced. If they have strong professional ambitions beyond simply wanting to work to earn a living, women sometimes find that men who are their equals do not want to be part of a "power couple"—or at least that there are not as many men as women who are comfortable with that type of relationship. If they are not willing to drop their professional aspirations, these women sometimes must consider "marrying down"—marrying men who are not their equal in terms of ambition and intellect—or not marrying at all. Larger numbers than ever before are choosing the second option.

No Regrets

The first time I went to Saudi Arabia, a colleague and I had both been invited by the same organization. She was Arab, but I am not. A quick Google search on me would reveal that I promoted gender equality as part of my professional life, and the forms I had to fill out required me to declare that I had a Brazilian ex-husband. A search on my colleague would show a public policy background focused on the Middle East, and her forms would show that she had never been married. Having traveled on my Pakistani passport to sixty countries, I was used to going through many hoops to get visas, and I expected nothing less for Saudi Arabia. I also thought the culturally conservative country would probably not approve of a woman from another Muslim country advocating for gender equality, and I expected delays or even a rejection.

To my surprise, in just three days I was approved for the visa, while my colleague was denied. We had both been given the same support from the inviting organization, which later told me that my age—I was thirty-three and she was twenty-eight—and divorce made me "safe"—that is, unlikely to be too attractive to a Saudi man. The visa process was just a small window into the complex set of biases and freedoms that arise for women in Saudi Arabia who get divorced.

Official statistics in Saudi Arabia claim that the divorce rate is highest in the Eastern Province (36.7 percent) and Tabuk (36.1 percent) and lowest in Jazan (17.9 percent). In Riyadh, the rate is just over 30 percent. Although no one seems to be able to give a source for this statistic, many Saudis quote a higher statistic offhand: 50 percent of all marriages end in divorce in Saudi Arabia, the same rate as in the United States.

A wide range of reasons are cited for these relative high rates. Some say that young people are marrying too quickly at the behest of parents and do not understand or prepare for marriage. This seems likely given that 60 percent of all divorces take place in the first year of marriage. Social conservatives in Saudi Arabia—and many in America too—blame the social outcomes of women's education, employment, and earnings for putting an end to the family, or at the very least for forcing a trade-off. For them, it is women being "too ambitious" that leads to marital trouble. Still others believe the opposite: that in fact it is too many women sacrificing their professional ambitions that leads to a growing divorce rate.

The reality is likely to be a mix. Research from other parts of the world shows that there are both positive and negative effects of women's labor force participation on the formation and dissolution of marital unions, on marital quality, on spousal health and well-being, and on the division of intrahousehold power relations.[4] This particular moment in countries like Saudi Arabia is a time of transition as families and communities adjust to the changing power balance.

Women and men are still making fairly rapid choices about marriage, even those who opt for an arranged marriage. Their expectations are high, shaped by ideals of love that they have not observed in their own homes because their parents chose very different models for entering marriage. Some are disappointed—and do not have a road map to manage their disappointment. Women's tolerance for bad marriages has declined as their opportunities outside of marriage have expanded in the form of education, employment, and exposure to the world. And some men, as their traditional roles are threatened, are now more willing to walk out of their marriage rather than adapt to the changing values of their wives—and society. A new divorce market is emerging in parallel to the marriage market, though it remains a relatively new phenomenon in Saudi Arabia.

This is not to say that divorce is accepted across all strata in society. It is still an unwanted option for the large majority, just as it is for much of the West. For many low-income women, divorce still brings economic vulnerability and social censure, particularly for those who do not receive economic and emotional support from their family.

I met one woman dealing with such censure at the head offices of Glowork, the placement agency and careers platform for women that promotes women's workplace participation with the support of the Saudi Ministry of Labor. She is one of the three receptionists working at the agency. A profoundly conservative woman, she did not want her name to be used here. Even with only me in the room, she wouldn't remove her niqab. From what I could see of her eyes, she might have been in her early forties. Hailing from a poor neighborhood of Riyadh, she had heard of a new program helping women get jobs and with nothing but that knowledge, she had come to the Glowork offices to be added to their pool of job candidates. The platform primarily caters to women with university degrees and interest in white-collar work. With her lack of higher education and refusal to work in a place where she might interact with men, Glowork decided she was unlikely to be placed externally. But they wanted to help. So instead, they offered her a place at one of their two reception areas, the one for women only. There she now sits for much of the day, signing in visitors and directing them to the correct offices and information. She spends nearly two hours commuting, using the dismal public transport that barely caters to women.

A few months after she started working at Glowork, her husband, who had been struggling financially, became resentful of her role outside the home. Her in-laws, who live next door, also started to object. One day he simply left; when I spoke with her, he had not been heard from for three months. Her income is now even more critical to her and her sons' future, yet she is constantly berated by her own parents and her in-laws for having driven away her husband. Left in the limbo of being married but without her husband around to be her "guardian," she is in a vulnerable position for a woman in Saudi Arabia.

But she has no regrets. When I asked her if her pursuit of employment came at too high a price—both socially and economically—she smiled for the one and only time during the hour we spent together. No, she said. She told me that she loves her work—it's her lifeline, and it makes her confident of her abilities for the first time in her life.

Islam has always allowed divorce and remarriage, although it is usually easier for a man to divorce his wife than for a woman to obtain a divorce. As divorce loses its taboo, it is becoming more common for women to marry again after a divorce, especially if they are educated, middle-class, or wealthy. As partner choice shifts from parents to young people, there is also more openness to taking on a partner who has been married before. And as economics changes the pressures on all young people, men have become more open to being with a financially independent woman; some even seek out divorced women, who are often more likely to want to continue working.

Divorce rates are also on the rise in other Gulf countries, the United Arab Emirates in particular. "We are starting to build a business out of divorce," a senior Emirati official told me. There are divorce parties to celebrate, rather than hide, new postmarriage lives. Particularly among wealthy women who divorce in their twenties or thirties, it has become a symbol of strength: *Not only did I survive,* divorce signals, *but I am thriving.* Women as well as some men are finding that personal fulfillment is more important to them than societal and family demands and expectations. Some women find that there can be a life after divorce, one that might involve professional fulfillment and even a new chance at love.

Amal Al Mutawa, the chief happiness officer from Dubai who divorced after a short marriage, expects to have such options. As the eldest of her siblings, she had the most guidance—or interference, depending on the interpretation—from her parents. Having made her first set of education, employment, and marital choices rapidly, under their guidance, she is more circumspect now, willing to take the time to find the right fit for her. "I would consider getting married again—I want to be a grandma!—but I need to surround myself with like-minded people, including my future partner."

The Degree Premium

Saudi Arabia and the Gulf countries are not the only Muslim countries that have undergone major transformations in marriage practices. Decisions about marriage, divorce, and staying single are wholly different for educated millennials throughout the Muslim world compared to their parents. Perhaps the most visible manifestation of this change is the premium now placed on education in the marriage market. From Kazakhstan to Morocco, higher education is now a prized attribute in a spouse. It already was for prospective grooms, as a marker of their earning capacity and ability to support their family. But it has now become a marker of prestige for prospective brides too.

Marriage used to be the only avenue for social mobility for women—a woman could move up (or down) in social class only by marriage. In this context, beauty, family background, youth, deference to male authority, and a pliable personality were the main features that enabled women to make a "good match." Education has now become a key lever of social mobility for women, in large part because of the new employment opportunities it generates but also because of the opportunities it now offers in the marriage marketplace.

In Islamabad, Rehana and Sania are both top-ranked students in the final year of their MBBS degree, the bachelor of medicine/bachelor of surgery degree offered in the British-derived education system in Pakistan. The next six students on the honors list are also women. But Rehana and Sania are very different—both in their reasons for being there and in their future outlook.

When asked whether she'll specialize or become a general practitioner, Rehana smiled shyly and said, "My parents will decide." That was a euphemism for "it depends on when my parents arrange a marriage for me." Today many urban families encourage girls to excel in their studies, first to get one of the coveted spots in medical college and then while they are working toward their degrees. In the past, families didn't want their sons' future wives to be educated. They believed that such daughters-in-law would be harder to control in the home, and in particular they didn't want young women who had interacted with men on a university campus. Now, having a more educated daughter-in-law is a mark of prestige and enlightenment, among urban families in particular, and many families recognize that their grandchildren will have a brighter future with an educated mother. After they graduate, medical students are in particularly high demand by potential suitors—or rather by their families. Word-of-mouth searches and local newspapers carry ads with some variation of: "Respectable family searching for fair lady doctor from decent family for son in civil service." Twenty years ago, these ads wouldn't have specified a woman with higher education. Even as archaic ideas around skin color still linger, there is a new desire for educated daughters-in-law.

The advantages of being educated gave Rehana's family an incentive to send her to medical school—in pursuit of a better match. She is not likely to work once she is married. In her parents' community—one to which her potential future in-laws are likely to belong—educated and smart daughters-in-law are prized, but not for their professional ambitions. Rehana knows that her degree will get her a better match than will be possible for the other young women in her community. But not if she wants to work.

Sania, on the other hand, has wanted to be a doctor for as long as she can remember. In particular, she is keen to become a cardiologist, a vitally needed specialization across Pakistan as cardiovascular disease rates skyrocket across South Asia. She wants to specialize as quickly as she can. When I asked her how she thought this plan would affect her marriage prospects, she hesitatingly told me about the man she wants to marry, a fellow student. He plans to have his family ask for her hand in marriage as they get closer to graduation, and then, as a married couple, they can begin a specialization residency together. For Sania's family, investing in her medical degree has always been about more than marriage—as long as the marriage also happens. Sania's future husband—and future in-laws—implicitly, if not explicitly, understand that two equals are coming together. A dual-career couple is acceptable to them, even desired, at least until there are children.

More educated women can attract more educated—and higher-income—men. For Sania as well as many other women, the degree premium goes hand in hand with a job premium in the marriage market. And both women and men have lost interest in reliving the traditional breadwinner and caregiver model of their own fathers and mothers. Both want new returns from marriage: values in common, a closer companionship, someone to share economic burdens. For many men, this new model includes hearing about their wives' day at work, something their own fathers have never done. For many women, the new model enables them to accomplish their own professional dreams while fulfilling the role of homemaker, aspirations their mothers never had. It's not equality yet, but it's closer than ever before.

Rehana's and Sania's choices and those of their families and future husbands' families have externalities for society too. In Pakistan, nearly 70 percent of all medical degrees go to women. They outperform men in the entry-level exams and thus enter medical school in higher numbers. They also work hard when they get there, securing the highest grades and nearly all the top honors at graduation. Yet they are only 23 percent of currently registered doctors.[5]

Although the premium on education in the marriage market indicates progress on gender norms, it also creates problematic societal consequences. When families do not want their qualified medical professional daughters-in-law to practice, they are essentially draining some of the best talent coming out of medical schools. In the market, "lady doctors" are a scarce resource—few in number and desired both by families searching for "good" daughters-in-law and by the medical community. Rehana's education investment will pay off for a couple of families. Sania's will pay off for the thousands of patients she might treat in her career.

In some ways, this range of choices is not so different from those of the elite young American women who went to women's colleges in the 1950s. It's the range of choices represented in *Mona Lisa Smile,* the film that Diajeng, the CEO of Hijup, likes so much. In both times and places, these women were often the first in their families to get a higher education, but not all of them sought to use that education in the workplace. Instead, for some it opened the door to meeting young men at nearby elite colleges so that they could "settle down" after college. The difference is that in most Muslim societies this change is under way at the same time as the other factors that are already bringing women into the workforce at an accelerated pace. Over time, more Sanias than Rehanas will be coming out of medical schools in Pakistan—and indeed, graduating from universities elsewhere in the Muslim world.

I've met nearly equal numbers of young female medical students who say they would like to actually use their medical degrees to practice medicine and those who say they have no such desire. Among those who do want to practice, most expect to do so easily, but others are tied in an epic battle of wills with their families or their prospective in-laws. In the short term, some will succeed and some will not. But the long term is likely to look very different in light of the fundamental changes now afoot. Young people everywhere, including in the collectivist cultures of the Muslim world, want to prove themselves and use the opportunities they are given. To some women, an opportunity to go to medical school is an opportunity to make a better match in the marriage market. But the exposure to new influences when they are in school can often change their aspirations, especially when they see other women making different choices about work and marriage than those expected by their own families. They meet young men, fall in love, and get their families to arrange marriages, often to men whose families are very different from their own. They may choose to keep working after marriage or to stay at home, but either way they will change the way they raise their own daughters. Whatever their path, many young women who graduate from medical school are fundamentally different from who they were when they entered five years before. Over time, there is much more change to come in the marriage market as not just education but also employment become markers of prestige.

Marrying into the Family

It is common across much of the Muslim world—and across all classes—for grown children to live with or close to their parents or extended family well into adulthood, even after forming a family of their own. And the norm for most of those who don't live with their parents is to visit them often. Family bonds have stayed strong even in the face of technological, economic, and social changes. As women have headed into the workforce, it is often grandparents, especially grandmothers, and aunts and uncles who provide a range of support related to child care, from looking after toddlers during work hours to handling school drop-offs and pick-ups for older children. Although most middle-income families in the emerging economies of the Muslim world can afford to hire domestic staff for cooking, cleaning, and child care, extended family support is still critical when it comes to child care and can take several forms. For Sara, the doctor in Pakistan, leaving her child at a nursery or with a nanny is not acceptable at all, and she relies wholly on her mother or mother-in-law. Mari, employed herself as a nanny in Jakarta, depends on her neighbor and sister for the help she needs in taking care of her daughter while she is at work. For Alya, an associate professor in Tunis, a nanny provides the main caregiving for her children, but extended family, usually her in-laws, oversee the nanny, providing a family presence at all times.

For now, this unique combination of women's integration into the workforce and a socially sanctioned care infrastructure is holding strong. But it comes with a price. Living close to or with extended family, particularly those in an older generation, comes with high expectations of what it means to be a mother, wife, daughter, or daughter-in-law—expectations, that is, about women's identities, not at work, but in the home.

Over dinner in Bahrain, a number of women from middle- and high-income households, all married working women with children, spoke of these expectations. One woman recalled a time when she was in the midst of a sales meeting for her high-end fashion business and her mother-in-law called to check whether her six-month-old daughter had been given her afternoon feeding. "Call the nanny if you are so concerned!" she said now, exasperated, but in that moment, she said, she had interrupted the meeting to patiently explain that all was well and the kids were being taken care of at home, including being fed on time.

The third way—neither overtly feminist nor wholly traditional and facilitated by the support of care workers and family caregivers—has helped women gain a footing in the workforce while still adhering to traditional norms around marriage and motherhood. The majority of women I spoke to want to keep this arrangement, and some are undisturbed by keeping up the appearance of being more traditional than they really are. "My husband helps me in the home and with our kids far more than my father ever helped my mother. My father never helped my mother in the home! But when we are visiting my in-laws or they are visiting us, my husband doesn't lift a finger. I am fine with this, it keeps everyone satisfied," one young Bangladeshi woman told me.

But extended family structures too are being changed by women's work and independence. Amir, a shop owner in Tehran, has a stay-at-home wife and two sons, both of whom are now married to working women. The extended family does not live together, but they all have dinner together at least three times a week. Amir said that he never thought much about the fact that his daughters-in-law work or that his wife doesn't until the evening his wife was taken ill at home and had to be rushed to the hospital. None of the men in the family were around, so one of his daughters-in-law drove his wife to the hospital; subsequently, she took care of his wife's regular hospital visits for checkups. "My wife doesn't even drive. Thank God for my daughters-in-law being independent women. Women need to be able to take care of themselves."

Because women's work hasn't upset the visible social order—particularly gendered roles—there are few vocal opponents of it, even as relatively dramatic change unfolds privately. Many women and men, caught between old and new mind-sets around their roles in the home, simply try to adjust their behaviors for different audiences. This is often a smart strategy, given the predominant culture, and they are likely to continue to use it in the near future—until new mind-sets prevail among the working population.

Who Pays?

Before marriage, women often have fewer financial obligations than men. So said Samira Negm, the ride-sharing entrepreneur in Cairo. "Men have to save a lot of money, but women don't need to. [Men] are expected to provide a fancy house, pay for the wedding, furniture, a room for kids not yet born. So people are wasting a huge amount of money for all this. Life could be simpler, but we are a consumer community. I saved money from my earlier work, but I spent it all on setting up the business. In some ways, we can take risks that men cannot. Yes, I need to get married, but I don't need to prepare for being married."

But this window of opportunity is a short one. "On the other hand," Samira continued, "while the situation for men is not fair before marriage, for women it's not fair after marriage. After getting married, men and woman share in expenses, so even after having a child they will go back to work to still earn money. So now women are working outside and inside while men are working only outside. For men, it's four to five years of working very hard. For women, it's the rest of their lives. A very small minority of men have started to help in the home. We cannot generalize that men don't contribute in the house, and of course there is cheap household labor. . . . But it's almost always women working on household chores, except the garden. They also have to manage the kids. And in many low-income families, women are in reality the main breadwinner. So she will be earning, cooking, cleaning, and sometimes having to take kids to work. This is very stressful."

Women's concerns about life after marriage are not limited to the double shift that many of them have to face. Traditionally marriage maintained women's financial dependence—or security, depending on one's perspective—as they became the financial responsibility of their husbands instead of their fathers. But as this situation has shifted to one of shared financial contributions to the household, it has also brought anxiety for women over what they might lose. Even in places in the Muslim world with some of the historically highest rates of women's workforce participation, work, marriage, and values around money form an uncomfortable trinity.

Dina works in the Economics Department of the University of Almaty. At just twenty-six, she heads the local examination board; when we met on a pleasant late spring afternoon at her office, she was greatly stressed about getting everything in place before exams started ten days later. Dina got a bachelor's degree in international relations in Kazakhstan and then went to the United Kingdom to get a master's in gender studies, focusing on violence against women. She sees evidence of the subtle challenges that women face in her own life and the lives of her students. "Women and men study the same amount, but there is gender segregation in the subjects, and even more so in the job market. The typical divide of women in the arts and men in the sciences. And when women are concentrated in a field, it becomes lower-paid—like accounting."

Kazakhstan became an independent nation when Dina was just a toddler, and her childhood was deeply affected by the economic transition that her parents faced after the fall of the Soviet Union. She thinks that structures like "child care and women's unions in the Soviet times" provided some protection for gender equality in the "Soviet generation" of her parents. "But these protections crumbled quickly during the post-Soviet economic collapse. When the government tried to optimize the remaining jobs, women were out first." She recalled her mother and other highly educated women like her trying other methods to earn money—cooking, selling small crafts in the streets—to take care of her and her siblings. "She had to work very, very hard. I too have been raised to be self-sufficient."

Dina explained, "The patriarchal model came back by the 2000s, and men occupied all the top positions in all important industries." Because of this, she thinks that parents have a preference for sons again—so that they can be taken care of in their old age. "But once sons are married, the wife is the boss. Daughters are much more likely to support their parents financially." Dina's own family is made up of three sisters—followed by two sons.

Economic shifts were followed by religious shifts in her family, and in Kazakhstan more broadly. "People need religion during hard times," Dina said. Her mother started to pray, asking Allah for things to get better. Her brothers grew up religious, and even she, between the ages of thirteen and seventeen, went through a period of praying five times a day, although she kept her head uncovered even while praying. This led to a revival of traditional ideas about marriage and motherhood. The wives of her uncles are stay-at-home mothers, and "they are covered of their own choice—no one forced them." Religion had been suppressed during the Soviet era, but there was a resurgence directly after the fall of the Soviet Union. Today the government, afraid of the risk of extremism, closely monitors religion's growth in the country.

These three sets of values—Soviet, Islamic, and globalized millennial—lead to complex trade-offs, ones that Dina feels acutely in her own life. "We say that the wife is the neck and the husband is the head. If you cut off the neck, the head cannot survive. I believe this, but I struggle with the economic aspect. I would expect a lot from a Kazakh guy—he would need to pay for everything. If I pay, I am not a woman. I am not feminine. But at the same time, I want to work too, and then how should we distribute spending in a household? Of course I should make a contribution too. We are having a war in our minds between traditional, Soviet, and Western influences."

Dina's slightly older friends are either Western-educated like her or graduates of "European-style" universities in Kazakhstan. After graduating, she said, they all spent their early twenties building up their own businesses and earning a lot for their age. But now they are "all married with three kids and sitting at home." She cannot understand them. And they cannot understand her. "Starting a business was for my development, but my goal is to get married and be secure," one told her. "Why do you need other projects?" asked another.

"Their mothers were more empowered," said Dina. But having lived during times of hardship and economic insecurity, these friends instilled in their daughters a need for the security offered by the old model of male breadwinners and female homemakers. Dina is torn. "I wonder, am I losing my youth to my career? Should I settle down and have kids now, then go back? But then what about my professional goals? I would need to be with a husband with whom together we can afford to have nannies at home. I am not sure what to do. I used to have a traditional Kazakh boyfriend who would pay for everything, but we were always in conflict because I couldn't be traditional. Now my boyfriend is more like me—but he wants to do a PhD." What Dina left unsaid is that she would then have to take on the full financial responsibility in their partnership in the foreseeable future, something that still sits uncomfortably with her.

Dina is not alone in being caught between new and old values around male and female roles when it comes to financial contributions in marriage. In countries like Bangladesh and Pakistan, both lower-middle-income economies, many in their large low-income populations prefer to "buy" a traditional marriage as their earnings grow. For example, in Bangladesh, while 32 percent of all married women are working or have worked in the last twelve months and 57 percent of all divorced and separated women work, only 25 percent of married women with a higher education degree work. And in Pakistan, while 29 percent of all married women work and 42 percent of divorced or separated women work, only 22 percent of married women with a higher education degree work. In these economies, where a large proportion of the population is uneducated and engaged in manual or low-skilled work, entire families—men, women, and their children—contribute to the household income simply to survive.[6] The ability of women to stay at home (and children to go to school) is thus treated as a luxury by those a rung higher on the income ladder. As families pull themselves out of poverty and into lower-middle-income brackets, women stop working outside and engage in unpaid labor in the home instead.

This phenomenon is partly what leads women like Rehana, the medical student in Pakistan, to choose a medical degree for better outcomes in the marriage market rather than in the labor market. Further up the income strata, however, among middle- and upper-middle-income families, work, marriage, and values become compatible again: women tend to use their higher education degrees for white-collar work.

By and large, however, across the Muslim world, more married women than ever before are continuing to work or are starting to work, indicating that the trade-off that women face between work and family is getting less costly and values around financial responsibility are evolving. In Jordan, 16 percent of married women ages fifteen to forty-nine are employed, while 23 percent of divorced, separated, or widowed women are employed. However, 40 percent of married women with a higher education degree are working. In Indonesia, the employment rates for all married women and for those with a higher education degree are the same—around 60 percent—but the rates for those who are divorced are higher, at 78 percent. In Egypt, 16 percent of all married women work, 26 percent of divorced women work, and 26 percent of married women with a higher education degree work.[7]

The New Breadwinners

As more married women from low-income and low-education backgrounds begin to work, marriage begins to look very different than it did before. On a sweltering humid day in the Bogor region of Indonesia, a couple of hours' drive outside of Jakarta, I visited a small hamlet where the majority of women are recipients of microfinance loans from Amartha Microfinance. Amartha is the brainchild of a young social entrepreneur, Andi Taufan Garuda Putra, who started it with just US$5,000 of his own money.

From the local field office, we hopped onto small motorbikes to travel muddy roads to reach this otherwise inaccessible rural area. All around us, equal numbers of men and women zipped past, also on motorbikes, the women wearing double head coverings—hijabs and helmets—and showing a freedom of mobility that is rare in much of the Muslim world, at least to this extent.

We started out at a payments session. As we sat on the floor in the courtyard of one of the women's homes, each of the fifteen or so women in this community, several with toddlers in their laps, made their payment as an Amartha representative recorded it in her notebook. The village was quiet as most of its residents gathered for the session. Nearby, on the veranda of another small house, some middle-aged men played chess, but otherwise the village was empty of both working-age men and school-age children. It was midday—most of the men were at work outside the village and the children were at school.

After the session, Ibu Nani, a youthful forty-five-year-old loan recipient, shared her story. Nani had completed junior high school, married, and had three children. Along the way, she began to sew wedding dresses, her passion, but eventually had to give up her small business as the women she employed were slowly lured away by the steady incomes of large factories in nearby towns that mass-produced clothing to supply to Western fast fashion brands. Sewing on her own, making wedding dresses was no longer a viable business. Nani showed me a few samples of her handmade designs that she still keeps at home—they are beautiful but clearly time-consuming and labor-intensive to make. This is what disruption through globalization looks like out in Bogor.

When Amartha came to town, Nani jumped at the chance to start afresh, especially as her husband's income was variable. Her husband had completed high school and was a driver, using his own truck to make deliveries for hire for local businesses. Currently out of work, he was one of the few working-age men in the village. As Nani and I talked, he sat in a darkened room in their home, watching TV. The loan was not large enough for the investment needed to restart the clothing business, so instead she had bought a stock of toys and small electronic goods and loaded them onto her husband's truck. She proudly showed me the truck, currently loaded with brightly colored balls, dolls, bats, and drums. She does not know how to drive the truck—her husband or son drive her to nearby villages to sell the goods door-to-door. When her husband gets work, they unload the toys and she keeps them at home.

Nani's heart remains, however, in one day reviving her creative pursuits. She hopes to sell her designs to a local factory, or find enough capital to start her own wedding dress business again. But for now she is proud of what she has achieved with the toy business. All three of her children completed high school. Her two daughters also work; one still lives at home and works in a factory, while the other works in an office and is married. Her son helps her or takes on odd jobs in nearby towns.

A second Amartha recipient, Ibu Latifa, was thirty-four and also a mother of three. Having completed junior high, she has the same level of education as Nani. With her Amartha loan, she started two businesses—one selling tiny fish for aquariums and the other selling clothing and other small consumer items door to door. Her husband is a motorcycle mechanic who works for a local repair shop. He completed high school.

She proudly presented the fish tanks in her backyard, and then, whipping out her phone, showed me some pictures of the type of clothing she sells. Latifa is a millennial and a near-native of Indonesia's telecommunications boom. In this nation of more than 250 million people, 20 percent of all women and 24 percent of all men use the Internet. Latifa uses the Internet to stay on top of fashion trends and better understand how to make her clothing and fish businesses more successful. Throughout our conversation, she was fiddling with her phone, much as a millennial in a café in Jakarta or New York might, but Latifa is a world away from those milieus.

Just over a decade apart, Nani and Latifa are markedly different in how they approach and understand their own role in their households. I asked both women, in private, what percentage of their household income they each contribute compared to their husbands. Nani's answer, 60 percent, surprised me—and from the surprise on her own face it was clear that it was the first time she had thought about her economic contribution this way. She had never before considered that her toy business brings in more to the household than her husband's unsteady income as a truck driver. She still saw her husband's role as that of the primary breadwinner and her own as a supporting one. That was how her neighbors and family saw her, how her children saw her, and how she saw herself. But she was in fact the primary earner.

Latifa, on the other hand, thought that she and her husband, through his motorbike repair work and her two microbusinesses, probably earned about the same. Like Nani, she hadn't really thought about her own share specifically—but in her case it was because she clearly assumed that they both were breadwinners. Latifa's hunger for success for her family and her entrepreneurial zeal were evident. She and her husband were using their three sources of income to build a house, but not to live in—it was another investment and the profits from it would be reinvested into a bigger house of their own.

Latifa's generation combines a strong work ethic with an ability to delay gratification—traits commonly associated with the baby boomer generation in the United States—and the technological dexterity of her fellow millennials. Some version of this awakening to economic power is happening across the entire Muslim world, especially among younger women. Older women, like Nani, are often unaware of the influence they have in their household through their financial contributions. Keeping the traditional norms and behaviors in place, they and their husbands downplay the importance of their informal work, even as it brings in a significant portion of the household income. Like many groups that have traditionally been out of power, these women are slow to recognize their newfound sources of influence.

But for a younger generation there has been a change in how they see themselves—and in how their husbands see them. Latifa assumes and embodies her co-breadwinner role, taking it in stride as she stays directed toward further economic gains. This subtle but profound shift in the mind-set of younger women is happening in both rural and urban areas and for low-income and middle-income women alike. And it is spreading as Indonesia's telecommunications boom has opened up new pathways for working women—from women like Latifa using online information to improve their products to those at the frontlines of the new "gig economy," such as women driving female-only motorbike-taxi services like LadyJek or those running ecommerce businesses buying and selling clothes, perfumes, electronics, and other goods to women in urban neighborhoods.[8]

Marriage as an institution is still one of the most fundamental cornerstones of society in the Muslim world, much as it was until fairly recently in most of the West. But marriage too is being rapidly redefined by the consequences of women's work. As women begin to exert more control over their marital choices, enter into more equal marriages, thrive despite divorce, or opt to stay single, they change perceptions of their own power and ability.

Sometimes women's changing roles and the economic forces behind them can lead to a loss of identity for men—as with Mozah's son, Ahmed, or men in the Rust Belt of the United States, or coal miners in the north of England. And many women in Muslim societies must still contend with forced marriages, child marriages, and deeply held traditions and taboos that can make their intimate lives difficult, even dangerous. However, the rise of the more equal marriage in many middle-class homes—stemming in part from women's more equal earning power—creates a sense of agency even for those women who do not yet share these privileges. What happens inside the home is increasingly shaped by what is happening outside of it— and these changing dynamics are redefining both work and marriage for generations to come.

∾ six ∾

Business at the Frontlines

Six months before I had consciously thought about writing this book, and a few years into the latest "Saudization" scheme launched by the Saudi Ministry of Labor to bring more local talent into the labor market, I was invited to speak at a conference in Riyadh. As I walked into a large conference hall in the five-star Al Faisaliah Hotel in Riyadh in April 2015, I saw a registration area where hundreds of young women in their anonymous black abayas, all of them either college seniors or recent graduates, were getting their badges and registration packets for Glowork's annual career fair. Just beyond registration were the eighty or so booths of local and multinational companies that were there to share information about openings in their businesses and, in some cases, recruit on the spot. Every corner of the hall was adorned in a bright fuchsia pink, the brand color of Glowork.

Khalid Alkhudair, the social entrepreneur behind Glowork, is a popular gender equality advocate in Saudi Arabia and increasingly across the Gulf who has won awards and appeared on magazine covers. This wasn't a likely scenario when he first started out. At the very first Glowork conference in 2013, the religious police tried to close down the event because of concerns about the large numbers of women descending upon the hotel. That day in 2015, however, the event was taking place with the government's backing, and the governor of Riyadh, an important member of the ruling royal family, was slated to open the conference. In fact, Glowork is now a public-private partnership with the Ministry of Labor of Saudi Arabia, and Khalid has expanded to for-profit ventures like Glofit (a series of women-only gyms) and GloCafe (a women-only restaurant), bringing new consumption options to women with disposable income in a culturally conservative environment.

Seated in the front row were the CEOs and senior executives of the eighty businesses participating in the fair—mostly men—along with political dignitaries, such as one of the thirty women who had been appointed to the Shura Council, a parliament of sorts. And at the back were the three hundred young women who had been selected to attend the conference, handpicked on the basis of their grades, out of the twenty thousand or so who were expected to attend the three-day fair. On two hours' sleep and a lot of coffee, Khalid was busy negotiating the governor's arrival at the conference, without which the proceedings could not begin.

I had been invited to make a keynote presentation on the position of Saudi Arabia in the World Economic Forum's Global Gender Gap Index. As I spoke from the podium, the governor, two federal ministers, and the head of the Human Resources Development Fund—all men—sat on the stage. It was a unique opportunity to be heard by the government and business leaders, and I wanted to make sure my message struck a balance between today's realities and hope for the future. But I was also concerned about how my message would be received by the young women at the back of the room—they were the people behind the data, and ultimately it was their views that mattered.

I concentrated my message on not only the currently low position of Saudi Arabia in the global rankings but also the enormous progress it had made and the type of public- and private-sector efforts that could further improve its performance. Despite its notoriety as a backward place for women—or perhaps because of it—Saudi Arabia has recently made significant efforts to address gender gaps. In fact, it has closed the economic gender gap faster than any other country in the world, relative to a decade ago.

Afterward, at the coffee break, it was mainly the male Western business leaders and the Saudi male business leaders working for Western companies who approached me first. They wanted me to know that they were among the companies making the changes that the data were capturing. At first they said they were instituting changes because the "Saudization" regulations requiring minimum percentages of local staff and an associated rating system compelled them to, but then they added that they often found Saudi women to be among their best workers and so were incentivized to recruit even more women.

As we were speaking, a young woman came toward me; she was a royal family member who had earlier helped open the conference by making the first remarks from the stage. She told me that she had a message from the governor, who was prevented from speaking to me directly by strict protocols. He had wanted me to know that he planned to make Saudi Arabia among the top twenty countries in the rankings in five years' time. In 2015, it was ranked 134th out of 145 countries. In my work, I have always found rankings to be an effective way of awakening a competitive spirit about change. Although making such a large jump in the rankings would be unrealistic given the starting point, anything that starts a conversation about gender equality—even one conducted by an intermediary—is one more way of chipping away at structural barriers.

I spent much of the rest of the day talking to some of the three hundred young women at the back of the room. For the most part, they wanted to know more about Saudi Arabia having made the most progress in gender equality out of any country in the world in the last ten years. They were surprised at learning that they were the foot soldiers of a small revolution—and they also took a fierce pride in it. They could see that the country had a long way to go in empowering women—whether they had ever traveled abroad or not, they knew enough about the world through their TVs and smart-phones to know that. But they also saw change unfolding around them and knew that they had opportunities their mothers would never have had. What they heard about themselves from the West didn't seem to match with the progress they saw around them, and they were proud—and relieved—that the progress was confirmed by objective data.

Unlikely Feminists

This moment in Riyadh highlighted for me some of the unique ways in which "womenomics" plays out in some of the most conservative parts of the Muslim world: men become the unlikely faces of work-force feminism, governments dictate how talent should be deployed, and businesses become the engines of social change. Men like the governor of Riyadh are in charge; they can decide how quickly—or slowly—to drive change. There are practical considerations too. Men like Khalid can find ways to obtain the required permits and govern-ment support to create an organization like Glowork, but a woman in Khalid's position might have had a harder time. Even though the company's mission aligns with the stated social and economic objectives of the government, a woman would need to have male support—her guardian, for example—in dealing with government offices; she would not be allowed to do it wholly on her own. Male business leaders—both Western and local—hold the keys and de-termine how quickly employment opportunities become available to women and whether they are set up for success in those structures.

In these environments, women trying to advocate for women's economic empowerment are viewed as upsetting a delicate balance.

Men, on the other hand, can be lauded as champions of those without a voice. Perhaps more than anywhere else in the world, to create a girls' club in the most conservative parts of the Muslim world, one must be part of the boys' club.

So who are these unlikely feminists? Some are like Fahd Al Rasheed, the group CEO and managing director of Emaar, The Economic City. The group is a publicly listed Saudi company leading the development of the King Abdullah Economic City (KAEC), an $86 billion mega-investment aimed at helping diversify Saudi Arabia's oil-based economy. While the City is not expected to be fully completed until 2020, some parts of it have been developed already, and as a government-backed venture, it has employed many Saudis along the way. Recently, those Saudis have begun to include women.

Fahd told me that approximately 10 percent of the people currently working in KAEC are women. "We are working to increase this level to 30 percent over the next five years and are running a number of programs to train women to take on a wider variety of roles." Women have already been successful in some key job functions. "The operations room at King Abdullah Port is staffed entirely by women who we recruited and trained from the towns surrounding the City. The training process took twelve months and provided them with all the technical skills they needed to do the job. The women who work at the port are between twenty and thirty-five years of age, and most of them hold college degrees. The fact that we invest in ongoing training and development to enable our employees to pursue rewarding careers has ensured that the turnover rate is very low. Within the City as a whole the labor laws are being designed to make it easier for women to work."

The City at present has only a few thousand people. By 2025, it's expected to have a population of two million. Although it is unclear how it will concretely function in the future, and even though the laws governing it are still being designed, the KAEC is likely to be a special statute area. In building a city from scratch with its own set of laws, there is an opportunity to set a different tone from the start.

The early experiments conducted by Fahd and the group to pave the way for women's employment did not go unnoticed by women, or by their families. "This was not an easy decision for many families in the area, but once they saw the efforts we made to create an environment that was culturally supportive and conducive to working women, they were more comfortable," Fahd said. And it resonated beyond the women and their immediate families. "The success of the initiative has meant that other women from around the area have been encouraged to seek roles in the City and receive the support of their families to do so."

Creating a new city from scratch is the type of major infrastructure project that tends to employ mainly men anywhere in the world, because of the traditionally larger pool of male talent for such work. In the West too, a project such as this one would be likely to attract a predominantly male workforce, from the manual laborers involved in construction to the engineers and architects leading the design. Fahd is conscious of the unique demographic, economic, and cultural forces that together have created such a strong momentum for change. A massive project such as his in an environment such as Saudi Arabia has made it necessary to address gender equality—and to speak about it.

"Saudi Arabia remains a very conservative society with ingrained attitudes about the workplace, and this can make it challenging to reach out to potential female hires," Fahd said. "However, the economic situation is changing, and this affects attitudes toward women in the workplace. Society as a whole is becoming a lot more accepting of women in the workplace. This is in part due to the rise of social media, which has made it easier not only for people to exchange views but also for women to set up businesses online. Saudi women are becoming more and more entrepreneurial and developing the business management and interpersonal skills which companies value. Industries also find new ways to use technology to support female employment, for example, through the establishment of virtual workplaces which allow women to work from their own homes and connect to teams and customers online."

The KAEC is being built during a moment when women's participation in the workforce is particularly valuable. To achieve the Saudi government's Vision 2030 plan, emphasizing human capital development and a diversification of the economy, all of the country's talent, including women, will need to be deployed. Fahd is hopeful: "The government takes the inclusion of women in the workforce very seriously, and I am confident these challenges will be alleviated in time."

Asked if he has a business or economic rationale for gender equality in his company, Fahd answered in a way that I had heard countless male—and female—Western CEOs respond. "Our company is a meritocracy," Fahd said, "and we seek to hire and develop the best talent we can, regardless of age or gender. I am actually proud of the fact that we don't need to have a specific rationale for hiring women. Our rationale is to hire the best people we can, and as long as we continue to ensure equal opportunities, we will see women playing an increasing role within the City. Cities are all about people and families, so having a female perspective in our operations is particularly important to us. There is a large population of highly qualified and extremely capable women in the country, and companies increasingly see the value of having a broader talent pool from which to select the very best candidates." Like many CEOs around the world, Fahd is willing to promote gender equality, not as a value in and of itself, but as a business virtue.

Whether it's in New York, London, Riyadh, or the King Abdullah Economic City, when it comes to the competition for talent and ideas, economics almost always trumps culture. And it is not just in Saudi Arabia that this rationale wins out. Elsewhere in the Gulf, a region that has made massive investments in women's education, the need for skilled talent is driving business leaders to push through cultural barriers. Most find a willing audience for their efforts.

Omar Alghanim is the forty-two-year-old CEO of Alghanim Industries, a multibillion-dollar business based in Kuwait. One of the largest privately owned conglomerates in the Gulf region, Alghanim Industries began with Omar's great-grandfather, Mohammed Alghanim, in the mid-nineteenth century. Like most Kuwaiti merchants, he started his business as a seafaring trading company; at the beginning of the twentieth century, it shifted to building materials and eventually general trading, including the first dealership for General Motors in the MENA region. I met Omar when he agreed to chair the New Vision for Arab Employment project at the World Economic Forum. Having created other such platforms over the years to provide a space for business leaders to act together, I was impressed by the particularly high level of passion and energy Omar brought to the role. I was even more impressed when he chose to personally join several discussions to shape the project directly, as his team and mine worked together. Over the course of a year, most of our efforts focused on education and employment initiatives. I was surprised when he asked to get involved in my team's work on gender parity, saying he simply wanted to listen in and learn.

A year later, I asked Omar if he would be willing to share more about his relatively recent personal journey on gender equality with me. And so, with temperatures soaring to 116 degrees Fahrenheit outside, I found myself facing him in his penthouse offices at the Al Hamra Tower, the tallest building in Kuwait. We were in a room used for the *diwaniyah*, a traditionally all-male gathering at which Kuwaiti men discuss politics and business.

Earlier in the day, his head of human resources and head of diversity had explained the changes the company has made in record time: extending maternity leave beyond the legal threshold (offering ninety days instead of seventy in Kuwait and forty in the UAE), tightening up sexual harassment policies, creating a diversity committee that reports directly to the CEO, and going as far as letting go managers who are not inclusive. A turnaround like that in the space of a year is hard to implement, anywhere in the world. But

Omar has a history of executing turnarounds. He told me that when he first took over the company from his father, who is still the chairman, he made sure he had complete freedom to ensure that he had the right talent. Soon he had replaced 75 percent of the top management team, and today he is justifiably proud of the meritocracy he created in the space of just a few years. "Arabs love rumor and innuendo," he explained. "We wanted transparency, candor, and straight-talking." This belief in meritocracy is new for a region that Omar described as a "wastocracy," derived from the word *wasta*, roughly meaning "connections."

Omar told me that the company's underlying meritocratic culture is what makes it easier for his company to implement gender equality. "I like to win," he said. "Our region has no shortage of financial capital. But we lack human capital. And young women are amongst the most talented. Sometimes we will lose one of these high-potential women to another company because they offer them a better salary. But they will often come back because of our culture."

After Alghanim Industries decided to tackle the issue more rigorously, one year before Omar and I talked, it began to understand and communicate the advantages to everyone. Alghanim had just acquired the dealership for Ford, and Omar placed two women among the five senior leaders in the new division. This was a deliberate choice. "We find we get better, more nuanced decision-making with these teams." It reminded me of something I had heard nearly ten years ago. Carlos Ghosn, CEO of Renault-Nissan, said that while cars are seen as the domain of men, in reality women and men both make the car-buying decision in most families—women just happen to look at different parts of the car when thinking about it. Diversity in the teams that make and market these cars is thus essential to selling them, and this logic applies in the heart of the MENA region as much as it does in Japan or France. In Kuwait, as it became clear at Alghanim that women who are economically empowered have their own cash to spend and are vocal players in their families' common consumption decisions, diversity in the company's leadership made business sense.

Both Fahd and Omar have good reasons for becoming unlikely change-makers for gender equality. Fahd is motivated by the changing priorities of the government as Saudi Arabia promotes its Vision 2030 plan to diversify away from oil. Omar's decisions around meritocracy, talent, and gender equality are driven by the bottom line and the goal of modernizing an eighty-five-year-old family business.

But I was curious about how these men feel about it personally.

Fahd admitted that his wife does not work, but he spoke enthusiastically about his daughter, the eldest of his three children, as being the sharpest. "People tend to view Saudi Arabia through a largely static lens, but this is a very dynamic country and one going through a historic period of change. When I returned to the country in 2005 [from graduate study in the United States], it was still very much a taboo to see women in the workplace and almost impossible to see women on corporate boards, acting as CEOs, or represented in major government bodies. Today, a decade later, we see more Saudi women graduate from college than men. Indeed, the largest women-only university in the world is here in Saudi Arabia. We have seen women elected to municipal councils and appointed to ministerial positions. The highest government body in the country, the Shura Council, which advises the king, is 20 percent composed of women. That's a higher level of female participation than in many Western democracies. It is particularly significant that Vision 2030, the road map laid out for the future of the country, has a specific goal to increase the participation of women in the workforce from 22 percent to 30 percent and, more importantly, to invest in developing their skills to make this happen. As a father, I hope my daughter's future will be everything that she wants it to be. I believe she has the potential to achieve anything she sets out to do, and I am confident that she and her female peers will have all the opportunity they need in Saudi Arabia. I, along with many other Saudis like me, work every day to make that a reality."

In Omar's view, the region has regressed over time and is only beginning to recover lost ground now. "Gender bias has gotten worse, in some regards, for my generation than that of my fathers—the '60s and '70s were a modern time in Kuwait. In the '70s, acceptable attire included clothing that would be considered 'risqué' in Kuwait today. Political Islam, [which] gained momentum during my generation, has in many ways widened the gender gap. There are strong efforts being made to reverse this across the region—a good development. A lot more needs to be done." He wants to be a part of that change. "I have two daughters and two sons. I want my daughters to have as much chance to take over from me as my sons." He paused and laughed, adding, "Or none of them, if they are not qualified." But always impatient for change, Omar is concerned that change is not happening fast enough, even when it has become possible that men in power can hand power to the next generation of women in family businesses. "Few male CEOs of family businesses are trying to open the path to leadership for their daughters. Even amongst some of my close friends and business associates, guys that I know well, there are some whose wives or daughters I have never met [because of gender segregation]." Among the scores of family business dynasties he knows personally, he could think of only five that are actively thinking about passing on their businesses to women in the next generation—but he granted that this is five more than there would have been a generation ago. In a region where private family-owned businesses and family-led governance structures are widespread, transferring power to the female half of the next generation is critical.

For men like Fahd and Omar, gender equality resonates personally because, having invested equally in their male and female children, they see the talent, curiosity, and intelligence of their daughters and have begun to dream of a different future for them. This pattern has been documented in other parts of the world. Researchers at Aalborg University in Denmark, the University of Maryland, and Columbia Business School studied Danish CEOs and found that those who had firstborn daughters closed the gender wage gap more than other CEOs. Another study, conducted by the University of Rochester and Harvard University, found that U.S. Court of Appeals judges with at least one daughter were more likely to vote in favor of women's rights than judges who had no children at all or who had only sons.[1] A new generation of male CEOs in the Muslim world who are fathers of daughters are also some of the most proactive if unlikely champions of gender equality.

"Do You Want to Eat Grapes or Fight the Caretaker?"

What happens when an intergenerational transfer of power puts a woman in charge? One of the most well-recognized female leaders of a family business across the Middle East is Lubna Olayan, CEO of the Olayan Financing Company (OFC). The company holds and manages all of the Olayan Group's businesses and investments in Saudi Arabia and the Middle East, including joint ventures with major multinationals. Overseeing a business started in 1947 by Olayan's father, Suliman, OFC controls a financial portfolio of private investments and public equities, and its subsidiaries handle products from more than two hundred suppliers and principals, while its distribution operations concentrate on fast-moving consumer goods, hospital supplies, office automation products, building supplies, telecommunications equipment, and industrial equipment. Other OFC companies are engaged in industrial services, project and construction management, real estate development, property management, and food services. Still others manufacture consumer, industrial, and medical products.

In 1983, when Lubna Olayan accompanied her husband on what was supposed to be a two-year stint in Riyadh, her father brought her into the company to work alongside him as his executive assistant. She and her husband never left, and today Lubna Olayan serves as the CEO of OFC. I have long admired Olayan and had the privilege to work with her when she joined the World Economic Forum's advisory group on gender equality for a number of years. Her approach to gender equality has always been one of quiet, but decisive, leadership, and the company is well-known for being one of the most progressive in Saudi Arabia, having opened up work opportunities for women, starting at a time when this was considered unlikely, if not impossible. I asked her why she (as a rare role model) and the company (as a leader in driving change) don't speak out more about the changes they are making on gender equality, in contrast to the way many Western companies might showcase their progress on gender equality.

"We are not a group that goes to the media," she replied. "We don't seek recognition. Instead, we focus on our internal audience and make sure that our partners and employees are committed to gender equality and support us. There are multiple forums for business leaders and the government to come together, including efforts led by the Ministry of Labor. We make sure to engage actively with them. There we share best practices, including all we have learnt at the Olayan Group through our efforts over the years. We are committed to these exchanges and to fostering change, and we will continue our efforts. But we will do it our way, by setting an example and creating a culture of change, a culture of equality and mutual respect. Is it our responsibility to help other companies? Absolutely. But we don't need the media to do it."

In part the hesitation to showcase progress is cultural—for example, many major philanthropic efforts in the Muslim world are not publicized the way they might be in the Western press, because of a religious and cultural stipulation for modesty in displaying generosity. But for the few women leaders like Lubna Olayan who attempt to tackle gender equality, it is also about preserving their license to operate. Women like Olayan are so rare that they are often in the spotlight simply for being women in leadership roles. They are keen not to draw unnecessary attention or a backlash, choosing instead to focus on making deep, lasting change.

This philosophy of quiet, resolute change has begun to pay off at the Olayan Financing Company. Working together at the company's head offices in Riyadh are both foreigners and Saudis, men and women, those in traditional dress and those in Western dress. At least in all the superficial ways that diversity can be observed, the office is as diverse as many offices in New York, London, or Tokyo, if not more so. But the diversity goes beyond appearances. When Lubna Olayan started working there in 1983, she was the only woman in the entire company. As late as 2001, she was still the only one. Today more than five hundred of the company's twelve thousand Saudi-based employees are women. In the historical context of the Saudi labor market, this is enormous progress.

Olayan said that when she first started working at OFC her biggest concern was to prove that she was good at her job and not serving in her role simply because she was an Olayan. As an Olayan, her skills and work ethic were much more important than her gender, because her father did not distinguish on the basis of gender, focusing instead on a person's dedication to the task at hand and the business. So she did not initially view either her work or OFC through a gender lens. But once she settled in and demonstrated that a woman could perform as well as a man, she looked around and realized that she was still the only woman, and she took the view that it was not "realistic, sustainable, or fair" that the company had no other women. So by the late 1990s, she had convinced her father to support the groundwork for change.

In the early 2000s, she began in earnest, hiring Hana Al Sayed as head of diversity to lead the way. But convincing partners to get on board with staff diversity has been as much a part of the change as convincing the company's own ranks. Olayan gave me the example of one line of business where she wanted to bring women into the factory and there were three partners: "a foreign one, another Saudi partner, and us. The other Saudi partner was not comfortable with the change and pushed back very hard against hiring women, and I couldn't convince him. So I went to enlist the help of some mutual friends, who happened to be in the government, to help persuade him. That worked, and now, ten years later, I am really pleased when I hear him say publicly that he is proud that our company was a pioneer in bringing women onto the factory floor." As Hana walked

me through the company's progress—and failures—in implementing gender equality, it became clear that it took both leadership from
Olayan at the top and methodical, quantifiable efforts from Al Sayed
to create a tangible change in mind-set among managers—and the
company's partners—to deliver results.

I asked Olayan about the broader changes taking place in Saudi
Arabia: Did she think they represented a momentary blip or signified
genuine long-term change? And what needed to be done to nudge
along the current momentum? "It may not be changing as fast as you,
myself, or Hana might like, but it is moving in the right direction.
There is no doubt about it. We see it in our own company as more
and more women apply to join us, but it's change growing out of a
real social need. Unmarried women want to be financially independent. Married women want to work because families need two incomes now. But if a woman comes from a conservative family, her
father, husband, or brother may insist that she can only work in a
women-only environment. It is very important that the family support a woman in the workplace. Quite frankly, I could not have done
it without the support of my father, my husband, and my siblings.

"Sometimes the women themselves will insist on a women-only
environment, and we should respect that. Every society has to do it
its own way. And we need to accommodate differences. We want to
push the envelope, but we don't need to break society along the way.
We have a saying here: do you want to eat grapes or do you want to
fight the caretaker? I totally believe in this. The number-one priority
is to give women opportunity, because that leads to financial independence and dignity. We want to push society towards this, but we
don't need to break society to do it."

On the subject of religion too, Olayan was unequivocal. "Religion
is not a barrier, but a skewed interpretation of any religion can be
used as a barrier by those who want to use it for an agenda. But as you
and I know, religion is not actually a barrier. And that's certainly true
when it comes to women in business. Where is a better proof than the
fact that the Prophet worked for his wife? If he can work for Khadija,

how can anyone say women are not allowed to work? More and more people are accepting that view, and the engagement of women in the Saudi economy is a feature of Vision 2030, the model for our future economic development. So there is movement, there is change. Though we would like things to change faster, we must exercise patience because you need to bring society along at a rate of change that is real and genuine. Otherwise, it's not a sustainable change. And when people push too hard, too quickly, things can backfire. Change needs to be responsible and steady."

Olayan's point on leading change toward gender equality cautiously, by pulling society along instead of antagonizing it, is reminiscent of the "third way" that many women in Muslim countries adopt as a strategy for joining the workforce while balancing their family care responsibilities, and it is echoed by many women leaders in prominent roles. This approach certainly seems like the most sustainable one in the context of the Gulf, particularly in Saudi Arabia. Those who take a more direct approach, even in the increasingly acceptable arena of economic empowerment, are often pushed back hard. It may be that the fight for equality in places like Saudi Arabia will first be won quietly in the workplace rather than loudly in the streets.

Leveling the Playing Field

On the other side of the world, in Kuala Lumpur, some of this equality has already been won. Women's rise in the workforce began earlier in Malaysia, and gender is becoming a less significant determinant of economic outcomes. And unlike in the Gulf countries, the remaining barriers stem from culture but are not enshrined in the law. If leading womenomics in corporate Saudi Arabia is about cautiously opening the tap to the large female talent pool, leading womenomics in Malaysia is about getting more women through that pipeline and onto a more level playing field for leadership. In this environment, for high-skilled women at least, the emphasis has shifted further downstream, from giving women a foot in the door for the first time to ensuring that they have equal opportunity once they are inside the room.

Aireen Omar is the CEO of AirAsia Malaysia, one of the two women heading a country operation for Asia's largest low-cost airline. I first met her at a World Economic Forum conference in China. It was during Ramadan, and despite being near the end of her fast, she was brimming with energy. Aireen's rise to the top of the Malaysian operations is due in part to her company leveling the playing field for women from its inception. "The cofounders, Tan Sri Tony Fernandes and Datuk Kamarudin Meranun, set up the company with the intention of meritocracy, regardless of gender, race, or religion. So gender neutrality has been a part of our DNA from the beginning. If a person is capable of the job, they will get the job and they will get paid the same doing it."

But gender equality at AirAsia Malaysia is also the result of a broader Malaysian context that has created a large female workforce pipeline. "Since we gained independence in 1957, if women have the right background, they are encouraged to be leaders in communities, companies, and government," Aireen said. "For example, we have had many female ministers. The minister of trade was chairman at AirAsia. The ex-governor of the Central Bank was a lady. There are lots of ladies who are CEOs in banks, even chairmen. So I think that we do embrace women to be part of the workforce here. The government has always been trying, in education, politics, the economy. The government has put in place a 30 percent quota for boards. But we shouldn't use it to simply fill in a quota—women should join boards because they are qualified."

Having lived and worked abroad before returning to Kuala Lumpur, Aireen is aware of the rarity of the corporate environment in Malaysia compared to elsewhere in the Muslim world. "The way I see it, unfortunately, not all Muslim countries have this kind of mind-set, but it has nothing to do with religion, it's the culture from thousands of years. In Islam women are encouraged to be leaders in their own right. They are encouraged to trade and be entrepreneurs and contribute to their community. Inequality is more of a cultural thing, not religious. You see, in Malaysia and Indonesia, we have strong women leaders. So I think that the governments of other countries need to work hard to change perceptions and traditional values. They need to show that a significant contribution would be created if women were to participate."

In the aviation industry, as it is in the West, the gender gaps are more pronounced in certain occupations. "We face the same external barriers as others," she said. "For example, pilots and engineers are generally dominated by men. But we encouraged women even in the first cadet pilot program. Today 6 percent of our pilots are now women. In comparison, Malaysian Airlines doesn't have any female pilots, but newer airlines now copy us too. We started a trend. And many women are in the top management besides me—for example, the group head of strategy and the chief commercial officer are both women."

Still, Aireen feels that women are not doing enough to lean in and lead, and this is where she chooses to intervene. "Women need to aspire to more. For example, the women pilots are often just grateful to be pilots. They could aim for being the director of all flight operations. In areas like that, where there are very few women, I try to create focus groups and personally encourage women. But in areas where there is no problem we shouldn't get too fixated on gender and instead encourage everyone to be the best that they can be."

Nezha Hayat, former head of the Casablanca Stock Exchange in Morocco and currently chair of the Morocco Capital Markets Authority, agrees that progressive business and regulatory efforts need to be supplemented by efforts to help women become better prepared mentally for leadership roles. "Young women today are not concerned about the glass ceiling—until they touch it. When they have just graduated, they don't think about it. Then all at once, ten years into their careers, they start coming to women like me for advice," Nezha said. "At that point, they have started facing expectations of being a wife and mother. They want to do it as perfectly as their mothers did it while not working. In their careers, they find that they have worked very hard but are not chosen to become the managers of their departments. That's when they ask me how to handle their private life and the glass ceiling."

Nezha thinks it's important to start earlier. "Very often, talking to them, you find out that they have put their own limits. They come to see me because they doubt they can make it. They are a minority, so they lack self-confidence." She advocates promoting visible role models and was part of one major effort to identify such women in different industries. "We found women in leadership roles across all sectors. They were just not visible. It made us and others realize they are extraordinary. So we made them visible. I don't think there were more than five hundred women in our list, but we could finally see them. Women were also being appointed as ministers at the same time. So the change became healthy and noticeable."

Nezha also talked openly and honestly about her own experience in *not* being able to have it all at the same time; she feels that it's important to show other women that it's possible to combine work and family but to not try to shoot for perfection in each area. She was present, she said, for the most important moments of her son's life and believes that she is a good mother, but she is also well aware of the hard work and time she had to put in to become one of the leading women in finance in Morocco. Nevertheless, she is at peace with having set her priorities and knowing that one cannot achieve perfection.

While Nezha tries to promote healthy role models, she also thinks there needs to be public infrastructure to provide support. She herself had support from her parents with the care of her son, but she's not certain this is a sustainable approach for the next generation. "There's still lots of cheap labor available in the home, and for now it's still possible to have help from grandparents. But as grandparents themselves live longer lives, they want to keep working and stay productive, not necessarily help with child care. So things are starting to change, and governments need to prepare for what might be a different society."

When it comes to the glass ceiling, she thinks affirmative policies are the way to go. "Unfortunately, I think quotas are not a perfect way, but they are a good way. While our constitution asks for equality so it's difficult to put quotas or other measures that are not just voluntary, we can show that diversity is good for better corporate governance. So in my new role at the Capital Markets Authority, I will try to do more to promote women on boards of directors. Once they have one, there is no problem having the second or third or more. The most difficult is to start."

Experiments with Equality

Although Malaysia and Indonesia are among the most progressive countries in the Muslim world when it comes to women in white-collar work, they also have large populations of lower-skilled women. For most of these women, labor market opportunities are deeply segregated by gender. Women's work and men's work—both paid and unpaid—look different. This gender segregation can be an advantage, however, for some businesses—and an opportunity to promote women's economic empowerment in the long term.

The biggest market today for Tupperware, an American company that makes food storage products, is Indonesia. The very factors that made Tupperware's business grow in the 1950s in the United States are now playing out in markets like Indonesia. Tupperware started by tapping into the availability of women in the United States who did not work outside the home but were looking for ways to make extra cash. They were encouraged to hold Tupperware "parties" in their homes, inviting other women among their friends and acquaintances to come over and buy Tupperware products. This model worked well in the United States and to some extent still does. "Housewives" who want to supplement their household income concurrently create both a massive salesforce and a massive consumer base, and Tupperware has given millions of women an opportunity to earn a living from their homes through traditional community networks. However, this traditional relationship-based sales model has declined in Western markets, and today the company's largest new growth markets are in the emerging world.

The Tupperware-style sales model is not limited to microbusinesses. Many women use the model to create larger businesses, hiring others—usually women—to sell for them. The top salesperson last year, across all of Tupperware's markets, was Fatima, an Indonesian woman who earned revenues in excess of US$2 million. She has turned her business into a family enterprise, hiring her husband to work for her in addition to hundreds of women on her sales teams. Neither Fatima nor her husband finished high school, and yet all their children have been to university.

I was invited by Rick Goings, the chairman and CEO of Tupperware Brands Corporation, to join his talk to the top-performing sales teams in Jakarta, Indonesia. Nearly two thousand women were packed into an auditorium, proudly wearing the coordinated uniforms of each sales team, complete with bright matching hijabs, to listen to Rick's three-hour, highly energetic talk and demonstration that ranged from global economic trends to deeply personal thoughts on family. The excitement, energy, and emotion in the room were palpable, with plenty of music, clapping, and dancing throughout the day, especially when the sales awards were handed out. Without warning, Rick asked me to join him onstage, where he praised me for becoming a leader in my profession in spite of "coming from a place where women are not expected to amount to much." The women clapped and cheered. Afterward, Rick explained why he did that spontaneously. For him, growing Tupperware in Indonesia—and in many emerging markets—has been about much more than business. He takes inspiration from being able to change mind-sets and provide opportunity. And part of changing mind-sets includes helping these women recognize their own power and possibilities for their future.

Addressing personal growth and resilience toward the end of his talk, Rick shared details about his family background, his love for his wife, and the loss of one of his children. The room was silent as two thousand Muslim Indonesian women from all walks of life sat mesmerized, listening to an American man discuss a subject so universally human that it resonated for all. Having expressed some of the most personal feelings and described his most painful moments, Rick switched the mood and began to talk about resilience through music and shared some of his favorite songs—two "fight songs" and a love song. Videos for his two fight songs—"Eye of the Tiger" from the 1982 movie *Rocky III* and "What a Feeling" from the 1983 movie *Flashdance*—played on the massive screen behind him.

As the actress Jennifer Beals danced in revealing clothing that none of these hijab-clad women would ever choose to wear themselves, they clapped and sang along. A sixty-year-old American company had brought a business model to their lives that worked for them, and a seventy-year-old American man was now sharing his own life lessons for inspiration. I was reminded once again that culture, religion, and values have little to no impact on the economic choices these women are making and the opportunities that have opened up for them.

There are certainly critics of Tupperware who would say that the company perpetuates traditional gender norms. It may look that way today, several decades after the model started in the United States and in light of the social changes that have unfolded in the West in that time. However, for anyone with the chance to listen to the women who were getting their first opportunity at micro-entrepreneurship, this seems a fairly detached criticism. In several interviews, through tears of happiness, Fatima, the top saleswoman, as well as many women who earn far less than her, insisted that work had transformed their lives—for the better—in immeasurable ways. It had brought them newfound respect in their families and communities, as well as a way to earn a living that allowed them to invest in their children while combining work and family in a way that was acceptable to society. And Rick himself looked less to me like the CEO I met at Davos and much more like an evangelizer of a brand of women's empowerment that could give low-skilled women in this part of the world an opportunity. Globalization has its winners and losers—but this seemed to be globalization at its best, bringing opportunity and creating bridges between cultures.

For many Western companies, however, success at promoting women's empowerment is not quite so certain. Nearly a decade ago, I was invited to present the World Economic Forum's Global Gender Gap Index to the Pakistan Business Council, a consortium of the CEOs of about twenty-five of the largest Pakistan-based businesses, both multinationals and local companies. One of the CEOs present told me about his experience in trying to integrate more women into his company. In the 1990s, a German energy and technology conglomerate started a pilot program to integrate more women into its workforce in Pakistan. The company had started with five hundred women in various skilled positions across the company. Five years later, only ten were left in the program.

Although they had made serious investments at this company in onboarding, training, and promoting these women, they had not thought through the social context. As soon as these women became engaged or married, which they invariably did within a year or two of starting work, they were expected to be at home. A decade ago, it was still difficult for their families or their in-laws to accept that they would continue in a corporate job after getting married. Often they would keep working, but in more flexible jobs like teaching, where they could combine marriage and motherhood. It was a win for science and business teaching in schools—but a loss for the company that had invested in them. The takeaway for this CEO at the time was that efforts to recruit and retain female employees would always fail in the local culture—and that the program was therefore not worth the investment.

Today things look different: local and multinational companies have become smarter about managing women's integration into their workforces and account for cultural constraints in the design of these efforts. A few years ago, McDonald's started a women's recruitment program in Pakistan with perhaps an even more difficult demographic pool than the German company had worked with—low-income women. Moreover, the company was recruiting for an even tougher role in terms of cultural acceptance—customer service jobs. Targeting recruitment efforts at women at age eighteen rather than those who were already closer to the average age at marriage of twenty-three, the company provided a path for them to combine work and college. Having learned from the experiences of those who went before them, McDonald's recruiters also took the time to speak to the young women's families, reassuring them that their daughters would be safe and protected from any unseemly behavior from male customers or coworkers, and provided a pick-up-and-drop-off service from their homes to the McDonald's restaurants. Saadia, whom we met in Chapter 1, is one of the beneficiaries of this carefully managed effort.

Amir is the regional manager for McDonald's for northern Pakistan. I asked him what the payoff is for McDonald's. "This started as part of our social responsibility efforts but soon ended up making business sense," he said. "Our female workers are usually also our best workers. They often complete traineeships faster, move into permanent roles, and rise through the ranks faster than the men."

After the initial hurdles and investments, many companies find that, when they get a chance for the first time, women tend to be model workers, even if they do not always stay as long as their male counterparts. The opportunity to work is so unexpected—and hard-won—that women workers treat it with the utmost rigor and dedication. Their bosses quickly realize that gender diversity is more than a Western notion, handed down from a local CEO or a faraway head office, and that it pays off. Nearly every business leader I have spoken to contends that their female workers are often their star performers even while their workforce remains predominantly male. This makes the investment in their recruitment worthwhile, especially when combined with the reputational returns.

In the past, Western companies may have avoided recruiting women to ensure that they were not seen as disruptive to the local culture, while local companies, caught in local norms and practices, may have never even considered it. Today, however, as the talent base around them changes and the aspirations of women and local governments change, all companies are rewarded, both directly and indirectly, for taking a progressive approach.

Most Western or multinational businesses have global diversity policies that would make it impossible for them not to hire women for their local staffs in the Muslim world. This makes them take bolder, more complex steps to integrate women. But it is not just a faraway edict that drives this change. The local managers they employ often want to drive change too, whether through human resource policy or corporate social responsibility (CSR) practices—or both, as Amir at McDonald's did. This creates a virtuous cycle for current and future staff, both male and female.

Local companies, particularly those with no global presence, may not be under pressure from global HR and CSR departments, but they know that they too are in the midst of culture change, and they also are increasingly conscious of the female face of their talent pipeline as more and more women become educated. Saudi banks have no choice but to hire women because women are beginning to hold the majority of finance degrees and MBAs. Private hospital administrators in Pakistan are often women, with their medical and public health degrees. In Kazakhstan, women are typically the majority in banks and the finance departments of companies because a majority of accounting, business, and economics degrees are acquired by women.

Women are a vital part of the talent base for some new technology businesses, much as they are for Tupperware's more traditional business model. The office of Kudo, a technology company, with its millennial workforce, ping-pong table, open-plan seating, and inspirational quotes on multicolored walls, could easily be located somewhere in Silicon Valley. Instead, it is in Jakarta, Indonesia. Kudo—its name is a Bahasa abbreviation of "kiosk for transacting online"—is a technology platform that bridges online ecommerce with traditional off-line retail, such as the ubiquitous *kirana* kiosks, the mom-and-pop shops scattered across cities and villages throughout Indonesia. In short, it's an assisted ecommerce platform. The Kudo app allows users to create their own digital store to sell phone credit, the ability to make utility payments, and ecommerce products like electronics and groceries. These Kudo agents then enable others who don't have credit cards, don't trust online payment systems, or are not tech-savvy to make online transactions. This is what the "Fourth Industrial Revolution" looks like across the emerging markets that make up the Muslim world.[2] Digital and analog expansion occurs side by side, new and old technologies coexist, and businesses like Kudo find profitable ways to bridge these worlds. From retail to manufacturing to telecommunications to transport, new business models—and new earning opportunities—emerge.

Unlike in many traditional businesses in Jakarta, nearly half of the suppliers and distributors of these new businesses are women. Agung Nugroho, cofounder of Kudo, told me that 40 percent of the agents using his platform are women—and of those, 60 percent are unemployed "housewives" seeking to supplement their household income. The other 40 percent are blue-collar working women or students. These women use Internet access to buy products online and sell them to others, many of whom are other men and women in their neighborhoods who can't or don't want to buy online and prefer to make purchases in person, with cash. Kudo's business model relies heavily on the mass entrepreneurship of these women.

For Agung, women are not just the primary users of his product—they are also the ones making the product. The two hundred or so twenty-something Indonesians with computer science, engineering, and business degrees in the Kudo office in Jakarta are a rare breed. "There are many young, productive people looking for opportunity and a chance to channel their energies into something they care about, but there are not that many who also have the skills we need, especially in engineering," said Agung. This skills gap creates an incentive for equality in the market for talent in a way that many voluntary company policies may not. Women make up 35 percent of Kudo's talent in total, even among the computer engineers who develop the technology behind the platform, and they fill 30 percent of the leadership roles. The head of product is a woman. For comparison, in Silicon Valley women make up 30 percent of employees in total and fill around 10 percent of technical roles and just over 10 percent of leadership roles.[3]

I got to meet about twenty of these young women, who hailed from different functions across the company, including marketing, engineering, and finance. Although all of them loved their jobs, some were unsure whether they would keep working after they had children or whether they would leave, as the women in the German company's Pakistan experiment had done over a decade earlier. But there is a difference between those women and the women working at Kudo. The latter want to fulfill their traditional roles as wives and mothers, but they also hold another set of values: they want to earn enough to afford the life they want for themselves and their families, and they want to fulfill their own professional ambitions.

Knowing this, and despite the possibility that they will leave the company in the future, Kudo competes for their talent through experiments tailored to retain this female workforce. Indonesia mandates ninety days of paid maternity leave, and the company complies with this policy, but its parental support policy goes further—the company provides a space for pumping breast milk and a partial nursery. Kudo policies also provide women with equal advancement opportunities to fill leadership roles. As a high-growth business, Kudo needs all the talent it can find and is willing to put in the effort to retain it.

Holding Up a Mirror

Not all corporate experiments with promoting gender equality focus inward. Some try to change mind-sets—or at the very least reflect the emerging mind-sets of working women—through advertising and media.

In the days preceding and following Donald Trump's inauguration as president of the United States on January 20, 2017, headscarves of all types—and the women who wear them—had a moment in the global limelight. France, Germany, and the Netherlands fully or partly banned the face-veil, and France tried to ban the burqini, a modest swimsuit, from seaside resorts. Meanwhile, Turkey allowed policewomen to start wearing the hijab, building on a 2013 law that had already permitted the hijab back into most of the country's state institutions after it had been banned for over eighty years. In the United States, at the women's march on the day after the inauguration, an image of a woman in a hijab made out of the American flag became a popular symbol. Soon after, the European Court of Justice ruled that banning the hijab in the workplace could be legal if a workplace banned all religious symbols.[4]

Far more riveting than the hijab's political aspects and the legal rulings associated with it—which had long been present—was its new image of empowerment. The image of an Egyptian beach volleyball player in a hijab and full bodysuit playing against a German player in a bikini at the 2016 Summer Olympics ricocheted around the globe. In the Muslim world, the social media conversation ranged from pride in the fact that a covered Muslim woman was competing internationally to surprise that her hijab was even a topic of conversation. In the West, views ranged from the opinion that the image was proof of a deep, unbridgeable cultural chasm to a view of it as evidence for the irrelevance of clothing. Some months later, Nike announced a new product—the Pro Hijab—and Nike Middle East produced an ad that shows a woman in a hijab going for a run, ignoring both her neighbors' judging glances and the voice in her own head asking, "What will they say about you?" Many working women—both those who wear the hijab and those who don't—lauded Nike for producing a practical garment that will help more women get into sports, the most male of pursuits. Others felt that the ad asks the right question ("What will they say about you?") but does not provide the right answers considering that running on the streets is unrealistic, even illegal, in places like Saudi Arabia. Instead, these critics pointed out, there need to be broader changes that give women the space to engage in sports and fitness without fear of judgment. Around the same time, *Vogue Arabia* launched its first edition, with American supermodel Gigi Hadid, who has Palestinian roots, on the cover with an embroidered garment covering her head and part of her face. Once again there was debate.

For all the divided opinions, however, it remains the case that these products, directly promoted to Muslim women, also create confidence. For the first time, many ordinary Muslim women looking out into the world are beginning to see themselves reflected back.

Many young women across the Muslim world bristle at being seen as downtrodden because they dress modestly. Some working women who wear the hijab—whether by choice, to conform culturally, or because of regulations—say that the West focuses on the wrong issues. In Saudi Arabia and Iran, the two countries where covering the head is mandated by law, many young women told me that they wanted an opportunity to prove themselves in the workplace rather than be "saved" from repressive clothing, whether they themselves believed in such laws or not. Yet others, including those who dress modestly as well as those who do not, said they were simply bored with what they perceive as an obsession with clothing, both locally and abroad. Many young women who would never wear the hijab themselves see the conversation about the hijab as a distraction from the real battleground of educational, economic, and political empowerment. Many conservative young women perceive the Western and sometimes local disdain for the hijab as an assault on some of their most deeply held beliefs.

The global attention on the headscarf has surfaced all of these views. Against a context in which the West is struggling to define the place of Islam in its societies, a conversation is now taking place that has never taken place before. Large Western brands are overtly recognizing that Muslim women, including those who cover, are a growing economic and social force, as workers and consumers, as sportswomen and icons. Nike's ad has struck a chord with many, not only because of its message of empowerment, but because the company is poised to make a profit off a large and youthful female population with a new-found interest in health and fitness and the means to pay for it. For many women in the Muslim world, this conversation has provided the perfect nudge, one based on economics yet providing a means to change culture. It has created an opportunity to show both the traditionalists at home and the broader world that women who cover are capable of achievement and that their hijabs are a choice that doesn't hold them back from their dreams.

Muna Abu Sulayman, who was one of the first covered women to have a spot on a prime-time show in the Arab world and who has recently invested in a couture modest fashion line, told me that working Muslim women who cover, as well as the ones who don't, need to see these images to feel recognized after decades of being invisible, both at home and abroad. However, she added, mainstream consumer and retail companies, both local and foreign, need to design better products for this new market. "I would design a headscarf for exercise very differently than the one from Nike. Companies need to get better advice and become more sophisticated in understanding the needs of all of the different types of *muhajaba* (women who cover)." Of course, many Muslim women choose not to cover at all, and with many other products the piety of the consumer is irrelevant. But who is considered a consumer has now expanded. "More and more covered women are represented in both the local and the international media," Muna pointed out, "and they are just as progressive and smart as everyone else. It validates someone's inner core and their hard work to see these images."

Holding up a mirror, even by way of commercial advertising, helps ordinary women—and men—who are living a new reality recognize the extraordinary change of which they are a part. And this strategy helps companies by making them more appealing to a new market that is hungry for recognition and validation that their beliefs and achievements need not be incompatible. Old methods of advertising to female customers that were relevant as recently as a decade ago no longer work with the working women of today's Muslim world. Products that sell an image of a woman only as wife, daughter, daughter-in-law, or mother hold less appeal than ever before to working women, who have other important parts to their identity today: employee, entrepreneur, boss. So companies, depending on their product, are becoming bolder with their messages and deriving both social and economic returns from shifting the narrative.

New Road Maps

Across the Muslim world, from Saudi Arabia to Indonesia, businesses are both cautiously and rapidly hiring, promoting, and retaining more women than ever before. As women make up nearly half—and in some cases the majority—of high-skilled graduates across the Muslim world, both global and local businesses have to adapt their talent strategy and change how they think about recruitment, hiring, leadership development, employee benefits, advertising, value chains, and broader conditions in their industry and how they work with government on labor policy and education reform that can meet their own talent needs and unlock opportunity for women.

Some are adapting by making special efforts to recruit in all-female universities. For others, the adjustment has been about hiring women on slightly different contracts—for example, with transportation stipends built in. Still others have taken an authoritarian approach to promoting women: CEOs directly appoint women into senior roles when standard talent development processes fail to bring women into senior roles owing to implicit biases and other factors. In some ways, there is nothing new about the fact that creating diversity takes effort. Many businesses across the globe are still learning to adapt to the influx of women into the workforce. The difference in the Muslim world is twofold: the speed of change and the lack of a locally adapted "how-to" guide.

Business leaders have to figure out how to strike the right balance between respecting culture and generating profit. Sometimes the trade-offs they face are daunting. Should they invest in recruiting women who might leave when they get married? Should they give women extra security? Should they give them separate parking spaces? Should they create their own sexual harassment policies where national policies are weak? When is the cost of accommodating a cultural norm too high? And when is it too costly to break cultural norms? Other changes are far easier. With women themselves—and the societies around them—pushing for a "third way," many businesses in the Muslim world are able to offer perks and practices that are specially designed for women. For example, it would be very difficult if not impossible for a company in the West to provide transport only to its female employees—such a practice would be grounds for discrimination—but in many companies in many Muslim economies it is perfectly normal, even expected, to offer this service to female employees. Leveling the playing field in the Muslim world can sometimes mean giving a leg up only to women.

But building these new road maps requires moving at a prudent pace. Lubna Olayan suggests that businesses, including Western multinationals, take a nuanced approach if they want to lead change. "It is like driving a standard car. You have to balance between the clutch and the gas. If you have the right balance, it works. But if you have too much gas, you crash, and if too much clutch, you will stall. There is a balance needed." In practice, this means engaging with those who may have a sense of loss from the changing economic, cultural, and social norms and may push back against change, including senior management, employees, and those in the value chain. "Our objective is long-term progress and how to get there by pushing as much as we can while upsetting people the least," Lubna Olayan said. "Find out what they don't like and how to bring them along. Understand that constituency. Small steps that don't take you back are much better than big steps forward that then send you back."

Unexpectedly, men are often the ones leading the charge on these efforts. Male leadership may suggest that there is bias even in the efforts to fight bias, but it also presents a strategic opportunity, one that many women in the Muslim world seem willing to use. Men still hold most of the power, and for now, men can open the doors to power for women faster than anyone else. These men are doing something new too, and have no road map to follow. Their own fathers began to lay the groundwork by integrating the first few pioneering female workers into the workplace two or three decades ago, but they did it quietly. The new generation is more outspoken in their advocacy.

As companies realize that their new talent pool looks more female than male, because the majority of university graduates are female, they will have to ensure that they are prepared to integrate this talent pool—and adapt their businesses accordingly. This is a new challenge for many companies, but often they find that these women, as the vanguard generation with the opportunity to work, are eager to apply their talent, skills, and leadership.

Although changing values and talent needs certainly drive business leaders—both male and female—to promote gender equality, so does the "women's market." No business can afford to ignore the female consumer segment because increasingly the women's market is simply "the market." From cars to soft drinks to fashion to transport, companies are realizing that women now have disposable income of their own and that they make their own consumption decisions. Even in joint purchases, they have a large if not equal share in decision making. And even when male family members are making the decision in public, often women have shaped those decisions heavily behind the scenes. Products once designed and advertised to appeal to men now have to be designed and advertised to have equal appeal to women. As companies experiment with ways to do this, they often learn that these efforts pay off for their bottom line. The new road map becomes the norm.

∾ seven ∾

Ministers and Mullahs

In 2012, Prime Minister Recep Tayyip Erdoğan of Turkey, speaking to a conference on population and development, said, "There is no difference between killing a baby in its mother's stomach and killing a baby after birth. I consider abortion to be murder. No one should have the right to allow this to happen." This was a regressive stance in a country that had begun to allow abortion up to ten weeks into pregnancy back in 1983 and that was one of the two countries in the broader Middle East, along with Tunisia, to have legalized abortion. Along with Erdoğan's statements, the Turkish health ministry was also preparing a bill proposing that abortion be allowed only in cases of rape or up to six weeks of pregnancy. Erdoğan's comments on reproductive rights didn't stop there. He added that he was "against birth by cesarean" because "unnecessary" elective cesareans were "unnatural."

Women's groups and liberals in the country were outraged, and thousands protested. Under particular scrutiny was the anticipated response of the only female member of Erdoğan's cabinet at the time, Minister Fatma Şahin, then the Turkish minister of family and social policies and one of the cofounders of the ruling Workers and Justice Party. Liberals and conservatives alike wanted to know what she would say, whose "side" she would take.

A few days later, Şahin issued a statement supporting the prime minister on both cesarean births and abortion. A chemical engineer by training, she tried to bring in a scientific rationale in addition to the ethical one. "The World Health Organization advises a rate of 15 to 20 percent of cesarean births," she said. "In Turkey, every one of two women gets a cesarean operation." She accused those who opposed Erdoğan's view of "distancing their critiques from science." She went further, arguing, "If you destroy a life and have an abortion after you ignore birth control methods beforehand, then this is a violation of the right to live."[1]

It was always unlikely that Şahin, as part of Erdoğan's cabinet, would have criticized the prime minister. But progressives were disappointed precisely because of her otherwise liberal views. In addition to the example set by her own career, Şahin had taken a stand on women's economic empowerment since she had become a minister. In fact, in the same year that abortion was being debated she and her staff had energetically supported a new task force to get more women into paid employment. I had begun to work with Şahin's team on the project, which would bring together some of the leading businesses in Turkey to work with the ministry to close 10 percent of the labor force gender gap.

Her clearly progressive views on women's integration into the workforce made her more conservative views on limiting abortion and cesarean sections surprising to me. I wondered whether her personal views were different from the public views she had shared. It is very possible that she truly believed in both workforce equality and more state control over reproduction decisions, even if these are fairly incompatible views. But it is more likely that, like politicians everywhere, Şahin was conserving her political capital in some areas in order to use it in other areas. The difference in the Muslim world is the sheer range of views and topics through which politicians have to negotiate a careful path when it comes to gender equality. Their bargains can appear at once hypocritical and the only practical way forward.

Polarized Societies, Patchwork Policies

Şahin's story is just one of many. Governments across much of the Muslim world often have deeply contradictory goals when it comes to women's labor market participation and the broader set of policies that determine whether women can actually enter the workplace in the first place. As they seek to support working women, many governments must try to appease religious conservatives who would rather see women stay in their homes. Both female and male politicians can find themselves presiding over such seemingly schizophrenic policies, although women often have to face both higher expectations and bigger hurdles in driving change.

The examples of such contradictions abound. The most familiar in the West is the driving ban in Saudi Arabia, which long prevented women from engaging in public life, including work. Even as the government enacted reforms for working women broadly, such as opening up women's access to previously prohibited or difficult sectors like retail, hospitality, law, and media, and appointed women to high-profile leadership roles—most recently, the Saudi Stock Exchange got its first female chair, Sarah al-Suhaimi—the driving ban remained firmly in place until September 2017 when the king announced that women would be allowed to drive by mid-2018. There are other examples of pushback from parts of the religious and political establishment. When the Ministry of Labor began working to get more women into retail positions in shops selling cosmetics, lingerie, abayas, and wedding dresses—motivated in part by the argument put forth by activists that women's modesty would be preserved if they could buy such intimate items from other women rather than men who are strangers—clerics declared that they would pray for the minister in charge to die of cancer, as had happened to his predecessor, unless he reversed the policy. The religious establishment was also in an uproar when one of their own, Sheikh Ahmed Al Ghamedi, former head of the religious police in Mecca, and his wife, Jawaher bint Ali, appeared on TV together, her face uncovered. Ghamedi declared that covering the face was not obligatory in Islam and make-up was not forbidden, adding to previous statements about women being able to go out unaccompanied and mix with men in "appropriate" settings.[2]

Such contradictions and inconsistencies are not limited to Saudi Arabia. Pakistan passed a sexual harassment act in 2010, for the first time recognizing sexual harassment as an issue in the workplace and making it a punishable crime. And yet it took much longer to pass a women's protection bill, which will help protect women who have been raped from being accused of *zina* (extramarital sex), and a law around honor killings, which prevents perpetrators from being able to walk free if the victim's family chooses to forgive them. Both tactics were previously used by rapists and by men who killed women in the name of honor to escape punishment. Although passage of the workplace bill indicates progress, women are unlikely to use it very often in a broader context where accusing a man of rape often still puts a woman at risk of being counter-accused of adultery. At the same time, it is not insignificant that policies to achieve gender equality in explicitly economic spheres are more progressive and more rapidly implemented than those seeking equality in social contexts. It's one more way in which economic change gets ahead of and then drives broader cultural change.

At times, the progress is not linear and previous gains can be reversed. In Kuwait, women finally won the right to vote and hold office, but within a few years new laws were passed that more strictly imposed gender segregation in education. These fractured approaches and contradictory policies represent deeply polarized societies when it comes to the role of women. Millions of Muslims hold very conservative views about economic, social, and political equality for women and men. Many believe that women's primary role is in association with family—as mothers, wives, sisters, daughters, and keepers of a family's honor.[3] They are thus to be protected, physically and mentally, from influences outside the home. When outside the home, they are to protect their own modesty.

The mass migration of women from home to schools and universities and then from educational institutions to workplaces has challenged these notions. As more women demonstrate full agency over themselves, intellectual engagement in their work, and their earning potential, and as their achievements are recognized, it becomes clear that there are economic advantages to these changes and that family structures and social bonds can indeed survive the move of women outside the home. And for some, there is a clear religious rationale for supporting equality and choice for women in economic, financial, social, and political matters—a budding Islamic feminism. For others, it is a case of traditional cultural practices becoming outdated and requiring reinterpretation, particularly as the Muslim world's exposure to the rest of the world increases.

Politicians are conscious of this new constituency of women (and their families) who have a broader view of what is acceptable for them. But they are also aware that in many pockets of their societies fear of the new and the unknown makes conservatives—another important constituency—dig ever deeper into their traditions. What constitutes majority opinion can be vastly different between countries and between issues.

But even those policymakers who recognize the new and still latent economic and political power of highly educated young women in their economies are playing catch-up. They have been caught off-guard by the vast numbers of women entering the workforce, and they are only now beginning to consider the needs of this new constituency. Some policymakers are trying to take a proactive approach, but most of them are not focused on working women, owing sometimes to lack of imagination and at other times to fear of upsetting a delicate balance with those who hold traditional values. Institutional inertia thus festers and laws go stale. In many Muslim countries, the laws are now behind the economic realities of their female—and male—citizens.[4]

These include but are not limited to laws and policies governing labor, tax, safety and harassment, access to finance, transport, and entrepreneurship. Whatever progress has been made on these fronts is highly varied across Muslim countries, resulting in very different enabling environments for the growing cohort of educated and working women.

When it comes to labor law, in only two Muslim-majority countries for which information is available—Indonesia and Kosovo—can women do the same jobs as men across the board.[5] In most countries, certain sectors and job types are off-limits to women, such as jobs in mining, metalworking, construction, and factories and jobs deemed hazardous or socially inappropriate. In thirteen countries, women cannot work the same hours as men and are prohibited by law from working in the evening or working night shifts, regardless of their personal situation or preferences. In ten countries, women cannot work in the same occupations as men, and twelve countries do not allow women to do the same job-related tasks as men with the same job type.

For example, while Pakistan's biggest exports include cotton and textiles, women are prohibited from "working in the same room as a cotton-opener in a factory; working inside any factory to clean, lubricate or adjust any part of machinery while that part is in motion, or working between moving parts or between fixed and moving parts of any machinery."[6] Women thus remain concentrated in the lowest-wage and most physically taxing work in the cotton industry—cotton-picking—and face great restrictions in accessing higher-paid and more skilled functions in factories further down the value chain.

The justification for most of these laws is either that they protect women or that they prevent morally unacceptable mixing of the sexes. Some women tend to agree that these laws are necessary. Maryam, a well-traveled, well-educated journalist in Cairo, told me, "Women are being treated with respect through restrictions on arduous or male-dominated roles." But such attitudes are changing as migration and the rising cost of living transform household structures and heighten the need for two incomes. In many towns and villages where the only source of work is the local factory and a small concentration of services, economic necessity drives women toward occupations they might not previously have viewed as feminine. In other cases, it is norms and behaviors that are changing as a new generation of women develop new aspirations and want access to traditionally male-dominated sectors. Laws can stand in the way of both groups.

Discriminatory laws and biases can also apply to white-collar work in urban areas. In 2014, the Tehran municipality arbitrarily announced that it would be firing a number of women in administrative and managerial roles for "their own comfort and well-being" because their work might require long hours and travel and interfere with their family lives. Some days later, this plan was modified and a new effort to segregate the municipality workplace was developed instead, one touted as a matter of "dignity." The proposals were never carried out, however. Soon after they were announced, the Labor Ministry expressed its misgivings and cited the need for nondiscrimination in the workplace. The ministry also cited, as a rationale, Iran's international obligations, such as its membership in the International Labour Organization, whose core principles include the end of unfair discrimination among workers.[7]

In the end, the Tehran municipality's move did not become law, but the bias behind it sent a clear signal to professional women. Over time both legally authorized discrimination and overt biases exacerbate pay disparity and leadership gender gaps within the sectors they directly target and have spillover effects in other sectors and professions.

Laws regulating hiring, firing, wages, and retirement create incentives—and disincentives—for women to work. In only six countries do laws mandate no gender discrimination in hiring: Azerbaijan, Kazakhstan, Kosovo, Mauritania, Morocco, and Tajikistan; in the other Muslim-majority economies, there are no such protections for women. And laws mandating equal remuneration for work of equal value are on the books in only eight countries: Algeria, Azerbaijan, Bangladesh, Kosovo, Libya, Morocco, Tajikistan, and Turkey. As is the case in many non-Muslim countries, retirement age tends to be lower for women than for men. In a bid to create more room for younger people—mainly younger men—in the workforce while also preserving traditional family structures, some Muslim countries have lowered the retirement thresholds for working women even further. For example, in Iran there is an ongoing debate about a new law that would allow women to retire after only twenty years in the workforce and keep the majority of their pension, a proposal at odds with trying to increase women's workforce participation and improve the country's fiscal situation.[8]

Some economic disparities arise from the uneven accumulation of wealth. Seven Muslim-majority countries—mainly former Soviet republics and Turkey—largely promote equal inheritance between sons and daughters, but most of them continue to follow traditional rules of inheritance for surviving children and for spouses: a greater share is assigned to sons because they are expected to support their female relatives. Some of today's working, educated millennials—and their parents—are starting to privately distribute their wealth equally between sons and daughters in their lifetimes. But under the law the distribution remains traditional, regardless of the earning capacity of the women and men involved.

When it comes to access to credit, the opportunity to manage assets through financial institutions, and regulations for starting a business, women are in a better position—at least on paper. According to the law, single and married women can set up a business, open a bank account, and sign a contract in the same way as single or married men across all large Muslim-majority economies discussed in this book. However, in only four countries—Azerbaijan, Kosovo, Kyrgyzstan, and Morocco—does the law prohibit discrimination by creditors on the basis of gender in access to credit. In only one country—Morocco—does the law prohibit discrimination by creditors on the basis of marital status in access to credit. So, while women are legally allowed access to the financial tools needed to start and grow businesses, the discrimination they face significantly increases the barriers to their entrepreneurship.

The tax code in many of these countries also differentiates between men and women in ways that hinder women's economic growth and independence. Among the thirty-eight Muslim-majority countries assessed by the World Bank, eight countries had tax deductions or credits applicable only to men, while there were no such incentives for women in any of these countries. Although it is easier to detect gender bias in personal income tax arrangements, gender bias—explicit and implicit—is also present in other taxes, such as consumption taxes and import duties. Gender bias can also be found in the way payments are linked to the receipt of benefits under social insurance programs.[9]

The limits that these outdated laws put on women's access to services that are important for their economic empowerment are only exacerbated by broader cultural factors that are harder to challenge. For example, even where women are allowed to open bank accounts, norms around male authority in financial matters and spillovers from other laws, such as uneven inheritance between sons and daughters, perpetuate the gender gap in access to bank accounts. As a result, women continue to have fewer accounts in financial institutions than men do in most Muslim economies. According to World Bank data, in only three countries—Kazakhstan, Kyrgyzstan, and Indonesia— do women and men have the same number of accounts in financial institutions in their own name—in fact, women have slightly more. In Iran, Uzbekistan, and Malaysia, women have a little over 90 percent of the number of accounts that men have. In Tunisia this ratio is around 60 percent, and in Turkey it is 64 percent. In Jordan, Sudan, Iraq, and Egypt, women have fewer than 50 percent of the number of accounts men have, and the ratio is only 21 percent in Pakistan and 15 percent in Yemen. Even in very high-income economies, women's penetration of financial institutions is much lower than men's. For example, while 90 percent of men over the age of fifteen in the United Arab Emirates and Bahrain have a financial institution account, just over 66 percent of women over fifteen do. Similarly, in Kuwait, 79 percent of men have an account while only 64 percent of women do, and in Saudi Arabia, 75 percent of men have accounts, compared to 61 percent of women.

Because their use of bank accounts is more limited, women are also less likely to use other financial services. The Global Findex, a database measuring how people save, borrow, and manage risk in 148 countries, found that "in developing economies women are 17 percent less likely than men to have borrowed formally in the past year." Even if they can gain access to a loan, women "often lack access to other financial services, such as savings, digital payment methods, and insurance." In addition, lack of financial education restricts women's access to financial services, limits its benefits for them, and compounds traditional views of men's primary responsibility in financial matters. For example, according to the World Bank, a study in Pakistan showed that while many women have access to bank accounts in name, the decision-making authority around the use of the funds in those accounts often lies with a male relative.[10]

For women who work, sexual harassment—in the workforce and during commutes—is a very real concern, but it can be prohibitive for those who do not work, preventing them from working or their families from allowing them to work. However, only ten Muslim-majority countries have legislation against sexual harassment in the workplace, and only half of these have criminal penalties. When it comes to transport and travel, the problem is even more acute. Only eight countries have legislation against sexual harassment in public places, and mobility is more restricted for women than men in nearly half of Muslim economies. As with financial equality measures, laws incentivizing the economic empowerment of women will fail unless they also support women in the broader aspects of their lives.

"Paradise Lies Under the Feet of Your Mothers"

One hadith of the Prophet, "Paradise lies under the feet of your mothers," was repeated to me by a very wide range of people during my travel and interviews for this book. Conservatives mentioned it to justify the importance they placed on women's roles as mothers above anything else. Liberals mentioned it to justify the overall importance placed on women in Islam, and thus the need to broaden all opportunities for them, including the workforce. Women and men, rich and poor, educated and illiterate, religious and secular—all brought it up.

In most Muslim societies, the most valued role of a woman is being a mother. Yet there is also a growing pride in women's education and, increasingly, their employment, which has compelled them to find solutions to manage the "double shift." Women spend far more hours than men on unpaid care work. Comparable international data are not available for most Muslim economies, but data from Turkey illuminate the point. Turkish women spend on average 377 minutes on unpaid work per day. By contrast, men spend 116 minutes on unpaid work, or one-quarter of the total time spent by women. Although Turkish men spend more time on unpaid work than men in Japan, Korea, and India, this average still places Turkey sixth from the bottom among twenty-nine OECD countries.[11]

Which women are able to find alternative solutions to manage unpaid work and how they do so are mainly dependent on class. Middle-income and upper-income women tend to hire household help—nannies, cleaning staff, and cooking staff—given the relatively low cost of low-skilled labor. In these families, additional care is often provided by their parents, grandparents, and in-laws. Low-skilled women who work as care providers rely almost exclusively on family and friends to manage their own care needs. The "care economy" in most of the Muslim world is thus private or unregulated, and cheap or unpaid.

Women like Gita, the environmental lawyer in Jakarta, or Sara, the founder of doctHERS in Karachi, talked openly about the limited and low-quality care infrastructure in their cities. Both made it clear that they would never use these facilities for their own children. Both of these women, however, have alternatives. Gita can afford to hire full-time private help. Sara has her mother and her mother-in-law to help. But for many other women, lack of care support is the key factor prohibiting them from joining or staying in the workforce after they have children. Rafika, a young professional at Kudo, the start-up in Jakarta, was five months pregnant when I met her. She was planning to leave the company before the end of her pregnancy. She couldn't afford full-time help and didn't have family in the city. So she, like many others, had decided that it made more sense for her rather than her husband to give up work—not only was she expected to be the primary caregiver, but her husband earned more than she did. Her computer engineering degree and four years of work experience would soon lie dormant.

There are many similar disincentives for women to work in societies where their roles as mothers and caregivers are more prized than their contributions as workers and breadwinners. This division of labor and care prevails around the globe, not just in the Muslim world. For the last decade in particular, as large numbers of women have entered the labor market, middle- and upper-income women have found market-based solutions by hiring lower-skilled, lower-income women to do care work. The position of lower-income women, meanwhile, becomes ever more precarious.

This fluid labor market, as imperfect as it is, may soon become even more constrained. In Indonesia, where over half of working-age women are active in the labor force—placing it in the top third among Muslim-majority economies—cheap household help is starting to disappear as education, economic opportunities, and aspirations grow for many low-skilled women who currently provide the household help to middle-income or higher-income women. This is the positive result of investments in education and economic development and millions more Indonesians being lifted out of poverty. However, if governments don't find a solution for the resulting gap in affordable care—for both high-skilled and low-skilled working women—there may be reversals in the gains in women's employment. Governments will need to proactively consider how to build a better public care infrastructure or regulate a private one. Formalization, regulation, and professionalization of domestic workers would also help protect low-income working women, raise the quality of services, provide pathways for career development, and make care professions more lucrative and stable rather than short-term stepping-stones.

Yet this is an area that governments are not tackling holistically, in part because of the ongoing tension between marriage and motherhood, on the one hand, and work, on the other. The current generation of working women have found creative solutions by themselves to blend their multiple identities, but systemic solutions remain unrealized for the next wave of educated, working women. Policies are still caught between the polarized views of society on the roles that women should prioritize. Even in economies where state-provided child care has been a norm in the past—for example, Kazakhstan, which currently has the highest rate of women's workforce participation of all Muslim-majority economies—state support is shrinking rather than growing. Some change is under way, however. Tajikistan now provides public child care services. Turkey enacted a new law that introduced one year of publicly provided pre-primary services. But wider change is needed.

In an environment where women are traditionally expected to prioritize marriage and motherhood, the workplace can discriminate— often legally. Unmarried women can get a job in the same way as an unmarried man in all Muslim economies, but in ten countries married women cannot access jobs in the same way as married men. Only in one of them, Kyrgyzstan, are prospective employers prohibited from asking about family status. In Algeria, Bangladesh, Iran, Iraq, Jordan, Kuwait, Qatar, Syria, the United Arab Emirates, and Yemen, the dismissal of pregnant workers is not prohibited by law. In six countries, women are not entitled to nursing breaks. Since women with babies are expected to stay at home, the reasoning goes, why would such provisions even be needed?

As policymakers have recognized the economic benefits of women's increasing participation in the workforce, they have sought to tackle parts of the challenge. All countries offer some maternity leave, and in 80 percent of the countries 100 percent of wages are guaranteed during the leave; in nearly all others, at least two-thirds of wages are paid. Who pays varies by country and can create very different incentives for employers. In eleven countries, including some of the most populous countries, such as Bangladesh, Indonesia, and Malaysia, the employer is solely responsible for wages during maternity leaves. In three countries, responsibility for wages is split between the government and the employer. The government fully covers mandated wages during the leave period in thirteen countries, including some of the former Soviet republics such as Uzbekistan and Tajikistan, high-income economies such as Bahrain, and upper-middle-income economies such as Turkey, Azerbaijan, and Iran, but also lower-income countries such as Pakistan and Jordan.

Maternity leave, however, can keep women out of the workforce if it incentivizes their caregiving role over their economic activity. In Iran, the length of paid maternity leave was recently increased from 180 to 270 days, in part to support women's caregiving for newborns and in part because of concerns about Iran's falling birthrate; Iran now joins Kosovo in offering the longest maternity leave in the Muslim world. Such efforts have been made in other countries, like Korea and Japan, but have backfired as these countries remained in a "fertility trap": both the rates of women's labor force participation and the rates of marriages and births remain low. Maternity leave can also be "too long." In Kazakhstan, Kyrgyzstan, Tajikistan, and Uzbekistan, unpaid maternity leave can be taken for a year or more. *Bloomberg* reports that parental leave policies that extend to a year or two often set women back professionally, and it cites Germany's example: German women can take off as much as three years per child with partial pay, but they often return to work part-time rather than full-time, earn less, and advance more slowly.[12]

A final factor affecting mothers is the role of fathers. Besides care infrastructure, other laws that allow both mothers and fathers to combine work and family are scarce in the Muslim world. The longest paternity leave in the Muslim world is fourteen days, offered in Iran. Men, however, are paid their full wages during their short leave. In only five countries must employers provide leave to workers who need to care for sick relatives, a role that also often falls on women. Paradise may lie underneath the feet of mothers, but both mothers and fathers will need better support in the modern economy to combine their many roles.

Religious Allies

Late one evening, after weaving through Cairo's unpredictable traffic, I arrived at the home of Dr. Amna Nosseir, a member of Egypt's Supreme Council for Islamic Affairs, a professor of comparative jurisprudence, and a former dean of the women's section at Al-Azhar University, the leading institution for Sunni Islamic thought. When I asked Dr. Nosseir if Islam and women's economic empowerment are compatible, she was contemptuous of the question at first, and then thoughtful. She believes that a false battle about what is the "right" form of Islam is the result of patterns of migration to the Gulf states that have led to the *fiqh* (customs) of Saudi Arabia mixing with Egyptian culture and damaging the situation for women in Egypt. She also feels that "the Western view, on the other hand, is too negative. We have to do what is suitable for us. Forget their voice, they are not fair to us." But she recognizes that, "as men developed an intellectual monopoly over religious texts in Islam, they chose antifeminist approaches," and that "because women were not encouraged to participate at all, no one was about to argue back."

It was as a young woman that Amna Nosseir found her calling: becoming a scholar of Islam herself. She grew up in a deeply conservative family in Upper Egypt, and she had to argue—and "cry hard"—to be allowed to delay marriage and attend boarding school in Alexandria back in the 1950s. A second round of arguments came when she wanted to move to Cairo for university. Both times she succeeded.

These early experiences gave her a taste for taking on the highly male-dominated field of Islamic scholarship. Her book on Islamic law versus practice takes on issues as combustible as polygamy and clothing. She takes issue with the dominant view about women working, writing, "Everything Allah gave to man, Allah gave to woman, so women should be able to work in any profession they want." She gives an example to back up her statement. "Women could work even as fighters, in the Prophet's time. Similarly, no one today would stop a woman from being a pilot." One part of her example related to the most male-dominated of professions in the early days of Islam, and the other referred to one of the most male-dominated professions in most countries today. But Dr. Nosseir is no feminist in the traditional sense and would probably balk at being called one, even as her work supports women's empowerment. She firmly believes that while work outside the home is a woman's choice, work in the home is fully her responsibility.

It is perhaps too much to expect that a woman of Dr. Nosseir's generation—and upbringing—would hold a view that equality in the labor market needs to go hand in hand with equality in the home. But promoting equality in the workforce is already revolutionary for her age and profession. Dr. Nosseir is often called upon to comment on TV about her knowledge, so she decided to leverage this recognition to run for the upcoming parliamentary elections. "It's time to turn books into practice," she explained. Her relatively moderate views backed up by a wholly religious argument have been essential to building the case for change: within the first year of winning her seat, Dr. Nosseir decided to tackle the niqab, seeking to ban it as an un-Islamic practice.

On another continent, in Almaty, Kazakhstan, the chief imam of the city's central mosque, Esmagambet Nurbek, is a similar ally for change: he, like Dr. Nosseir, uses Islamic scripture as evidence to support women working. He gave the example of his own daughter, her love of math, and his belief that she should be able to choose any profession she wants. In his view, the dialogue about women and work from an Islamic viewpoint is fairly straightforward: there is no religious rationale preventing women from working.

As these and other scholars have stated, according to most interpretations, Islamic scripture contains no restrictions on women with
regard to having a career, profession, or work; nor does it imply that
a woman's place is only within her home. In the area of economic
rights, a woman who chooses to work, according to scripture, is entitled to equal pay for work of equal worth (not necessarily equal
work). Once a woman gets married, she keeps her own last name
and therefore her own identity. Property that she owned prior to
marriage remains her property after marriage. Scripture spells out
that any earnings a woman makes during her married life, either by
way of investments of her property or as a result of work, do not have
to be spent on the household. Both her property and her income remain under the control of a woman, and she is not obligated to share
them with her husband. Islamic scripture considers the maintenance
and support of a married woman wholly the responsibility of her
husband, even if she possesses more wealth than her husband. Prior
to marriage, it is the father's responsibility to provide for a daughter.
During her engagement, a woman is expected to be on the receiving side of gifts. At the time of marriage, it is the husband's duty
(not that of the bride's family) to pay for a marital gift that will be
exclusively the possession of the woman, who may choose to spend
it as she wishes. Scripture puts no obligation on her to spend it on
the household or to give it to her father or anyone else. Similarly,
scripture sets out financial obligations during a period of divorce and
beyond. A divorced woman or a widow with children is entitled to
child support. Some scholars maintain that it is because Islamic law
is more favorable to women in terms of financial security before,
during, and after marriage that men inherit more than women do
under laws pertaining to inheritance.

Using a religious rationale to promote women's employment and
broader economic rights is not unprecedented. Religious grounds
have often been used very successfully to enhance women's social,
educational, and economic freedoms. In Iran, it was the Ayatollah's
"jihad against illiteracy" that brought many women into schools and

universities, and the spirit of the Islamist revolution brought women out of their homes. Even in more controversial areas that relate to the home, religion has been used as a support rather than a barrier for change. For example, in Saudi Arabia, even as some preachers suggested that violence within marriage is condoned by religion, the government successfully worked with other religious authorities to enact its first law on domestic violence, which it defines as physical, sexual, or psychological violence. The law provides criminal penalties and protects spouses and family members. In Turkey, the Islamic political movement had an advantage over secular alternatives in overcoming barriers to female participation in voluntary education institutions among the poor and pious and over time, ironically but not surprisingly, reduced Islamic political preferences.[13]

How policymakers promote gender equality is often a complex task of trying to stay in power while meeting the needs and demands of their increasingly globalized—and polarized—economies and societies. Alliances with religious leaders and scholars, however unlikely or impermanent, are vital for broadening the constituency for women's economic empowerment. Civil society organizations and grassroots women's groups are making such alliances too. But it is not just advocates for change who need to bring religious perspectives into their case for normalizing and enhancing women's economic rights. Such partnerships are mutually beneficial. Religious leaders themselves have growing constituencies of working women who do not want to be alienated from their faith yet often do not see their choices reflected and celebrated in the world of faith and religion. Religious leaders need a better narrative for working women in order to catch up with the changes that are under way.

All Eyes on Her

In 116-degree heat one morning in Kuwait City, I met seventy-year-old Dr. Massouma Al Mubarak at her home in a quiet suburb. In some ways, her story is like that of suffragettes around the world: she is a woman who drove change through an unbending will. But hers is also a uniquely local story in which local culture and customs were fundamental to winning the right to vote and hold office.

Kuwait is a tiny, oil-rich parliamentary monarchy in the Arabian Gulf. Despite being progressive on women's education, and even employment, relatively early compared to its neighbors, Kuwait gave women the right to vote and run for office only a little over a decade ago, in 2005, thus becoming one of the last countries in the world to grant this right. Kuwait is a semidemocratic system with an emir and appointed government as well as an elected parliament. It took nearly twelve attempts for women to finally get the vote, through the efforts of Dr. Al Mubarak and many others. "At times, conservative and liberal men actually joined forces and voted to prevent women's suffrage, even against the wishes of the emir," she said.

Ironically, Kuwait's semidemocratic process resulted in women there receiving the vote later than the women of Kuwait's more autocratic neighbors, who received the vote earlier by royal decree. For a period of some years, Kuwaiti women were unable to get universal suffrage passed through the male-only parliament, whereas women in other Gulf countries had been "given the right by surprise." Dr. Al Mubarak recalled an incident in 1999, when Kuwaiti women didn't yet have the right to vote. She was asked to go help women in Qatar, who had finally been awarded the right to vote along with men as the country made a small but important step toward combining more agency for citizens with the royal family's rule. She said that some Qatari women didn't know how to react to the new right to vote and to run for political office. "How can we put our photos in the street?" some asked her, in reference to campaign posters. Some potential female candidates considered putting up photos of their husband instead. By contrast, Dr. Al Mubarak thinks that Kuwaiti women were more ready for change because they had been more empowered socially and economically for longer. Even so, today there is little difference between the two countries.[14]

Soon after women won the right to vote, Dr. Al Mubarak became minister of planning, the first woman in the country's history to hold a ministerial role, and in 2009 she became one of the four women who ran for office and won a spot in parliament. Her path to these achievements was a circuitous one. Born in 1947 to a mother who was uneducated and a father who was a clergyman, Dr. Al Mubarak lost her father while still in high school, and her eldest brother took over as head of the household. When it came to making a choice about university, she wanted to study political science, which she felt passionate about. Her brother tried to dissuade her, saying it was not an appropriate subject for a woman to study, but she was determined and said she would rather stay at home than go to university and not study political science. Her brother gave in.

Soon after college, Dr. Al Mubarak married, and the young couple went to the United States, where both earned advanced degrees and they had children. Upon returning to Kuwait, she became the first female political science professor, and then the first female head of the Political Science Department, at Kuwait University. Dr. Al Mubarak may have broken through many glass ceilings in her life, but she said that as a child and young woman, the concept of gender equality was foreign to her. It was in the United States as a graduate student that she learned about the women's movement. Coming back, she immediately joined the local women's association and thus started on her journey in the quest to shape Kuwait's long and ongoing march toward equality.

Working with the culture and with men in authority became one of the most effective strategies employed by leaders like Massouma Al Mubarak. After the difficult battle over the vote, as the first-ever female minister, her every move was under scrutiny. Early in her tenure, it became clear that while women had been granted the right to vote, they were not registered to vote and polling stations simply didn't have the capacity to register the more than two hundred thousand women who were now eligible in the short time before the next elections were scheduled. She was also concerned that women who were new to the political process might be hesitant to seek out registration themselves. She knew that the conservative forces that had resisted the vote for women for so long might be content with poor participation rates at this first historic election and would prefer to avoid the additional expense of expanding registration services within the required time. And she knew that if she was going to address these concerns, she couldn't risk pushing solutions as part of a "women's agenda." Instead, she needed to look for a solution that worked for everyone. So she came up with an efficient, technology-driven alternative whereby women would be automatically registered through their ID cards, thus removing hurdles for women and reducing costs for the state. She took the idea to the prime minister and then the emir to build support from the top before the question was discussed in parliament. Presented as a matter of efficiency for the state—not as a women's rights issue—and with strong support from the top, the proposal passed.

Dr. Al Mubarak applied the same principle when it came to reforming the arbitrary assignment of jobs to a particular sex (usually only to men) in the civil service. Using a combination of economic rationales and religious ones, and building a coalition of supporters, she argued for women to be able to access most civil service roles. "Women can be anything they want to be according to religion," Dr. Al Mubarak said. "No job needs to be reserved wholly for men or women, with two exceptions. Only *muazzins* (those who broadcast the call to prayer) must be men, and the teachers in girls' schools must be women." She was able to open up hundreds of civil service roles to educated, skilled women who wanted to do them.

Being a trailblazer in any field means carrying the expectations of many, and the risk of disappointment or failure can be high. For women in the Muslim world who have recently broken barriers to reach the top of political leadership, every public gesture they make to promote greater gender equality risks a potential political minefield. So building coalitions and partnerships with male leaders becomes critical, as does an angle of attack that presents change for women as a matter of gain and efficiency for all. This is the strategy Dr. Massouma Al Mubarak has used, and it's one that other women have used effectively too, whether in leading their businesses or driving change in their families.

Hearing Dr. Al Mubarak's story and its parallels with the experience of women in politics in other Muslim countries and elsewhere, I was left wondering: Do trailblazers in politics effect change for other women, particularly for women's economic empowerment? Or do they represent individual success stories that have little to no impact on ordinary women's lives?

At one level, it is clear that trailblazers do matter—as role models. Simply by being women in positions of authority, they have the power to change mind-sets around them. One clear impact of having women in a country's highest office is simply demonstrating that women can lead in the highest office in the land—so why wouldn't they be able to lead elsewhere? This "passive" role model effect is well recognized and works at many levels in political, economic, social, and cultural leadership. In India, researchers studied the impact of a quota system that randomly assigned villages to reserve village council positions for women. They found that exposure to female leaders changed villagers' beliefs about female leader effectiveness, reduced their association of women with domestic activities, and significantly reduced male villagers' association of leadership activities with men.[15] They also found that both fathers and mothers increased their aspirations for their daughters, and the desire for a daughter to become a village council leader was particularly enhanced in fathers. Girls' own aspirations for themselves increased as well: they were less inclined to be a housewife or to allow in-laws to choose their occupation for them, and they were more inclined to delay marriage and to want a job requiring an education. The education gender gap closed, girls' performance in school improved, and the amount of time they spent on household chores decreased.

As Sheryl Sandberg, author of *Lean In,* often says, "You can't be what you can't see." In the Muslim world, where female role models for caring, nurturing, and home-based roles abound, highly visible female leaders in the public space, even if rare, are vital to shaping the mind-sets of the next generation, and they have already influenced a new wave of working women.

So who are these role models? Seven Muslim-majority countries have had nine women as heads of government: Sheikh Hasina is prime minister of Bangladesh, and Khaleda Zia twice served as prime minister of that country; Benazir Bhutto was prime minister of Pakistan twice; Megawati Sukarnoputri was president of Indonesia; Roza Otunbayeva was president of Kyrgyzstan; Cissé Mariam Kaïdama Sidibé was prime minister of Mali; Mame Madior Boye and Aminata Touré have been prime minister of Senegal; and finally, Tansu Çiller was prime minister of Turkey.

There is a correlation between these women's leadership and the rise of the fifty million new women entrants to labor markets in the Muslim world. In the years since the first of today's millennial generation was born, among the economies covered in this book, Pakistan has been led by a woman for five years, Indonesia for three years, Bangladesh for twenty-two years, Kyrgyzstan for two years, and Turkey for three. Is it coincidence that these countries have subsequently seen a major rise in women's workforce participation? Perhaps, but that is unlikely. It is more likely that while major economic factors have driven the shifts under way today, perceptions have also played a subtle but important part. Whether these leaders were loved or hated, they unwittingly demonstrated to millions of young girls—and their parents—that women could be independent, women could be vocal, women could work, and women could hold positions of leadership.

Referring to Benazir Bhutto, Pakistani journalist Bina Shah writes: "She emboldened the heart of every girl and woman in Pakistan who was ever told that being a woman precluded her from a lifetime of accomplishment, service and worth. This was her greatest legacy."[16] At the end of 1988, when Benazir Bhutto first became prime minister, I was eight years old. It is impossible to describe the sense of possibility I felt for myself once a woman ran the country. And it was not only me. Girls in my school talked about what they would do when they grew up in a wholly new way. Perhaps it was something we would have started talking about at that age anyway, but Benazir Bhutto became a lightning rod for channeling those dreams and aspirations.

The power and platform of some women leaders in the Muslim world and elsewhere is partly the result of their association with a male leader, a husband or a father, and this fact is sometimes used by their critics to suggest that their power is less legitimate than that of men. But power derived from family connections is certainly not restricted to women: in many developed and developing countries, when democracies and civic institutions are not strong, power propagates within families, and many male leaders also receive power this way. Women politicians, being rarer, simply tend to receive more of the scrutiny.

What is more remarkable perhaps is that power was transferred to women in these political dynasties at all, given the traditional imbalance in how economic inheritance was and often still is distributed between sons and daughters in Muslim societies. Megawati Sukarnoputri is the daughter of Indonesia's first president. Benazir Bhutto was the daughter of a former prime minister. Sheikh Hasina of Bangladesh is the daughter of the founding father of the country. Khaleda Zia is the wife of former Bangladeshi president Ziar Rahman. Regardless of how they came to power, how they performed in office, and how they eventually lost power, their impact on girls and women by simply being in a position of leadership cannot be underestimated.

Then there are the symbols and role models who are slightly less visible than presidents and prime ministers—the women parliamentarians, ministers, mayors, and judges.

When it comes to parliaments, Algeria, Sudan, and Tunisia are the only three countries among the thirty covered in this book that have crossed the 30 percent threshold beyond which researchers say diversity starts to pay off. Another eight countries have crossed the 20 percent threshold, like the United States, or are just above it: Bangladesh, Iraq, Kazakhstan, Mauritania, Morocco, Pakistan, Turkmenistan, and the United Arab Emirates. At the other end of the spectrum are countries whose parliaments are less than 10 percent women: Bahrain, Iran, Kuwait, Oman, Qatar, and Yemen. The larger countries of Egypt, Indonesia, and Turkey have around 15, 17, and 15 percent women in their parliaments, respectively.

Some of the better-performing countries have used quotas to increase the representation of women in their parliaments. Sudan has a reserved seat quota for women in its national parliament of 30 percent. Tunisia's new constitution specifies gender as a protected category in its nondiscrimination clause, and the government has also introduced quotas for candidate lists in national elections. Pakistan introduced a 22 percent quota for women in local governments, while Saudi Arabia introduced a 20 percent quota for women at the national level. Overall on average, the percentage of women in parliament in the Muslim world has risen from 6 percent back in 1990 to nearly 17 percent today, ahead of Brazil (5 percent to nearly 10 percent) and India (5 percent to 12 percent). During the same time period, the numbers in China rose from 21 percent to nearly 24 percent, and in the United States from just under 7 percent to 21 percent.

Ministerial positions also create a "role model effect" because of their high visibility and perceived power in the media and in public debate. Globally, women hold on average just over 18 percent of ministerial roles. In the Muslim world, Indonesia and Mauritania lead the way with 23 percent and 27 percent female ministers, respectively, according to the latest globally compiled data. The UAE has recently joined this rare group of countries with more than 20 percent female ministers. Morocco and Sudan have between 15 and 20 percent women ministers, and another six countries have between 10 and 20 percent women ministers. At the other end, Saudi Arabia currently has no female ministers.

These numbers are an improvement from just over a decade ago. Back in 2005, none of the thirty countries covered in this book had more than 20 percent female ministers, only two—Iraq and

Kazakhstan—had between 15 and 20 percent female ministers, and only three had between 10 and 15 percent female ministers.

When it comes to the justice system, Mali is the only country among all Muslim-majority countries where the chief justice is female. None of the thirty larger economies covered in this book have a woman in this role. In Kyrgyzstan, there are 45 percent women justices on the constitutional court, while in Algeria, Azerbaijan, and Kosovo there are 22 percent women in this role—the same as the global average. In thirteen of the countries covered—Egypt, Iran, Iraq, Jordan, Kuwait, Libya, Mauritania, Morocco, Pakistan, Qatar, Turkey, the UAE, and Yemen—there are no women on the constitutional court.

Many women trailblazers in the Muslim world are highly conscious of their pioneering role and its potential impact on perceptions of women's leadership. Between 2005 and 2007, Massouma Al Mubarak led three ministerial portfolios—communication, planning, and health. The night before my meeting with her, I had dinner with a group of young professional Kuwaitis, both women and men. They spoke admiringly of Dr. Al Mubarak and suggested that I ask her about an incident that had stood out for them. After a fire at a public hospital that resulted in the deaths of patients, she chose to resign as minister of health, even though she had just taken over the position and the problems at the hospital could not have been created under her watch. These young men and women said that a man in her position would not have resigned and only a woman would have had the sense of political responsibility to do so. When I asked her about this episode, she was adamant that resigning had been the right thing to do and that it had been important to set the right example: "All eyes were on me."

Beyond the role model effect, women's leadership is not always better for other women. Some women political leaders do put in place more policies that foster broader positive changes for women and proactively promote gender equality, but the record for most leaders is mixed. Women leaders in the Muslim world, like women leaders everywhere, often try to walk a fine line between maintaining their broad acceptance and pushing a "women's agenda." For instance, a posthumously created fund, the Benazir Income Support Fund, transfers cash directly to low-income women, but during Benazir Bhutto's two terms in power her government made little effort to get more women into employment or empower them financially. And Sheikh Hasina of Bangladesh may have done more harm than good. Grameen Bank gives 90 percent of its loans to women to run micro-businesses, and its founder, Muhammad Yunus, won the Nobel Prize in 2006. In 2011, Sheikh Hasina forced him out and increased government control over the bank to 25 percent, at the expense of its 5.5 million small-time shareholders, almost all of them women, who used to own more than 95 percent of the bank. This was widely regarded as a political move to prevent Yunus from gaining any further popularity and assert control over an institution that impacted millions of lives, without regard to the beneficiaries of the institution.[17]

In some parts of the Muslim world, queens, sheikhas, and first ladies hold significant cultural influence, but often they too have been cautious advocates for women's *economic* empowerment. Queen Rania of Jordan has focused primarily on education, although the Jordan River Foundation, which she chairs, has also sought to expand economic opportunities for women from low-income households. Sheikha Mozah, the third wife of the former emir of Qatar, has taken a strong stance on higher education but has not advocated strongly for employment opportunities for the women who come out of the higher education system. Suzanne Mubarak of Egypt and Leila Ali of Tunisia, who are now mostly reviled after the Arab Spring of 2010–2012 sent their husbands out of power, were engaged in some efforts toward women's empowerment through foundations and charities, but they were not deeply focused on broadening economic opportunity for women.

There are too few data points from which to draw clear conclusions about whether women political leaders have driven women's economic empowerment in any significant way beyond the passive role model effect. Anecdotal evidence would suggest that women in power in the Muslim world are particularly sensitive to cultural norms and are sometimes more constrained than men in making changes that push the boundaries of traditional gender roles. Instead, they form alliances and become adept at compromise and negotiation.

For women's economic empowerment to be taken seriously in politics, Dr. Al Mubarak believes, more women have to actually be in politics. Otherwise, men, even liberal men, will shy away from dealing with "women's issues." There is plenty of research to back up her view, including the research conclusion discussed earlier: that it takes a critical threshold of 30 percent for groups to benefit from diversity.[18] It is only beyond this threshold that nondominant groups can be themselves and represent the views and experiences of their group.

The Changing of the Guard

During a trip to Dubai in the spring of 2016, I met many women from around the world who had found opportunity in Dubai's melting pot, but it was difficult to get meetings with local Emirati women who were professionals or entrepreneurs. Instead, I came across one expat after another and was slightly disappointed at not being able to interview more local women. So it was with some hesitation that just a few hours before flying out, I set up a meeting with Maysa Al Mani, introduced to me by another young woman I had interviewed simply as a "Saudi activist" who she thought would "be interesting" for my book.

With no background on her besides her first name, and having had a long and tiring day at a conference, I went into the meeting with little enthusiasm. My low expectations turned out to be wholly unjustified. Twenty-eight-year-old Maysa started by telling me about her work as a consultant with PricewaterhouseCoopers, particularly her work on Saudi Arabia's Vision 2030, the current regime's economic development and diversification plan. She told me about late nights spent working in government offices with armies of other consultants and showed me how she used the Global Gender Gap Index, which my team and I produce for the World Economic Forum, to build her case for integrating more women into the economy. In particular, she had worked on proposals for legislative change to improve women's access to education, health, transport, and the workforce and had also proposed changes to family law. She hoped to create a behavioral economics "nudge" unit, similar to one created by the United Kingdom's government to influence health, education, and other public goods. She said that she had left banking to join public-sector consulting so that she could begin to change government after realizing, "If you can't beat them, join them."

All of this was interesting, certainly, but not as extraordinary as what she said next. Almost casually, Maysa mentioned that she had run for municipal elections in Saudi Arabia. I had read profiles of some of the women who had run for the elections held at the end of 2015, but I had not imagined I would meet one of them spontaneously. To be among the first women to ever run for office in a country that still had so many restrictions on women's agency—with the very public risk of failure—required guts.

Of the several hundred women who registered as candidates, only twenty were elected. Maysa said that she ran, "not to win, but to show the government that if you allow women to participate in any public arena, women will be there. I wanted to be an added number, to show women are there, especially young women. My campaign started virtually. Twitter was the main domain. I wanted to increase the level of communication between the residents of the district and the Majlis al-Baladi [the municipal council]. I wanted to make a website for my district for citizens to send photos and recommendations, or anything related to the municipality's work or even violations. My slogan was 'as-sukan shuraka al-tanmiya' ('citizens are partners in development'). I did not only want to focus on the accountability of the elected members, but also the people—to tell them you have a big role to play."[19]

Although she did not win herself, she is happy she participated and even happier that in this historic election women voted, were candidates, and were elected. Three changes that were simply not possible until now happened all at once. "When women won, it shocked a lot of people in a good way, especially in underdeveloped areas. To have women winning there is huge. I think it gave people a reference: to say, 'Yes, we have women in Majlis as-Shura [the national consultative council], we have women in the municipal council, and hopefully we can have women as ministers and even judges.' I love to see women in decision-making positions. Even if the municipality is a tiny entity, it is a body which makes decisions and is representative of people, men and women. Women participating in these elections and winning offices broke a lot of the stigma. Now in some councils they have separate rooms for the women with cameras [so that they can communicate with the male counselors]. This recently happened in Jeddah, and Representatives Rasha Hefzi and Lama Suleiman fought it and had serious discussions over the separation. This is extremely healthy. Yes, let's push the men! I'm really happy with the struggle that is happening for women to get their seats next to men. I hope all women representatives, if they want it, know they have the right to sit next to the men."

Maysa represents a new wave of women considering careers in politics and public service across the broader Muslim world. If more of them follow through on these aspirations, they have the potential to open the gates to greater economic and social agency for women. Women's growing power in the economy is bound to influence politicians, male and female alike. And policymaking to bring more women into the workforce is a critical economic challenge, so male and female policymakers must take charge of this agenda. One pathway to changing policies to meet the needs of working women and promote further gender equality is getting more women into politics itself. If more of the fifty million new entrants to the workforce in the last fifteen years channel their education and experience toward politics and the public sector as a profession, they will be able to represent others like themselves and pave the way for a next generation of women politicians *and* workers.

For now, neither traditional nor modern values fully prevail, so politicians are trying to optimize the delicate mix that will give them the most power and legitimacy to govern, sometimes acting against their own values, whether liberal or conservative. Fatma Şahin in Turkey eventually left the national government and ran and won as mayor of Gaziantep, a city at the frontlines of managing the influx of Syrian refugees into Turkey. The business-government task force for gender parity that she started with the World Economic Forum was continued by the ministry staff, who saw it through to its final stages, surpassing its initial target. Erdoğan's abortion bill was withdrawn owing to the public pushback, but women's activists say that most doctors in public hospitals, worried about running afoul of government views, have stopped performing abortions altogether.

An uneasy, polarized, and polarizing conversation continues around the idea of what it means to be a woman. On International Women's Day, March 8, 2016, Erdoğan declared that "woman is above all else a mother," compounding his earlier statements encouraging women to have at least three children—especially as things like disposable diapers have now made it "easier" to raise children—and chastising women for "denying their womanhood" when they say they won't have children because of work.

Yet on May 30, less than three months later, his wife, Emine, said something quite different at an event promoting women's employment in mobile technologies. The event brought together 141 female university graduates who had completed their 220-hour training program on mobile technologies and mobile design. The three projects awarded that day by Emine Erdoğan, all designed by women, included a location-sharing app for people experiencing violence or abuse, an app to help seniors with reminders for their medical treatments, and another app to find registered cleaning staff for white-collar working women. She also noted that the "elimination of barriers such as wage differentials and glass ceiling obstacles are requirements for equity."[20]

Regardless of what either Mrs. Erdoğan or her husband may personally believe, disposable diapers, mobile technology, and a professionalized care economy are likely to bring more women—mothers or not—into the workforce, not drive them out.

Future-Ready Interventions

Governments play a crucial role in accelerating—or slowing down— the rise of working women in the Muslim world. It is beginning to dawn on some policymakers that they cannot ignore the talent and skills of the most educated segments of their young population or the consumer power of a new and growing group of breadwinners. Some are now trying to catch up in places where women have already joined the workforce in large numbers. A very wide range of policies could support the movement that is under way and enhance its returns for society, but seven areas in particular are important to preparing for the future: broadening Internet access; providing education and train- ing for science, technology, engineering, and mathematics (STEM) and information and communications technology (ICT) fields and ensuring that talent is used in the labor market; leveraging the gig economy; providing training and financial support for entrepreneur- ship; developing a professionalized care sector; expanding transport options; and workplace legislation.

If economic growth in the future is likely to be based on tech- nological know-how and technology-driven business models, then investing in the education and skills of a technology-savvy workforce and broadening access to high-quality digital tools and mobile com- munications are critical elements of setting up all citizens—women and men alike—for success in the future. These inputs are even more critical for women, who, as the newer entrants into the workforce, have fewer traditional networks and role models to rely on.

Access to technology is the basis on which the opportunities of a technologically driven economy are built. However, both cell phone penetration and Internet access are more limited for women than for men across much of the developing world and emerging markets, including many Muslim-majority economies. For example, while a higher number of women than men have used cell phones in the last three months in the United Arab Emirates, in other Muslim economies for which data are available fewer women than men have done so. In Azerbaijan, only 76 percent of women have used cell phones compared to 91 percent of men. In Egypt, 72 percent of women have used cell phones compared to 83 percent of men, while in Iran, 56 percent of women have used cell phones compared to 78 percent of men. These differences also exist for Internet access. In Bahrain, all women accessed the Internet in the last three months compared to 82 percent of men, according to the latest available data, but most countries have a wide gender gap in favor of men. For example, in Bangladesh, only 5 percent of women accessed the Internet in the last three months compared to 8 percent of men. Even in countries with higher Internet penetration overall, the numbers for women can be markedly lower. For example, in Iran 34 percent of men accessed the Internet in the last three months compared to 26 percent of women, while in Morocco 58 percent of men did compared to 45 percent of women.[21] Broadening the base of Internet and mobile access is a fundamental strategic intervention that all governments across the Muslim world must take, including ensuring gender-equal distribution. For women like Mozah, the cook in Cairo, a combination of web access and short-term training could change her market access and thus her income and her quality of life.

Governments also need to take a proactive approach to ensuring that women are not simply users and consumers in the digital world. They should also have a level playing field in becoming the leaders who are developing new technologies. Here, many Muslim economies have an advantage compared to the Western world, where the numbers of women going into STEM fields are traditionally lower. These upstream advantages need to be expanded to more women, however, and then channeled to ensure that women can use their knowledge further downstream in the labor market. There is precedent for such lost opportunities in the past, including the wasted medical degrees of women in Pakistan despite the strong demand for doctors, or the wasted engineering degrees of women in Kuwait despite strong demand from the petroleum industry. Governments will need to ensure that they convert their gender advantage in STEM education to labor market returns for women by broadening access to finance, encouraging female entrepreneurship, and incentivizing tech companies to transparently hire, retain, and promote women.

In many Muslim-majority economies, as in other emerging markets, a significant portion of the workforce is already engaged in independent work in comparison to the West, where a traditional job has been both the most prevalent model and the middle-class ideal. The digitization of independent work through the "gig economy" allows for broader access to markets, more efficient delivery of services, and flexibility, which is often valued by women given the multiple demands on their time. What is considered precarious work or a "side hustle" in the West is often seen as a welcome new opportunity and the main revenue source for many women in the Muslim world. There are countless examples of women using social media platforms to sell products such as clothing and food or even offer medical services. Although the overall outcomes are dependent on the type of platform and the type of market covered, online platform models such as Mumm in Egypt, Glowork in Saudi Arabia, and doctHERS in Pakistan that seek to connect a supply of female talent with potential demand are particularly successful because they combine appealing economic incentives with concessions to local cultural requirements.

As governments notice these new work formats, they are also beginning to find ways to facilitate better outcomes for the people who use them. For example, in a government-led program in Saudi Arabia women are being trained in mobile phone repair, a service they can then offer individually from their homes through social media and gig platforms or by working for companies and shops that specialize in providing these services. This program is complemented with a women-only telecommunications complex. In Malaysia, the government is proactively encouraging more households in the bottom 40 percent to develop digital entrepreneurship skills and use online tools and platforms to generate more income. Such approaches are still rare, however, and governments across the Muslim world would do well to combine training and digital access for women to open up new economic opportunities to them.[22]

Entrepreneurship should not be limited to online gig work. Currently, the percentage of firms with a woman among the principal owners is low in most Muslim economies, both poor and rich ones. The numbers are as low as 4 percent in Azerbaijan, 13 percent in Morocco, and 13 percent in Malaysia, while at the other end of the spectrum, they are higher than 30 percent in five countries: Tajikistan (33 percent), Egypt (34 percent), Indonesia (43 percent), Kyrgyzstan (49 percent), and Tunisia (50 percent). This number is just over 50 percent in Brazil, over 64 percent in China, under 11 percent in India, and 28.5 percent in Russia. In some countries, like Tunisia, women-led start-ups fail more often than those led by men.[23] Important elements of support for different types of entrepreneurs, such as access to finance and training, flexible labor markets, transparent tax regimes, and bankruptcy rules, must be developed taking both gender and income into account. It is critical that governments consider the different needs of not only highly skilled female entrepreneurs but also the millions of women who are low skilled.

Governments must broaden economic opportunity, often through fostering entrepreneurial activity, for low-skilled women, many of whom belong to the poorest households. Some governments are doing so directly, while others are partnering with or encouraging civil society institutions to fill the gaps where markets and governments have failed. The Al-Nahda Philanthropic Society for Women, an entity under the patronage of the Saudi royal family, aims to empower women through financial and social support, training and employment services, and advocacy. Rasha Al Turki, the CEO, says that the group's goal, development rather than charity, is what makes it sustainable. The all-female team provides support to low-income women, helping them develop new skills or use existing skills to earn income and turn a profit. They connect these women to markets—or help create markets where there are none. The women, limited by social constraints from venturing out into public to take their goods to market themselves, often run their microbusinesses from home. Al-Nahda gets their products—food, embroidery, clothing—out to markets for them. Such models help create a virtuous cycle in these households, which tend to make a greater investment in education for the next generation of children, including girls, and to place a higher value on the women themselves. There are countless examples of models such as Al-Nahda's that support women's micro-entrepreneurship across the Muslim world, from small private philanthropic efforts to larger-scale government-backed efforts, and they will continue to be critical until the education deficit is fully eliminated over time.

Another core area where governments will need to take a proactive approach, preempting the challenges on the horizon, is the care sector. In order to balance home and work, many middle- and high-income women are using private, informal solutions to get support for child care, elder care, and household chores, often by hiring lower-skilled women at very low wages to provide these services. Governments have the opportunity to boost growth, provide stability for families, and lift millions more out of poverty by investing in a public care infrastructure and professionalizing and regulating the private care sector. For many low-skilled women, training and certification as well as minimum wage floors in this sector could go a long way toward providing a viable and dignified livelihood, and stricter laws could prevent child labor, such as Jamila's work with her mother providing domestic help to other households. For some middle-income women, the added costs of professionalization could make the price of private care support prohibitively high, driving them out of the workforce. Therefore, governments also need to think about providing subsidized, high-quality public care facilities at scale through crèches, day care centers, and early childhood education centers. As a high-employment sector, the care sector can create a lot of economic opportunity, particularly for women, who provide the majority of the labor in this field, especially when coupled with professionalization.

Such a literal nanny state holds some cultural resonance. As Dia-jeng, the CEO of Hijup pointed out, not only was Prophet Muhammad's wife a CEO, but he was raised by a nanny for the early part of his life. It was customary in the privileged tribes of Mecca to send infants out into the desert to be looked after by women who were professionals in providing such care. They were reunited with their mothers later on in life. Halima Al-Sa'diyah raised him for the first six years of his life and would be among the early converts to Islam later. From the very founding of Islam, then, outsourcing child care has been normalized, for women who can afford it, and compared to the "mommy wars" in the West carries less stigma and is less polarizing. Through the use of online intermediaries, the nature of care work is already changing for workers and consumers alike as middle-class families hire household help by the hour. Governments have an opportunity to regulate and professionalize this work, supporting workers through training, certification, and safety regulation and enhancing the consumer experience over time.

Finally, a broader enabling environment is also needed, including policies related to mobility and transport. In many economies, safe and efficient public transport or private transport infrastructure is missing for all, but particularly for women. Although Saudi Arabia's recently modified driving ban may be the most notorious globally, women in most Muslim economies face travel constraints. Monis Rahman, an entrepreneur in Pakistan who runs one of the largest job-matching platforms in the country, calls the lack of mobility for women in Pakistan a gender-based "transport apartheid" that puts women at an immediate disadvantage in the labor market. Women who can afford it find private solutions, such as drivers, but the cost is prohibitive for many. Online platforms and apps are also providing some solutions, such as Careem's women-only car services in the Middle East and LadyJek and Sister Ojek motorcycle services in Southeast Asia. But governments have a role to play in solving some of the underlying concerns, such as addressing sexual harassment on public transport and providing even lower-cost options for those who cannot afford wholly private or sharing-economy solutions. In several countries, governments have designated women-only sections on trains and buses, while others have created wholly segregated transport systems, but these remain options limited in number and few are tackling safety concerns on mixed public transport.

This broader enabling environment also includes laws that forbid women from working in similar roles to men and the absence of laws stipulating wage equality, protection from sexual harassment in the workplace, and job protection for pregnant women. There has been recent movement in some Muslim-majority countries on these issues, which are particularly pertinent for the formal workforce. Egypt adopted a law that criminalizes sexual harassment in employment, education, and public spaces. Kazakhstan is gradually removing gender differences in retirement ages for men and women so that they will be equal by 2027. In some countries, governments are putting in place affirmative policies—both the United Arab Emirates and Malaysia have announced quota policies for corporate boards, and Turkey offers tax breaks to companies that provide jobs to unemployed women—but much work remains to be done given the unequal playing field for working women and men.

No one approach on its own will be enough. In the words of Mari Elka Pangestu, a former minister for trade and industry in Indonesia (which has among the highest rates of women's labor force participation in the Muslim world): "It has to be a package. You can't just address the finance issue, you can't just address the market issue. You've got to address it as the financing issue, the market issue, and then the capacity of the woman herself—how to build up the capacity and empower them through that process."

Government also cannot act alone. Massouma Al Mubarak, the former minister in Kuwait, said, "Business would have the most to gain from such efforts because they need this talent. And yet not a single business ever voiced their support for women or provided any funds to support any campaigns." Dr. Al Mubarak thinks that businesses speaking up would incentivize politicians and policymakers to take a closer look at women's economic empowerment. In her view, in places like Kuwait where even the right to vote was very recently seen as violating the stability of society and destroying the family, tackling workforce integration is a step too far for politicians and policymakers without a clear economic rationale laid out by the business community.

How such interventions are made is even more critical. They will require a measured, careful approach that blends economic and cultural needs and brings a variety of stakeholders on board, not just the women they seek to uplift or those who are already supportive of them. This applies just as much to local governments as it does to foreign ones that wish to accelerate the rise of working women: investment and opportunity rather than charity, and working with the culture rather than against it, should form the base of any such efforts.

As a start, policymakers should lay out an economic case for promoting women's economic advancement. It is not hard to build a case for the scientific breakthroughs that lie dormant in the minds of the women with biology PhD degrees in Iran, the sustainable cities in the minds of Emirati women with urban planning degrees, the novel ideas for revolutionizing the child care sector in the minds of Tunisian women, or the algorithms in the minds of Kazakh women with computer science degrees.

But the arguments for innovation and growth do not convince everyone. A socially and culturally appropriate approach is also essential to addressing the needs of new constituencies while reassuring traditional ones. This requires making change at a pace that society can handle. Cross-sector advocacy and collaboration are one important way to ensure that many constituencies buy into the change under way. For many governments, it is not just in the broader interest of their economies to address the concerns of working women but also in their narrower self-interest, owing to the rising political power of these women. As voters—and potential revolutionaries—young, educated working women have an equal if not greater stake than young men in seeing change and opportunity come to their countries.

What's Next?

I WAS WALKING PAST AN INCONSPICUOUS BUILDING IN SHIRAZ, close to the tomb of the Persian poet Hafiz, when I noticed a group of young women huddled by the door. One of them broke into a smile and waved at me to come in. It turned out to be the Department of Architecture at the University of Shiraz, and these students were a group of aspiring architects from all over the country. They were eager to share their dreams and ambitions with a visitor, one of the many they were expecting would be coming to their country as tourism begins to pick up thanks to Iran's cautious opening to the world. In particular, these young women saw an opportunity for their soon-to-be-acquired architecture credentials in the growing tourism sector. "I want to restore more of Shiraz's historical buildings so the world can see them," said one. "I want to go back to Mashhad and help build hotels so more people come to visit my city," said another, referring to the city's significance to Shia Muslims and its inadequate infrastructure for coping with the more than two million visitors, mainly religious tourists, it receives every year. "Have you been to Mashhad yet? You must go to Mashhad!"

As Iran opens up to the world, its neglected infrastructure will need the skills and enthusiasm of these young women more than ever, just as the other emerging markets of the Muslim world will also need the talent of their female workforces to power their growth and development. These countries will find willing contributors. The new generation of young Muslim women see problems around them they want to solve and new opportunities they want to harness. They have pride in their communities, cities, and countries and want to be economically, politically, and socially engaged and to actively shape their economies and societies. They have the tools to do so. In just a generation or two, women have become a formidable economic force. But what happens next?

Exponential but Not Inevitable

The next wave of educated women is going to be even larger than the current generation of working women, based on current school and university enrollment numbers. If those women join the workforce at similar rates as the current cohort did, they will collectively form the largest group of young working women ever to join the labor force in Muslim-majority countries.

They are very likely to do just that. Efforts at economic diversification and fairly high growth rates in many emerging markets in the Muslim world are creating new opportunity for educated women to channel their knowledge into productive activities. Large emerging markets such as Bangladesh and Pakistan are trying to diversify production beyond low-value-added goods and services based on cheap, low-skilled labor. In the Middle East, there are efforts to broaden the growth base beyond oil and gas. Local consumption is growing rapidly in Southeast Asia, where efforts are being made to diversify exports beyond commodities. With this growth in higher-value-added production and services, more businesses will need access to skilled talent—and are willing to pay for it.[1]

There are other economic forces at play too. The growing consumption of families, which incentivized women to leave their homes and join the paid workforce, is also likely to continue and to bring yet more women into workplaces. Young families across the Muslim world want reliable health care, good schools for their children, transport, consumer goods, and leisure activities. In most economies, especially in urban areas, these goods and services are not affordable without both the women and men in families bringing in an income.

These working women will become the role models for a new generation. A much larger proportion of these young women—those still in schools and universities today—will have seen their older sisters, their neighbors, and in some cases their own mothers work outside the home. Thus, unlike the women before them, they will have role models and mentors who will ease the navigation of their next steps.

Most of the fifty million who recently joined the workforce are already parents or soon will be. Their expectations and aspirations for their daughters will be greater than the expectations their parents had for them. They are living proof that more is possible. Men's mindsets are shifting too. Few educated fathers see a good marriage as the only ideal—as they might have just a generation or two ago—for their daughters. In fact, those women who have managed work and family—and most of the men around them—no longer see these two elements as incompatible or the combination of them undesirable. The fact that women are still expected and willing to manage both spheres has given them a license to go ahead and do it.

Neither overtly feminist nor wholly traditional, this "third way" has helped women gain a footing in the workforce while still adhering to traditional norms around marriage and motherhood, facilitated by the prevailing social infrastructure. Familial bonds have remained strong between generations despite the remarkable changes that have occurred between one generation and the next, and despite rapid urbanization and internal migration. These bonds, driven by a mix of culture and convenience, are unlikely to disappear soon, and they provide working women with a private safety net for managing their care responsibilities.

Some women—especially urban, middle-income women, in both white-collar and service work—supplement the family safety net with paid services, usually provided by lower-skilled women. This further accelerates women's integration into the workforce by creating opportunity for low-skilled women who have not received sufficient education for higher-skilled work and lack other employment opportunities. Over the next decade, as some of the older cohort of today's middle-income millennials start facing the dual load of growing children and aging parents, demand for these services will only increase.

Of the two hundred people I spoke to, nearly all forecast that women would rise even more rapidly in the workforce in the coming decade across the Muslim world. A few, however, recommended caution. "Just because more women are joining the workforce doesn't mean we can take the shift for granted," said Ghada Barsoum, an assistant professor at the School of Global Affairs and Public Policy at the American University in Cairo. Her caution is not unwarranted.

Trends are not inevitable and can be reversed. The war in Syria is devastating a generation of relatively well-educated young people. As in many conflicts, not only does economic activity get disrupted for women and men, but women often bear the brunt of the worst atrocities of war. In the late 1970s and early 1980s, the rise of Islamist regimes in Afghanistan and Iran led to a loss of social and economic freedoms for women, the effects of which women are still feeling today. Conservative politics or conflict could undo the gains of the last years. Today's positive trends are also not universal. There are vast differences within countries when it comes to women's education and economic empowerment. Geographical limits, especially the urban-rural cultural and income divide, could stall progress in some countries. For example, in some provinces of Pakistan, the literacy rate for women is under 5 percent, while in some regions of Saudi Arabia it is unthinkable for women to leave the house at all, much less for work.

Most importantly, supporting policies are needed to speed up progress. Although the current rise of women in the workforce will help lift other women in the future, this momentum alone will not be enough. Education and economic opportunity for women will need to be brought to geographies and communities where they are not the norm. Regulations and policies that create a strong enabling environment will be needed, ranging from access to finance and new labor laws to family policies and care infrastructure. Governments will also need to ensure that women and men have equal access to the new technologies that are shaping our economies and societies and to the skills needed to apply them. And finally, business, government, and religious leaders will need to create a more positive narrative that speaks to and for the new working women of the Muslim world, legitimizing their place in society. In other words, most emerging economies of the Muslim world are well positioned for women to become major economic players, but policymakers, business leaders, and young women themselves would be wise not to count on the power of trends alone; instead, they must take steps to seriously address the challenges while seizing the new opportunities. They all stand to benefit from it.

For now, however, the factors that encouraged women to enter the workforce, and remain there, show no signs of abating. If anything, they are getting more powerful and compounding each other.

A New Home for an Old Dream

If the rate of change since the turn of the millennium is projected into the future, it is likely that by 2025 yet another 50 million women will have joined the workforce in Muslim-majority countries, bringing the total number of working women to 210 million. But this is likely to be a conservative estimate. It is more likely that progressively more women will make the choice—and have the opportunity—to work in the years to come and that their numbers will grow exponentially, particularly if policymakers and businesses begin to take a more proactive stance.

As I was writing this book, Donald Trump was elected president of the United States, the United Kingdom voted for their nation to leave the European Union, and nationalist sentiment was growing across Europe. The protectionist, anti-trade, anti-immigrant narratives that legitimized these movements stem at least in part from both real and perceived losses from globalization and the fear of growing technology-driven unemployment in the future.

But the very same forces that are making some advanced economies close themselves off from the world—technological change and the global flows of goods, services, labor, and ideas—have been central to the rise of fifty million women in the Muslim world. An education revolution provided a basis for many young women to embrace the opportunities offered by exposure to new tools, ideas, and technologies. Having little access to public life in the past, a cohort of young women in the Muslim world have eagerly seized the openings given to them now. Women use their smartphones to conduct their businesses, as Ibu Latifa does to figure out the best feeds for her micro fish farm and the best fashion for her clothing business, and they are at the forefront of developing technology-driven solutions to old problems, as Samira has done in tackling Cairo's decades-old traffic problems. Diajeng has used technology to build a fashion empire catering to other practicing young women like herself, and Saadia's work for an American fast-food chain is bringing her access to a meritocratic path for professional engagement. Women like Fatima dream of working for European brands so their ingenuity is seen by the world. And multitudes of young women on the streets of Jakarta are driving and using local transportation network companies, powered by apps, while young women in Riyadh are using social media to create catering businesses.

In many advanced economies, the rise of temporary work, often enabled by new platforms, has given rise to fears of a growing "precariat." These are just concerns given that for decades good work has provided stability and a safety net. But there is a difference between an Uber driver in the United States or Europe and a driver for Raye7 in Cairo or Careem in Jeddah. In many emerging markets, including the majority of those in the Muslim world, most work has always been precarious; generations of micro-entrepreneurs have functioned with little to no safety net and poor public infrastructure. For many young women—and men—the platform workforce and other technology-driven opportunities for earning a living are more economic opportunity than they have ever had before, and they provide more stable work than anything their parents had. The digitization of independent work offers more security than before in the form of better access to markets. Women in particular, as the traditionally marginalized group, are eagerly leveraging these opportunities and the flexibility they offer both as customers and workers.

Underlying this embrace of technology and globalization is grit, resilience, and a hunger for achievement. As very recent migrants from home to work, with uncharted waters to navigate, young women are eager to succeed and eager to use all the tools at their disposal. Their traditional invisibility in the public space has made their ambition particularly potent as they have finally come to be noticed. Business leaders often put this another way: they think that women are not just more qualified, but that they are also more keen for professional accomplishment after having been denied this opportunity in previous generations. White-collar professional women have thrived in the private sector of their countries, a sector that is relatively meritocratic compared to their countries' public sectors. Mimicking their route to success in school, millions of young women across the Muslim world are in the early stages of finding satisfying careers in workplaces that their mothers would never have dreamed of working in. Whether this relative meritocracy can follow them to senior levels as their numbers swell in junior and middle ranks remains to be seen, but it has opened a potential pathway for demonstrating their know-how.

Although there is vast inequality in many of these emerging markets, the growth of the middle class has instilled a sense of optimism about the future and about the potential for intergenerational transfer of income and opportunity that is rare in the West's working class at present. For working women in particular—especially white-collar professionals, entrepreneurs, and medium- and lower-skilled service sector workers—the new opportunities offered by technology and globalization have combined with their own determination to use them to enhance a sense of progress and prosperity across generations. Most working women believe that the next generation will do even better than them, both economically and in terms of social freedoms. They plan to open even bigger doors for their children, especially their daughters, recognizing and building on the investments made by their own parents in their education. This combination of appreciation for the past, hope for the future, and real investment can create a self-fulfilling virtuous cycle. If you have done better than the previous generation through a combination of education, economic opportunity, and exposure to ideas and tools from around the world, you try to ensure that these assets will be available to your own children. This cycle is unfolding in the homes of fifty million women and will unfold in the homes of at least another fifty million in the next decade.

Capitalism, globalization, and technology have had harsh impacts on the working class in the United States, in the United Kingdom, and elsewhere in the West in recent years. On the other side of the world, these same forces have empowered millions of women, with far-reaching consequences for their families, communities, and countries. The American dream is alive and well—among the working women of the Muslim world.

Powering a New Golden Age

This dream has the potential to fuel more than just prosperity for those who have it. It could help revive a lost narrative, in a new form, and fuel the growth of Muslim economies.

From the eighth to the thirteenth centuries, Islam enjoyed a golden age when science, mathematics, medicine, economic development, and culture flourished. When Islamic advances in these fields were subsequently transferred to the rest of the world, they became the basis for many discoveries and inventions in the West too. The reasons for the perceived Islamic ascendance and its later decline are still debated, but meanwhile the period holds a near-mythical status in the minds of Muslims today, and many leaders argue for rebuilding that lost era in the modern world, sometimes as a counter to extremist ideologies.

Central to the last golden age was a concentration of talent, new technology, and globalization. Today the Muslim world once again has many educated people, more than ever before; talent is prized as never before in the workforce, and globalization and new technologies are more welcome than they have been before.

But the current moment is different from the past in one important respect: it has propelled women into the workforce and given them new opportunities for the first time.

Women are now the majority of those who are being educated and a growing proportion of those who are working, creating, building, thinking, and leading. As discussed earlier, the literature on gender diversity deems 30 percent to be the number at which diversity begins to pay off in the aggregate. With women now making up over 31 percent of the total workforce across the Muslim world, this tipping point has been reached. The percentage of working women is distributed differently across Muslim countries: ten of the thirty economies covered in this book are at or well over the 30 percent threshold, while the other twenty range between those that are only halfway to 30 percent and those that are very close. If the momentum of the virtuous cycle continues, especially if it is supported by policymakers and business leaders, most economies in the Muslim world could get to this threshold and beyond.

The new golden age may already have arrived for some Muslim working women, and as their countries pass the tipping point they have the power to unleash broader change across the Muslim world. This newly empowered labor force represents tremendous opportunity for communities to prosper, for companies to address their needs for skilled labor, for governments to broaden their tax base, and for economies to grow. Muslim working women are not a monolithic group, but all are a new class of woman who has never existed before in the history of Islam. They are hungry for opportunity, having been barred from it in the past, and yet they also carry with them a different social experience, one they are keen to preserve. This will lead to new policies, new workplaces, new products, and new values. This is how diversity pays off.

The future these young women will shape is likely to be far more prosperous, dynamic, and peaceful than anything that came before. As one of the young architecture students in Shiraz put it, "It is impossible to send us back into our homes again now that we have tasted success ourselves. I want to help change everything around me." A drive for achievement, once experienced, is hard to give up. These young women are just at the cusp of beginning to recognize their own power and the profound change they are a part of.

As I was nearing the end of writing this book, my paternal grandmother passed away, the last of a generation who could recall a time before Pakistan—and many other countries of the Muslim world—came into existence as a sovereign nation. Her limited but rare education contributed to raising a son who chose to marry a woman, my mother, who was as well educated as him. Together, they raised daughters, my sister and me, who would come of age just as broader changes were unfolding for working women across the Muslim world. Looking at the arc of this transformation from my grandmother's perspective, the magnitude is astonishing. Late in her life, even though she could not fully understand my choices and ambitions, she was proud that I had made my own way. In some ways, I imagine her pride resembles what I felt for Nazia, the inspiring field engineer who was confusingly present in the barren landscape of the gas field where I met her over twenty years ago.

Just as Nazia, once seen, could not be unseen, millions of young girls now see Khadija's modern-day daughters. Fifty million new working women in the Muslim world are making an indelible mark on the economic and social fabric of their countries through their resilience, determination, and pioneering spirit. That progress can't be undone. And as another generation joins them, the start of this millennium may well be the most profoundly transformative quarter century for women in the history of Islam—and for the Muslim world itself.

Acknowledgments

Writing my first book has been both a challenging and deeply fulfilling process as I learned something new at every turn. The most revelatory aspect of writing was how much it is a communal activity rather than a solo one.

I wrote this book over the course of a year during weekends and holidays from a demanding but inspiring job. While this meant time was limited, the people at the World Economic Forum—both colleagues and constituents—provided much stimulation for this book. I am immensely grateful to Klaus Schwab, founder and executive chairman of the World Economic Forum, who has been a mentor, challenger, and inspiration for more than a decade. Our wide-ranging conversations have led to several of the reflections in this book and ideas about books still to come. As I worked on two parallel creative processes over the last year—writing the book while building out a new practice on education, gender, and work—I was probably a more challenging colleague than usual. I am grateful to my whole team for their understanding and in particular to Valerie Peyre, Till Leopold, and Vesselina Ratcheva for their curiosity and encouragement. Thanks also to the colleagues who were early supporters, particularly Mel Rogers, Adrian Monck, and Oliver Cann, and to those who helped me in obtaining access and material for this book, particularly the MENA, ASEAN, and Europe and Central Asia teams. Additionally, the World Economic Forum's Global Shapers network, composed of young leaders below the age of thirty, was almost always one of my first ports of call in every country I traveled to thanks to the Global Shapers team. Finally, thanks to my colleagues Nicholas Davis and Oliver Cann for taking the time to read drafts of this book and provide invaluable suggestions and edits.

I am indebted to my agent Eric Lupfer, first at Williams Morris Endeavour and now at Fletcher and Company, for seeing value in this book and navigating me skillfully through all the steps needed to get it out into the world. I am also grateful to my excellent editor, Katy O'Donnell, and the whole team at Nation Books for their thoughtful edits and for patiently initiating me into the process of publishing. I may never have made it to the agents and publishers stage, though, had it not been for the *Financial Times* and McKinsey's Bracken Bower Prize, given to an aspiring author under the age of thirty-five for a topic related to the challenges and opportunities of economic growth. Without its financial support and recognition, this project might never have gotten off the ground. Andrew Hill from the *Financial Times* was instrumental in providing advice and contacts, including my eventual agent, Eric. Professor Herminia Ibarra and Professor Lynda Gratton, involved in judging the Book of the Year and the Bracken Bower Prize, respectively, were very generous with practical advice. Dominic Barton and his colleagues at McKinsey also gave regular encouragement and access to their research.

A vast number of very busy CEOs, executives, and entrepreneurs, some of whom are quoted in this book, gave me access to their networks and their personal time, candidly sharing their own stories, their thoughts about the future of the female workforce in their companies and countries, and their hopes for their own daughters and sons. They include Ozlem Denizem, Sharan Burrow, Tim Noonan, Aireen Omar, Lubna Olayan, Huda Al Ghosson, Khalid Al Ahmed, Alanoud Hamad, Rick Goings, Loay Elshawarby, Fahd Al Rasheed, Khalid Alkhudair, Muna Abu Sulayman, Nezha Hayat, Waleed Abd El Rahman, Monis Rahman, Salma Abou Hussein, Amanda Witdarmono, Andi Taufan Garuda Putra, Intan Pramesthi Satriyandini, Andreas Harsono, Azita Berar Awad, Hala Yateem, Nadia Boulifa, Diajeng Lestari, Fara Askari, Aitosik Ilyassov, Pavel Koktyshev, Dana Abikeyeva, Arailym Ashirbekova, Asset Abdualiyev, Dari Al Bader, Abdullatteef Al Sharikh, Sarah Akbar, Shaikha Al Bahar, Hana Al Sayed, Omar Alghanim, Massouma Al Mubarak, Siham Al Razaki, Lubna Al Kazi, Ghada Barsoum, Sahar Al Sallab, Amira Azzouz, Amna Nosseir, Mari Pangestu, Zainah Anwar, Sara Khurram, Rasha Al Turki, Hawazen Al Dokheed, Elissa Freiha, Maysa Al Mani, Lubna Qassim, and Amal Al Mutawa. Their staff, too countless to name and often young millennial Muslim women themselves, not only facilitated my research in sixteen countries but offered me a glimpse into their own lives. I have also relied on data from several international organizations, including but not limited to the International Trade Union Confederation, the World Bank, the International Monetary Fund, the International Labour Organization, and the United Nations Educational, Scientific, and Cultural Organization.

This book benefited from the journalistic steering of Adam Ellick back when it was just a proposal and from his network of friends who are authors and journalists, including Pamela Druckerman, Nicholas Kristof, Elmira Bayrasli, Lauren Bohn, Andrew Blackwell, Parag Khanna, and Dexter Filkins, who all agreed to advise me because he asked. Professor Ricardo Hausmann, Professor Laura Tyson, and Borge Brende, whom I count as friends and mentors, have long been role models. My classes with Professor Ronald Heifetz have been a key influence in helping me find my voice. I am also grateful to my old classmates Maleeha Malik Qader, Sharmeen Obaid Chinoy, Bibi

Al Sabah, Vusal Isayev, Magzhan Ilyassov, Abang Rahmat Yusuf, H. B. Qermane, Ruba Al Hassan, and Chingiz Dosmukhambetov for opening up their networks in their home countries. I thank Elena Mayer Bestig for her precise research assistance at the start of this project and Jill Swenson for excellent editing on the earliest drafts of this book.

Balancing work with research and writing left very little time for family and friends over the course of more than a year. I am grateful to all of them for their patience. My wonderful parents are muses for this book because of how they invested in their own two daughters. I am thankful for the advice and support of my sister, Sara, and for her help in researching many parts of this book. My grandmother passed away as I was nearing the end of this book, before I could share it with her—I am glad I got to tell a little of her story. Valmina Prezani, Camilla Kappeler, Chris Cooper, and Emanuel Amon are among the beautiful friendships I have come to rely on, as well as Damaris Papoutsakis and Rabab Fayad, who gave lots of support to ensure that I finished this book as professional and personal events sent me far off the timelines I had originally set for it. Thanks to my friends Irene Mia, Shannon McAuliffe, Ruba Al Hassan, Sarah Tamimi, Hector Escamilla, Sushant Palakuthri Rao, Annette Heimlicher, Fiona Paua, and Katherine Tweedie for inspiring me, sometimes unknowingly, to enjoy the ride.

My gratitude is most profound for the scores of ordinary women who agreed to share their journey of education and employment with me. As an economist and first-time author, I was more comfortable with data and policy than storytelling, so learning how to interview people came through a lot of trial and error. For some of my earliest interview subjects, it meant two years of exchanges as I came up with better questions. All of them continued to respond, taking precious time from their busy lives. I am in awe of what these women have managed to achieve by renegotiating skillfully their own loyalties and those of others around them in pursuit of their dreams. I hope this

book has captured just a little of their enormous power and will inspire others to tell more stories about them. Being allowed into the
homes and workplaces of hundreds of these women, with hospitality,
candor, and kindness, has been a gift I couldn't have imagined at the
start of this journey. Understanding their story has helped me understand my own.

Notes

Introduction: Khadija's Daughters

1. Education data are from the United Nations Educational, Scientific, and Cultural Organization (UNESCO) and the World Bank. Employment data are from the International Labour Organization (ILO) and the World Bank.

2. Employment data are from the ILO and the World Bank.

3. In 2017, low-income economies were defined as those with a gross national income (GNI) per capita, calculated using the World Bank Atlas method, of $1,025 or less in 2015; lower-middle-income economies were those with a GNI per capita between $1,026 and $4,035; upper-middle-income economies were those with a GNI per capita between $4,036 and $12,475; and high-income economies were those with a GNI per capita of $12,476 or more.

4. Only high-income, upper-middle-income, or lower-middle-income countries are included. Low-income countries with a GNI below $1,026 per capita are not included.

5. GDP figures and growth rates are from the World Bank.

6. Goldman Sachs Global Economics Group, *BRICS and Beyond* (New

York: Goldman Sachs, 2007), ch. 11, "The N-11: More Than an Acronym"; and ch. 13, "Beyond the BRICS: A Look at the 'Next 11,'" available at www .goldmansachs.com/our-thinking/archive/archive-pdfs/brics-book/brics-full -book.pdf.

7. In this book, "womenomics" broadly refers to the rise of women in the workforce and its subsequent benefits to businesses and the economy. The term was coined in 1999 by Kathy Matsui, an executive at Goldman Sachs in Japan, to refer to the potential for Japanese women to bring much-needed talent and dynamism to the Japanese workforce and economy. A 2009 book by Katty Kay and Claire Shipman by the same name took a more personal approach to the topic and laid out how the rise of women in the workforce allows working women to redefine success.

8. Jonathan Woetzel et al., *The Power of Parity: How Advancing Women's Equality Can Add $12 Trillion to Global Growth* (McKinsey Global Institute, September 2015), available at www.mckinsey.com/global-themes/employment -and-growth/how-advancing-womens-equality-can-add-12-trillion-to-global -growth.

9. More than 80 percent of the 200 women and men agreed to share their stories under their own names, often proudly. The 20 percent who preferred anonymity were mainly those who were in highly public positions—CEOs or royalty—and who did not want their comments about their countries' broader policy environment or religious authorities attributed publicly. A few were ordinary working women, both poor and rich, who did not want to share information publicly about the impact of their professional lives on their personal lives.

Chapter 1: Education Pioneers

1. Michael Lipka, "Muslims and Islam: Key Findings in the US and Around the World" (Washington, DC: Pew Research Center, May 26, 2017), available at www.pewresearch.org/fact-tank/2017/05/26/muslims-and-islam-key -findings-in-the-u-s-and-around-the-world/.

2. Education data are from UNESCO and the World Bank.

3. Ruchir Sharma, "People Matter," ch. 1 in *The Rise and Fall of Nations: Forces of Change in the Post-Crisis World* (New York: Norton, 2016).

4. Education data are from UNESCO and the World Bank.

5. Education data are from UNESCO and the World Bank. In Turkey in 1970, only 5 percent of young people were enrolled in university—2 percent of women and over 8 percent of men—and three out of every four university stu-

dents were male. By 1990, 13 percent of the population was enrolled in university: about 9 percent of women and 18 percent of men. Today the overall rate of university enrollment in Turkey is nearly 80 percent: 84 percent of men and 73 percent of women. This means that there are now nearly nine women for every ten men enrolled in university. This pattern implies a more accelerated pace for women than men in the acquisition of university education. Similarly, in Egypt ten years ago, there were three women for every four men in university; today those numbers are nearly equal. In Pakistan, where the average enrollment rate is around 10 percent, female enrollment rates have grown more than the rates for males.

6. According to the latest data, in Algeria, Azerbaijan, Bahrain, Indonesia, Jordan, Kazakhstan, Kuwait, Kyrgyzstan, Libya, Oman, Pakistan, Qatar, Sudan, Syria, Tunisia, and United Arab Emirates, there is a reverse gender gap: more women than men are enrolled in university. In Egypt, Iran, Morocco, Saudi Arabia, Turkmenistan, and Uzbekistan, women are only a few percentage points behind men. Countries like Saudi Arabia are returning closer to parity after nearly a decade of women enrolling in much higher numbers than men. Data are from the World Bank.

7. Education data are from UNESCO and the World Bank. Although in the majority of countries there is parity, near-parity, or better outcomes for girls than boys in primary and secondary education, in five countries—Iran, Libya, Oman, Saudi Arabia, and Syria—there are still secondary enrollment gender gaps of between five and ten percentage points. Six countries don't have enough recent data.

8. For example, in Indonesia in 1970, around 20 percent of secondary school teachers were women. Today just a little over half of all secondary school teachers in Indonesia are women. In Jordan, which is more socially conservative, this number rose from 34 percent in 1970 to nearly 60 percent today. In Iran in 1970, before the Islamic revolution, around 26 percent of teachers in secondary schools were women. Today over 54 percent are. Data are from the World Bank.

9. World Economic Forum, *Global Gender Gap Report 2016* (Geneva: World Economic Forum, October 2016).

10. International Labour Organization (ILO) and Asian Development Bank (ADB), *Women and Labour Markets in Asia: Rebalancing for Gender Equality* (Geneva: ILO and ADB, April 2011); Jad Chaaban and Wendy Cunningham, "Measuring the Economic Gain of Investing in Girls: The Girl Effect Dividend," World Bank Policy Research Working Paper 5753 (Washington, DC: World Bank, August 2011).

11. Education data are from UNESCO and the World Bank. Seven countries don't have enough recent data.

12. First five verses from Surah Al Alaq, available at Quran in English, translated by Talal Itani, www.clearquran.com/096.html; See, for example, Raheeq Ahmad Abbasi, "Women and Education in Islam," *Minhaj-ul-Quran International* (May 27, 2009), available at www.minhaj.org/english/tid/8535 /Women-Education-in-Islam-article-by-dr-raheeq-ahmad-rahiq-ahmed -abbasi-nazim-e-aala-mqi-minhaj-ul-quran.html.

13. Carla Power, "A Secret History," *New York Times Magazine,* February 25, 2007; Mohammad Akram Nadwi, "Al-Muhaddithat: The Female Scholars of Islam," videotaped talk at Cambridge Islamic College, published May 2014 at www.youtube.com/watch?v=qwihHlqqvqI; Abbasi, "Women and Education in Islam"; "Khadija bint Khuwaylid," Wikipedia, available at https://en.wikipedia .org/wiki/Khadija_bint_Khuwaylid (updated June 5, 2017); "Aisha," Wikipedia, available at https://en.wikipedia.org/wiki/Aisha (updated June 8, 2017).

14. After oil and gas, the automotive industry is Iran's biggest industry, accounting for about 10 percent of GDP and employing about 4 percent of the labor force. There was a boom in local car manufacturing between 2000 and 2013, driven by high import duties and a growing middle class. After the imposition of fresh sanctions in July 2013 prevented Iranian companies from importing the vehicle parts upon which domestic cars rely, Iran had to cede its place to Turkey as the region's top vehicle manufacturer. Kioomars Ashtarian, "Iran," ch. 15 in *UNESCO Science Report: Towards 2030* (Paris: UNESCO Publishing, November 2015).

15. Philipp Grosse Kleimann, Santiago Castillo, and Alexander Brenner, "Back to Business: Iran, a New Emerging Market," *Automotive World,* July 12, 2016, available at www.automotiveworld.com/analysis/back-business-iran -new-emerging-market/.

16. Saudi Arabian Cultural Bureau in Canada, "The King Abdullah Scholarship Program," available at www.saudibureau.org/en/inside.php?ID=16.

17. Abdul Hannan Tago, "5 Divorces Every Hour in KSA," *Arab News,* July 3, 2016, available at www.arabnews.com/node/948551/saudi-arabia.

Chapter 2: Workforce Trailblazers

1. Education data are from UNESCO and the World Bank.

2. Population data are from the World Bank.

3. Employment data are from the ILO and the World Bank.

4. Employment data are from the ILO and the World Bank.

5. See the website for the 30% Club at https://30percentclub.org/; in a study of more than 150 German firms over five years, researchers confirmed that boards need a critical mass of about 30 percent women to outperform (as measured by return on equity) all-male boards. See Catalyst Information Center, "Why Diversity Matters," July 2013, available at www.catalyst.org/system/files /why_diversity_matters_catalyst_0.pdf.

6. Education data from UNESCO and the World Bank. In Jordan during the same time period, the share of university-educated men in the workforce rose from 15 to 21 percent—still dwarfed by the blue-collar workers who make up the majority of the male workforce.

7. This is a 70 percent increase over the 4 million women in the labor force in the year 2000. During the same time period, there was a higher absolute increase of men in the labor force, but relative to the year 2000, this represented a 42 percent increase, smaller than that for women.

8. According to the latest figures, labor force participation for women grew in all economies in the MENA region except Syria.

9. Michael J. Silverstein and Kate Sayre, "The Female Economy," *Harvard Business Review* (September 2009); The Female Factor, "Women in the Economy," available at www.thefemalefactor.com/statistics/statistics_about_women .html.

10. Sandra Lawson and Douglas B. Gilman, "The Power of the Purse: Gender Equality and Middle-Class Spending," Goldman Sachs Global Markets Institute, August 5, 2009, available at www.goldmansachs.com/our-thinking /investing-in-women/bios-pdfs/power-of-purse.pdf.

11. Growth rates are from the World Bank.

12. Fertility rates are from the World Bank. In developed economies, the replacement rate is just over 2.0 children per woman, but in developing economies it can be much higher owing to higher mortality rates. The global average is estimated to be 2.33. Thomas J. Espenshade, Juan Carlos Guzman, and Charles F. Westoff, "The Surprising Global Variation in Replacement Fertility," *Population Research and Policy Review* 22, no. 5 (2003): 575–583.

13. Esra Gürmen, "How Turkish Soap Operas Took over the World," *Fader* (May/June 2017), available at www.thefader.com/2016/03/01/turkish-soap -operas.

14. Labor force data are from the ILO and the World Bank.

15. Education data are from UNESCO and the World Bank. Data by country showing the age-cohort distribution of the stock of education in the

economically active and inactive parts of the population are not available for most Muslim-majority economies.

16. Government of Balochistan, "Literacy and Education," Multiple Indicator Cluster Surveys (MICS) report, 2010, available at www.balochistan.gov.pk /mics/MICS-4-Web/4-1-Results-Literacy%20&%20Education.pdf.

17. World Economic Forum, *Global Gender Gap Report 2016* (Geneva: World Economic Forum, October 2016); UN Women, "Economic Empowerment of Women," available at www.unwomen.org/-/media/headquarters/attachments /sections/library/publications/2013/12/un%20women_ee-thematic-brief_us -web%20pdf.pdf.

18. Stephen Klasen and Francesca Lamanna, "The Impact of Gender Inequality in Education and Employment on Economic Growth: New Evidence for a Panel of Countries," *Feminist Economics* 15, no. 3 (2009): 91–132.

19. Derived from analysis in Jonathan Woetzel et al., *The Power of Parity: How Advancing Women's Equality Can Add $12 Trillion to Global Growth* (McKinsey Global Institute, September 2015), available at www.mckinsey.com /global-themes/employment-and-growth/how-advancing-womens-equality -can-add-12-trillion-to-global-growth.

20. Rachel Dunifon, Anne Toft Hansen, Sean Nicholson, and Lisbeth Palmhøj Nielsen, "The Effect of Maternal Employment on Children's Academic Performance," Working Paper 19364 (Cambridge, MA: National Bureau of Economic Research, August 2013), available at www.nber.org/papers/w19364; Sylvia Walby and Wendy Olsen, "The Impact of Women's Position in the Labour Market on Pay and Implications for UK Productivity," report to Women and Equality Unit (London: UK Department of Trade and Industry, November 2002); UN Women, "Economic Empowerment of Women"; Susan Harkness, "The Contribution of Women's Employment and Earnings to Household Income Inequality: A Cross-Country Analysis" (Bath, UK: University of Bath, Centre for Analysis of Social Policy and Department of Social and Policy Studies, June 2010).

21. While the relative impact of maternal education on child mortality is three times stronger than female labor force participation, excess female child mortality has an inverse relationship with the length of mother's education *and* female labor force participation. In other words, women's employment has a more significant effect on lowering excessive deaths of baby girls than it does on absolute child mortality. See V. B. Tulasidhar, "Maternal Education, Female Labour Force Participation, and Child Mortality: Evidence from the Indian Census," *Health Transition Review* 3, no. 2 (1993): 177–190.

22. UN Women, "Women Working for Recovery: The Impact of Female Employment on Family and Community Welfare After Conflict" (2012), avail-

able at www.unwomen.org/~/media/Headquarters/Media/Publications/en/05BWomenWorkingforRecovery.pdf.

Chapter 3: Uncharted Waters

1. ILO and Gallup, *Towards a Better Future for Women and Work: Voices of Women and Men* (2017), available at www.gallup.com/reports/205127/gallup-international-labour-organization-report.aspx.

2. Tariq Khokhar, "Women More Often Work Unpaid in Family Firms," World Bank, July 3, 2016, available at http://blogs.worldbank.org/opendata/chart-women-more-often-work-unpaid-family-firms.

3. Arlie Hochschild, *The Second Shift: Working Families and the Revolution at Home* (New York: Viking Penguin, 1989).

4. Johannes P. Jütting, Christian Morrisson, Jeff Dayton-Johnson, and Denis Drechsler, "Measuring Gender (In)equality: Introducing the Gender, Institutions, and Development Data Base (GID)," Working Paper 247 (Paris: OECD Development Centre, March 6, 2006), doi:10.1787/354470443614.

5. Leila Hoteit, Ted@BCG, Paris, May 2016, available at www.ted.com/talks/leila_hoteit_3_lessons_on_success_from_an_arab_businesswoman.

6. See, for example, Rise, a wealth management platform for migrants, at www.gorise.co/.

7. Ghufran El-Katatney, "Stop Making Fun of the 'Lower-Class' Egyptians Enjoying Their Summer Vacation," ScoopEmpire, July 27, 2016, available at http://scoopempire.com/stop-making-fun-lower-class-egyptians-enjoying-summer-vacation/#.V6SsoPl95D8.

8. Hindra Liauw, "Muslim Conservatives Boo 'Jilboobs' in Indonesia," Rappler, August 8, 2014, available at www.rappler.com/world/regions/asia-pacific/indonesia/65619-muslim-conservatives-jilboobs-indonesia.

9. "Kyrgyzstan in War of Words (and Billboards) over Women's Clothing," GlobalVoices, July 29, 2016, available at https://globalvoices.org/2016/07/29/kyrgyzstan-in-war-of-words-and-billboards-over-womens-clothing/.

10. "Kyrgyzstan: President Throws Weight Behind Anti-Veil Posters," Eurasianet.org, July 14, 2016, available at www.eurasianet.org/node/79661.

11. Claire Cain Miller, "Millennial Men Aren't the Dads They Thought They'd Be," *New York Times,* July 30, 2015; Nika Fate-Dixon, "Are Some Millennials Rethinking the Gender Revolution? Long-Range Trends in Views of Nontraditional Roles for Women," Council on Contemporary Families, March 30, 2017, available at https://contemporaryfamilies.org/7-fate-dixon-millennials-rethinking-gender-revolution/.

Chapter 4: A Digital Opportunity

1. According to World Bank data, over 50 percent of the female workforce is engaged in self-employment in Azerbaijan and Indonesia, and in Bangladesh, Egypt, Iran, Kazakhstan, Malaysia, Turkey, and Yemen, the figure is over 25 percent.

2. "The Pitfalls of Islamic Fashion," *The Economist*, April 20, 2017.

3. Data are from the Malaysia International Islamic Financial Centre (MIFC).

4. Mikelle Street, "5 Things to Know About Vogue Arabia's First Editor-in-Chief," Observer, May 7, 2016, available at http://observer.com/2016/07/5-things-to-know-about-vogue-arabias-first-editor-in-chief/.

5. Data are from the Pakistan Medical and Dental Council, available at www.pmdc.org.pk/Statistics/tabid/103/Default.aspx.

6. "Are Pakistan's Female Medical Students to Be Doctors or Wives?" *BBC News*, August 28, 2015, available at www.bbc.com/news/world-asia-34042751.

7. Sadaf Jabeen, "Doctor on Call," *The News International*, December 27, 2016, available at www.thenews.com.pk/magazine/you/174565-Doctor-on-call.

8. In *Homo Deus: A Brief History of Tomorrow* (New York: HarperCollins, 2017), Yuval Noah Harari predicts the rise over the long term of a "useless class" of people who will be displaced by technology and have no function to fulfill in the modern world. The economist Guy Standing talks about the shorter-term challenge of a growing "precariat" in *The Precariat: The New Dangerous Class* (London: Bloomsbury Academic, 2011).

9. Michael A. Osborne, Carl Benedikt Frey, Craig Holmes, et al., *Technology at Work v2.0* (Citi Research and Oxford Martin School, January 2016), available at www.oxfordmartin.ox.ac.uk/downloads/reports/Citi_GPS_Technology_Work_2.pdf; World Economic Forum (WEF), *The Future of Jobs: Employment, Skills, and Workforce Strategy for the Fourth Industrial Revolution* (Cologny, Switzerland: WEF, January 2016), available at www3.weforum.org/docs/WEF_Future_of_Jobs.pdf.

10. Osborne et al., *Technology at Work v2.0*, 19.

11. WEF, *The Future of Jobs*, 33.

12. Osborne et al., *Technology at Work v2.0*, 37.

13. "Untraditional Choice," *The Economist*, July 13, 2013; Laurence Chandy, ed., "The Future of Work in the Developing World: Brookings Blum Roundtable 2016 Post-Conference Report," January 31, 2017, available at www.brookings.edu/wp-content/uploads/2017/01/global_20170131_future-of-work.pdf.

14. Claire Cain Miller, "Why Men Don't Want the Jobs Mostly Done by Women," *New York Times*, January 4, 2017.

Chapter 5: A New Marriage Market

1. The Dammam metropolitan area is formed by the "triplet cities" of Dammam, Dhahran, and Al Khobar.

2. Sarah Kershaw, "Saudi Arabia Awakens to the Perils of Inbreeding," *New York Times,* May 1, 2003; Regan Doherty, "Young Gulf Arabs Question Tradition of Cousin Marriages," *Reuters,* April 4, 2012; Jocelyn Kaiser, "Saudi Gene Hunters Comb Country's DNA to Prevent Rare Diseases," *Science,* December 8, 2016.

3. Aya Batrawy, "Saudi Women's Changing Attitudes Toward Marriage," *The National,* January 21, 2015, available at www.thenational.ae/world/middle-east/saudi-womens-changing-attitudes-toward-marriage.

4. Glenna Spitze, "Women's Employment and Family Relations: A Review," *Journal of Marriage and the Family* 50, no. 3 (August 1988): 595–618.

5. "Are Pakistan's Female Medical Students to Be Doctors or Wives?" *BBC News,* August 28, 2015, available at www.bbc.com/news/world-asia-34042751; data are from Pakistan Medical and Dental Council, available at www.pmdc.org.pk/Statistics/tabid/103/Default.aspx.

6. Katrin Elborgh-Woytek et al., "Women, Work, and the Economy: Macroeconomic Gains from Gender Equity," Staff Discussion Note 13/10 (Washington, DC: International Monetary Fund, September 2013), available at www.imf.org/external/pubs/ft/sdn/2013/sdn1310.pdf.

7. There are no data for unmarried women in these countries.

8. Fransiska Nangoy, "Demand for Women-Only Motorcycle Taxis Soars in Indonesian Capital," *Reuters,* January 19, 2016.

Chapter 6: Business at the Frontlines

1. "Like Daughter, Like Father," Columbia Business School, Ideas and Insights blog, February 22, 2011, available at www8.gsb.columbia.edu/ideas-at-work/publication/733/like-daughter-like-father#.U6rnTO8g_IU; Adam Glynn and Maya Sen, "Identifying Judicial Empathy: Does Having Daughters Cause Judges to Rule for Women's Issues?" *American Journal of Political Science* 59, no. 1 (2015): 37–54.

2. Klaus Schwab, *The Fourth Industrial Revolution* (New York: Crown Business, 2016).

3. T. L. Andrews, "Silicon Valley's Gender Gap Is the Result of Computer-Game Marketing 20 Years Ago," *Quartz,* February 16, 2017, available at https://qz.com/911737/silicon-valleys-gender-gap-is-the-result-of-computer-game

-marketing-20-years-ago/; Jack Linshi, "6 Charts Showing Tech's Gender Gap Is More Complicated Than You Think," *Time,* March 26, 2015.

4. "The Islamic Veil Across Europe," *BBC News,* January 31, 2017, available at www.bbc.com/news/world-europe-13038095; "Turkey Allows Policewomen to Wear Muslim Headscarf," BBC News, August 27, 2016, available at www.bbc.com/news/world-europe-37205850.

Chapter 7: Ministers and Mullahs

1. Anatolia News Agency, "Family Minister Backs Turkish PM on Abortion, Caesarean Births," *Hurriyet Daily News,* May 27, 2012, available at www.hurriyetdailynews.com/family-minister-backs-turkish-pm-on-abortion-caesarean-births-.aspx?pageID=238&nID=21684&NewsCatID=338.

2. Thomas W. Lippman, "Saudi Women Shatter the Lingerie Ceiling," *New York Times,* January 21, 2012; Katherine Zoepf, "Shopgirls," *The New Yorker,* December 23 and 30, 2013.

3. For some, it is interpretations of the Quran and sayings of the Prophet that suggest that women and men have highly differentiated roles in society and that men should work outside the home and women inside the home. For others, it is not religion but rather culture that dictates their views on gender. These include men who insist that wives, sisters, and daughters must stay within the home after puberty, women who prohibit their daughters from pursuing a higher education lest they become too independent, and, in extreme cases, men who would rather see their daughters die than bring "dishonor" upon the family by making their own marital choices.

4. According to a 2016 World Bank report, "the Middle East and North Africa region is home to 11 of the world's most restrictive economies, namely Saudi Arabia, Jordan, Iran, Yemen, Iraq, Bahrain, the United Arab Emirates (UAE), Oman, Syria, Qatar, and Kuwait. Along with Afghanistan, Sudan, Mauritania, and Brunei, these are the 15 most restrictive economies in terms of women's ability to work or establish a business, as measured by the report." World Bank, "Despite Progress, Laws Restricting Economic Opportunity for Women Are Widespread Globally" (press release), September 9, 2015, available at www.worldbank.org/en/news/press-release/2015/09/09/despite-progress-laws-restricting-economic-opportunity-for-women-are-widespread-globally-says-wbg-report; World Bank, *Women, Business, and the Law: Getting to Equal* (Washington, DC: World Bank, 2016), available at http://wbl.worldbank.org/~/media/WBG/WBL/Documents/Reports/2016/Women-Business-and-the-Law-2016.pdf.

5. World Bank, "All Indicators," in *Women, Business, and the Law,* available at http://wbl.worldbank.org/data/exploretopics/all-indicators.

6. Ibid., 14.

7. Arash Karami, "City of Tehran's Female Workers Fired for Own Well-being," *Al-Monitor,* July 16, 2014, available at www.al-monitor.com/pulse /originals/2014/07/tehran-municipality-fires-women-staff.html; Arash Karami, "Tehran Mayor Says Gender Segregation a Question of Dignity," *Al-Monitor,* July 18, 2014, available at www.al-monitor.com/pulse/originals/2014/07/tehran -mayor-responds-segregation.html; Arash Karami, "Labor Ministry Opposes Tehran's Proposal for Gender Segregation," *Al-Monitor,* July 30, 2014, available at www.al-monitor.com/pulse/originals/2014/07/iran-labor-ministry-opposes -sex-segregation.html.

8. "Vote for Women's Early Retirement Sparks Heated Debate in Iran," *Financial Tribune,* January 31, 2017, available at https://financialtribune .com/articles/economy-business-and-markets/58575/vote-for-women-s-early -retirement-sparks-heated-debate.

9. Janet G. Stotsky, "How Tax Systems Treat Men and Women Differently," *Finance and Development* (International Monetary Fund) 34 (March 1997), available at www.imf.org/external/pubs/ft/fandd/1997/03/pdf/stotsky .pdf.

10. John Isaac, "Expanding Women's Access to Financial Services," World Bank, February 26, 2014, available at www.worldbank.org/en/results/2013/04 /01/banking-on-women-extending-womens-access-to-financial-services.

11. OECD, "Gender Equality" (OECD Gender Data Portal), available at www.oecd.org/gender/data.

12. Laura Colby, "Can You Have Too Much Maternity Leave? In Europe, Maybe," *Bloomberg,* February 28, 2017, available at www.bloomberg .com/news/articles/2017-02-28/can-you-have-too-much-maternity-leave-in -europe-it-s-possible.

13. Erik Meyersson, "Islamic Rule and the Empowerment of the Poor and Pious," *Econometrica* 82, no. 1 (January 2014): 229–269.

14. There are two women in Qatar's central municipal council and one female minister, but no women in Qatar's parliament (*Majlis as-Shura*). Today there is only one woman in the Kuwaiti parliament (national assembly), after a peak of four female ministers in 2009; she occupies the sole "woman's slot."

15. Lori Beaman, Raghabendra Chattopadhyay, Esther Duflo, Rohini Pande, and Petia Topalova, "Powerful Women: Does Exposure Reduce Bias?" *Quarterly Journal of Economics* 124, no. 4 (2009): 1497–1540.

16. Bina Shah, "The Legacy of Benazir Bhutto," *New York Times,* December 26, 2014.

17. Although Bhutto seemed to do little to empower women while she was in power, Clinton Bennett concludes that Bhutto's record speaks for itself in terms of empowering women's organizations and inspiring more women to get into politics (Bennett, *Muslim Women in Power: Gender, Politics, and Culture in Islam* [London: Continuum, 2010]); Joseph Allchin, "Grameen Bank Set to Go Under Full Government Oversight," *Financial Times,* February 15, 2015.

18. Catalyst Information Center, "Why Diversity Matters," July 2013, available at www.catalyst.org/system/files/why_diversity_matters_catalyst_0.pdf.

19. Samyah Alfoory, "Setting the Agenda: Reflections of Saudi Women on the Campaign Trail," The Arab Gulf States Institute in Washington, February 8, 2016, available at www.agsiw.org/setting-the-agenda-reflections-of-saudi -women-on-the-campaign-trail/.

20. "First Lady Emine Erdoğan Calls for Gender Equality, Ending Exploitation of Women's Labor," *Daily Sabah,* May 30, 2016, available at www .dailysabah.com/politics/2016/05/30/first-lady-emine-erdogan-calls-for -gender-equality-ending-exploitation-of-womens-labor; "Turkey's First Lady Calls for Workforce Gender Equality," *Hurriyet Daily News,* May 30, 2016, available at www.hurriyetdailynews.com/turkeys-first-lady-calls-for-workforce -gender-equality.aspx?pageID=238&nID=99858&NewsCatID=339.

21. ITU, "World Telecommunication/ICT Indicators Database 2017," available at www.itu.int/en/ITU-D/Statistics/Pages/publications/wtid.aspx.

22. Data are from World Bank World Development Indicators.

23. Lilia Blaise, "Two-Thirds of Women-Led Start-ups Fail in Tunisia," Wamda, March 26, 2017, available at www.wamda.com/2017/03/thirds-women -led-startups-fail-tunisia-report.

Conclusion: What's Next?

1. According to the World Economic Forum, local businesses rank Bangladesh ninety-seventh in the world in ease of finding skilled talent, Pakistan ninety-third, Turkey eighty-third, Saudi Arabia seventy-ninth, Kazakhstan sixty-fifth, and Indonesia forty-third.

Index

SAADIA ZAHIDI is head of Education, Gender, and Work and a member of the Executive Committee at the World Economic Forum. Her team works with leaders from business, government, civil society, and academia to develop and implement strategies to close skills gaps, prepare for the future of work, promote lifelong  learning, and foster gender equality. Ms. Zahidi founded and coauthors the Forum's *Future of Jobs Report*, *Global Gender Gap Report*, and *Human Capital Report*, and several other publications. She was selected as one of the BBC's "100 Women" and won the inaugural *Financial Times*/McKinsey Bracken Bower Prize for prospective authors under thirty-five. Ms. Zahidi is a frequent speaker at conferences and in the media. She holds a bachelor's degree in economics from Smith College, a master of philosophy in international economics from the Graduate Institute of International and Development Studies in Geneva, and a master's in public administration from Harvard University's John F. Kennedy School of Government. Her current interests include the future of work, the impact of technology on employment and income inequality, skills gaps, social safety nets, and new education models and services.

# The Nation Institute

Founded in 2000, **Nation Books** has become a leading voice in American independent publishing. The imprint's mission is to tell stories that inform and empower just as they inspire or entertain readers. We publish award-winning and bestselling journalists, thought leaders, whistle-blowers, and truthtellers, and we are also committed to seeking out a new generation of emerging writers, particularly voices from underrepresented communities and writers from diverse backgrounds. As a publisher with a focused list, we work closely with all our authors to ensure that their books have broad and lasting impact. With each of our books we aim to constructively affect and amplify cultural and political discourse and to engender positive social change.

Nation Books is a project of The Nation Institute, a nonprofit media center established to extend the reach of democratic ideals and strengthen the independent press. The Nation Institute is home to a dynamic range of programs: the award-winning Investigative Fund, which supports groundbreaking investigative journalism; the widely read and syndicated website TomDispatch; journalism fellowships that support and cultivate over twenty-five emerging and high-profile reporters each year; and the Victor S. Navasky Internship Program.

For more information on Nation Books and The Nation Institute, please visit:

www.nationbooks.org
www.nationinstitute.org
www.facebook.com/nationbooks.ny
Twitter: @nationbooks